Power, Politics and the Emotions

How can we rethink ideas of policy failure to consider its paradoxes and contradictions as a starting point for more hopeful democratic encounters?

Offering a provocative and innovative theorisation of governance as relational politics, the central argument of *Power, Politics and the Emotions* is that there are sets of affective dynamics which complicate the already materially and symbolically contested terrain of policy-making. This relational politics is Shona Hunter's starting point for a more hopeful, but realistic understanding of the limits and possibilities enacted through contemporary governing processes. Through this idea Hunter prioritises the everyday lived enactments of policy as a means to understand the state as a more differentiated and changeable entity than is often allowed for in current critiques of neoliberalism. But Hunter reminds us that focusing on lived realities demands a melancholic confrontation with pain, and the risks of social and physical death and violence lived through the contemporary neoliberal state. This is a state characterised by the ascendency of neoliberal whiteness; a state where no one is innocent and we are all responsible for the multiple intersecting exclusionary practices creating its unequal social orderings. The only way to struggle through the central paradox of governance to produce something different is to accept this troubling interdependence between resistance and reproduction and between hope and loss.

Analysing the everyday processes of this relational politics through original empirical studies in health, social care and education the book develops an innovative interdisciplinary theoretical synthesis which engages with and extends work in political science, cultural theory, critical race and feminist analysis, critical psychoanalysis and post-material sociology.

Shona Hunter is a Lecturer in Sociology and Social Policy Governance at the University of Leeds, England and a Research Associate at the Research Centre into Visual Identities in Architecture and Design at the University of Johannesburg, South Africa.

Social Justice

Series editors: Kate Bedford, *University of Kent, UK*, Davina Cooper, *University of Kent, UK*, Sarah Lamble, *Birkbeck College, University of London, UK*, Sarah Keenan, *Birkbeck College, University of London, UK*

Social Justice is a new, theoretically engaged, interdisciplinary series exploring the changing values, politics and institutional forms through which claims for equality, democracy and liberation are expressed, manifested and fought over in the contemporary world. The series addresses a range of contexts from transnational political fora, to nation-state and regional controversies, to small-scale social experiments. At its heart is a concern, and inter-disciplinary engagement with, the present and future politics of power, as constituted through territory, gender, sexuality, ethnicity, economics, ecology and culture.

Foregrounding struggle, imagined alternatives and the embedding of new norms, *Social Justice* critically explores how change is wrought through law and governance, everyday social and bodily practices, dissident knowledges, and movements for citizenship, belonging, and reinvented community.

Titles in this series:

Chronotopes of Law: Jurisdiction, Scale and Governance
Mariana Valverde, 2015

Law, Environmental Illness and Medical Uncertainty
Tarryn Phillips, 2015

Global Justice and Desire: Queering Economy
Nikita Dhawan, Antke Engel, Christoph H. E. Holzhey and Volker Woltersdorff (eds.), 2015

The Sexual Constitution of Political Authority
Aleardo Zanghellini, 2015

Power, Politics and the Emotions: Impossible Governance?
Shona Hunter, 2015

Forthcoming:

Protest, Property and the Commons
Lucy Finchett-Maddock

Regulating Sex After Aids: Queer Risks and Contagion Politics
Neil Cobb

Law Unlimited
Margaret Davies

Power, Politics and the Emotions

Impossible Governance?

Shona Hunter

Routledge
Taylor & Francis Group
a GlassHouse Book

First published 2015
by Routledge
2 Park Square, Milton Park, Abingdon, Oxon, OX14 4RN

and by Routledge
711 Third Avenue, New York, NY 10017

a GlassHouse Book

Routledge is an imprint of the Taylor & Francis Group, an informa business

First issued in paperback 2016

British Library Cataloguing in Publication Data
A catalogue record for this book is available from the British Library

Library of Congress Cataloging-in-Publication Data
Hunter, Shona.
Power, politics and the emotions: impossible governance? / Shona Hunter.
pages cm. -- (Social justice)
Includes bibliographical references and index.
ISBN 978-0-415-55510-4 (hbk) -- ISBN 978-0-203-79804-1 (ebk) 1. State, The.
2. Political culture. 3. Critical psychology. I. Title.
JC11.H86 2015
320.01--dc23
2014047302

ISBN13: 978-0-415-55510-4 (hbk)
ISBN13: 978-1-138-68584-0 (pbk)

Typeset in Galliard by
Servis Filmsetting Ltd, Stockport, Cheshire

For my large, loving and unruly family, but especially for my grandmothers Masie Swift and Jean Hood who taught me the difference between melancholy and melancholia.

Contents

Acknowledgements

As one of the governing subjects whose experiences I consider in *Power, Politics and the Emotions* it would probably not be surprising for me to say that I have an ambivalent relationship with my insider institutional positioning. But it is this ambivalent insider-outsider positioning which has given me access to all the outsider-insiders that have made the book's writing possible. Given the length of the book's gestation, the thanks go back a long way . . .

I benefited from two sets of substantial research council support which I could not have applied for or held without my institutional positioning. The first was part of a funded UK Economic and Social Research Council (ESRC) studentship (2000–2003 ref R422012425) which enabled me to undertake the health service based empirical work. Tony Maltby and Lena Robinson, my supervisors, both nurtured the independence of thought that allowed me to move well out of the established confines of mainstream social policy which laid important ground-work for my future intellectual directions. The second tranche of personal funding was a five year Research Council's UK Fellowship in the New Machinery of Governance (2006–2011 ref 460293) which enabled me to undertake much of the writing but also the development of the theoretical ideas begun in that earlier doctoral work and then continued in the work that I subsequently undertook as part of the Integrating Diversity Research Team (2003–2006). Working as part of that team and especially with Sara Ahmed and Elaine Swan was person-ally and professionally nourishing at an important formative stage of my career. Their energy, commitment and friendship as well as their approach to politically engaged scholarship have been crucial to this book's development as well as my own. Even though it is now a while since we worked alongside one another, I want to thank them and other members of the Integrating Diversity Research Team for a hugely intellectually and personally freeing experience which fed directly into the empirical work that I talk about in Chapters 5, 6 and 7.

The work of Fiona Williams, Gail Lewis and Janet Newman has also been enor-mously nourishing to my academic development in general and the thinking in this book. Fiona and Janet have both inputted directly into the book itself. Fiona encouraged me to think big at the very earliest stages in the book's planning and enabled me to understand the potential power of my arguments as a contribution to a much broader feminist postcolonial project. Janet has generously read and commented on a number of the chapters in the manuscript. Her most recent book was an important influence in the final stages of this book's work-up. Her ongoing warm encouragement of me and my work is greatly appreciated. The work of all three has been crucial to opening up the confines of social policy analysis to important interdisciplinary influences that have fuelled the more innovative developments in social policy. The ongoing importance of Gail Lewis's work to positioning Black feminist work into mainstream social policy cannot be underestimated.

The final stages of writing this manuscript were like being dragged playfully, but still pretty traumatically, through an academic hedge backwards, with and by a range of my friends and colleagues. Lisa Garforth has diligently read all of the manuscript as it was written and much of it more than once, her encouragement and enthusiasm for my ideas has been central to my ability to finish it and her theoretical insight has been crucial at important points. Rachael Dobson has been the most amazing intellectual and emotional processor for some of my deepest fears for the writing. It is through discussions with her that I became most able to understand my own ideas on the relational. Hopefully she has transitioned as much as me through the process! For the last few years Lisa and Rachael as well as Say Burgin, Shirley Tate and Teela Sanders have been my friends; central to my ability to resist the perils of academic life as well as my ability to enjoy its many many fruits. Being part of the editorial collective of *Critical Social Policy* (*CSP*) has been similarly sustaining throughout the whole period spanning all of the empirical projects and the book itself! The collective is one of my most valued academic spaces because of the way it continues to prioritise political and intellectual discussion as core to the process of 'getting the work done'. It is still a fine example of difference being generative rather than stifling. As well as Lisa, Janet, Shirley and Rachael, John Clarke, Paul Hoggett and Helen Lucy have all read and commented on chapters at different stages. Nirmal Puwar commented on an earlier paper in ways which have had an impact on the arguments in Chapter 5 in particular. Marian Barnes, David Taylor and Paul Stenner commented on the arguments now forming the main part of Chapter 7 when this chapter was published in another incarnation as part of a special issue on 'Psychosocial Welfare' for *CSP*.

It is common to hear academics grumbling about the time teaching takes away from their ability to write. I feel very differently. Writing and teaching are so completely intertwined for me that I am not sure that this book would have seen the light of day, or certainly not in a way that I could feel proud of and nourished through, without the deep engagement of students on my third year 'Governing Cultures Identities and Emotions' course. For 12 weeks of the year over the last five years we have pored together over published papers, the emerging chapters and 'raw' empirical material that have ended up here. In the final year Ashley Bullard, Sisi Chan and David Page have made the pain of writing seem worth it through especially interesting and fun class discussions. Amanpreet Aluwhalia who was also a dissertation student writing brilliantly about relationality and with whom I have since developed a deep and rewarding friendship deserves a very special mention here. I have also taught parts of the book in South Africa at Rhodes University School of Journalism, and in Germany at the University of Mannheim's Department of English and American Studies, and most recently in Geneva at the Conférence Universitaire de la Suisse Occidentale (CUSO) Doctoral School at the kind invitation of Noemi Michel and Rahel Kuhnz. Each experience has enabled a deeper engagement with the ideas I present here. In particular reading Himadeep Muppidi's latest book after a fabulous few days teaching with him in Geneva helped me to gather the guts to go all the way with neoliberal suicide! The result is no reflection on his fine book, of course.

Without the editorial support of Kate Bedford and Davina Cooper I am sure that this book would never have seen the light of day. Together, they have read all of the manuscript. Their intellectual generosity and collegiality is such a rare thing in contemporary academic contexts that I am hugely lucky to have encountered them, and then had the pleasure of learning from them. Their commitment to the book and their belief in my ability to deliver it have meant its completion. I have learned so much from both of them not only about the process of writing but about the generosities of academic life. They have enabled me to be brave, hopefully not stupid. Even when her work with the series had finished, Kate saw the book through to the end. Latterly, I have also benefited from the input of newer members of the editorial team, Sarah Lamble and Sarah Keenan. Colin Perrin and Rebekah Jenkins at Routledge have both been immensely flexible and patient in the face of significant delays.

Roland Mizon has read and commented on much of the manuscript, at least as much in the hope that this would hurry it into being as any interest in considering *yet again* the risk of neoliberal suicide which he faces down every day at work. Finally, my parents have provided me with more intellectual, emotional and practical support than I could ever deserve. I know that this is fine with them, but I think it's worth saying how much I love them for it. I hope that this book and what it says about them as much as what it says about me makes them very proud.

Some of the material included in this book has appeared in an earlier form elsewhere. An earlier version of Chapter 2 was published under the same name in *The Journal of Psychosocial Studies* (2012), *6*, 3–29. A previous version of Chapter 7 was published as 'Living Documents: A Feminist Psychosocial Approach to the Relational Politics of Policy Documentation' in *Critical Social Policy, 28*(4), 506–528. Sections of Chapter 5 were published in *Doing Diversity Work* in the paper 'Adult and Community Learning: Leadership, Representation and Racialised "Outsiders" "Within"', *Policy Futures in Education, 4*(1), 114–127.

Part I

Governance from a feminist psychosocial perspective

Chapter I

Governing subjects, repression and equality

Uncertainty and instability characterize these times. Nonetheless, success and progress endure as a condition to strive for, even though there is little faith in either. All individuals and societies know failure better than they might care to admit – failed romance, failed careers, failed politics, failed humanity, failed failures. Even if one sets out to fail, the possibility of success is never eradicated, and failure once again is ushered in.

(Le Feuvre, 2010)

On May 1, the people entrusted me with the task of leading their country into a new century. That was your challenge to me. Proudly, humbly, I accepted it. Today, I issue a challenge to you. Help us make Britain that beacon shining throughout the world. Unite behind our mission to modernise our country. There is a place for all the people in New Britain, and there is a role for all the people in its creation. Believe in us as much as we believe in you. Give just as much to our country as we intend to give. Give your all. Make this the giving age. "By the strength of our common endeavour we achieve more together than we can alone." On 1 May 1997, it wasn't just the Tories who were defeated. Cynicism was defeated. Fear of change was defeated. Fear itself was defeated. Did I not say it would be a battle of hope against fear? On 1st May 1997, fear lost. Hope won. The Giving Age began.

(Tony Blair, Labour Party Conference, 30 September 1997, Brighton, England)

Energetic, future oriented, hopeful and rousing; Tony Blair's comments to the Labour Party Conference in his first few months as British Prime Minister are typical of the heady optimism characterising a range of late 1990s Western liberal democratic state projects. Australia, Germany, Italy and the United States all had their own versions of such future oriented new deal, third or middle way social democratic projects. The promise of these projects was the reconciliation of the principles of social equality and economic success. All had high hopes for social renewal through cohesion and harmony within the nation; a harmony to be created through an economically enabling and socially inclusive state. The cynicism, fear and social division associated with previous governmental failures to achieve such a socially and economically inclusive vision could be defeated within this consensus driven social democratic project. Following Blair here, the British project clearly fits this bill. The barely muted neo imperial tone conveys a sense of worldly omnipotence. Anything and everything appears possible within such a cohesive and united liberal democratic mission. There is no question about the direction of progress. Defeat over internal as well as external enemies has been achieved.

Viewed retrospectively the sort of heady optimism associated with this social democratic project might be understood as a hopeful blip, struggling to establish itself within the broader context of the sorts of governmental anxieties, paranoia and fears more often considered characteristic of late modernity's 'structures of feeling' (Williams, 2009). These are fears fuelled by terrorism, natural disasters, spread of disease, the speed and unpredictability of technological advance, economic crisis and energy and general resource scarcity amongst a range of other social 'threats' (Hoggett, 1989, 2009). They are fears which attest to a fundamental human consciousness of mortality which makes citizens fearful about death, fears against which states claim to protect (Stevens, 2011).[1]

In the English[2] context an overt sense of governmental anxiety was very firmly re-established by the time the Labour Party was voted out of office to the Conservative Party's familiar tune of the left's legacy of governmental failure. According to this Conservative mantra Britain was 'broken', in social and economic decline (again) as evidenced by ongoing inequality, falling prosperity and increasing social unrest. This decline is positioned as the result of 'the poisonous legacy of thirteen years of Labour misrule' (Cameron, 2010; Lister, 2011), where markets were allowed to run themselves rampant and overzealous bureaucracy tightened its grip in the wrong places or in the wrong ways. As the current Conservative-Liberal Coalition Government's first term of office draws to a close, hopes rescind again. Potential for pending election success depends on the ability to re-establish these faded hopes. Thus, regardless of political hue, this circular story of governmental failure goes on; characterised by the pendulum swing between triumphal victory, accompanied by promises of democratic and social renewal, and crushing defeat, accompanied by cries of despair at (still) unfulfilled governmental promise.

What is it that is going on here that makes it so apparently impossible to learn from our governmental mistakes? And in particular why, in spite of a range of governmental efforts at inclusion, is it that some people always seem to be included and others are always excluded? And then following that; why is it that it so often appears to be the same people who appear to occupy these positions of included and excluded? For Chantal Mouffe (2000) this circularity of governmental failure is predictable from within the context of a consensus seeking liberal democratic project which fails to recognise its underlying paradox: that equality and freedom, or inclusion and differentiation in the terms I am using in *Power, Politics and the Emotions*, are not reconcilable. There are plenty of analysts who have come to the conclusion that the irreconcilability of core liberal democratic ideals suggests the redundancy of the liberal democratic state project itself (Dean, 2009). My aim in this book is not to argue for or against such a project. It is to engage with its lived enactments and the challenges and prospects presented through them. My sympathies are very clearly against the neoliberal drift in contemporary Western liberal democratic state projects because of the way they tend to be presented in terms that value the generation of profit over the protection and enhancement of life. However, I do not view any such drift as fundamental to the enactment of the state. This is mainly because I do not see the state, whether conceived of as liberal democratic, neoliberal or otherwise, as a thing in itself.

From my feminist psychosocial point of view the state comes into being through the everyday processes of relational contestation that I call 'relational politics'. By relational politics I mean the everyday actions, investments and practices of the multiple and shifting range of people and other material and symbolic objects that make up the state. One of my core concerns in *Power, Politics and the Emotions* is to highlight this everyday relationally contested nature of the state because, if this is not recognised, then we run the risk of seeing a contemporary neoliberal drift as definitive of the liberal democratic state project's nature. If the only manifestation of the state is the neoliberal, then the only option for those against neoliberalisation would be to give up on the idea of the state altogether, letting it wither on the vine, or killing it off by other more violent methods. But, if, as I am contending in *Power, Politics and the Emotions*, neoliberalisation is not all that there is to the state, then this killing off would be misguided at best. Indeed, if we understand neoliberalism itself as in some way hostile to the state, or at least to a state which engages with human subjectivity and agency in life enhancing ways, then such a killing off of the state by neoliberalism's critics only serves to support neoliberalisation. Killing off, abandoning or otherwise giving up on the state project is a potentially self-defeating practice. It is for this reason that I conceptualise this risk of giving up on the state as part of a neoliberal suicide. This is a form of state suicide which, though it may be usefully contemplated, should not be acted upon. In the rest of this chapter I begin to elucidate the reasons why contemplating, *but not acting on*, the state's suicidal tendencies is useful in rethinking the state in a more life enhancing form than the current English enactment of the (neo)liberal democratic model. At the end of the chapter I turn to overviewing the book's content.

A very neoliberal suicide

The issue of suicide is fraught, controversial and contested (Jaworski, 2010, 2012). Its psychodynamics are complex, multifactorial and variously related to sadism, masochism, altruism, narcissism and, occasionally explicitly, to ideas of rationality (see Akhtar, 2009; Lees and Stimpson, 2010; Mikhailova, 2006). For David Webb, an analyst and survivor of suicidality, suicide is the acute expression of a crisis within the self, a 'storm in the mind' (2010, p. 6). The lived experience of contemplating and attempting suicide is 'chaotic and confused, full of ambiguity and doubt. Anger, fear and other passions are also tangled with the paralysing hopelessness and helplessness' (2010, p. 6). Yet, 'contrary to the assumptions behind the [predominant] mental illness approach, it is possible to see thinking about suicide as a *healthy* crisis of the self, full of opportunity despite its risks' (2010, p. 8; emphasis in original). Approaching suicide in this way does not mean downplaying the dangerous, life threatening and ultimately, for some, life taking risks, but it does mean refusing to either suppress or indulge painful suicidal feelings. It also means understanding that not all suicidal thoughts lead to suicidal actions, but that they *could* do. Following Webb's argument such feelings should be honoured and respected as real, legitimate and important, as a central part of an agonising struggle for the self for some people. These feelings tell us as much, if not perhaps more, about the struggle for life as they tell about the desire to die.

The struggle for life central to suicidality is a struggle over relationality. It is essentially a struggle for belonging. This struggle becomes especially hard where there is an obvious tension between the subjective and objective senses of self, how the self is experienced 'inside' as the 'real me', and the way this 'real me' feels it is misrecognised or not seen at all by others. Stories about suicidality are often bound up with a subjective sense of passionate curiosity, a 'passionate yearning' (Webb, 2010) and a willingness to explore boundaries and to engage in adventure. Such stories tend to communicate a great passion for connection with others and the world around which is mismatched with the limited ability of that external world and the others that make it up to recognise and engage such a thirsty desire for community and belonging. This inability of the external world to match the love and affection of the subject is experienced as a deep grief, triggered by a sense of loss.

Suicidality points to the central human paradox considered within psychoanalysis which understands loss to be at the heart of the process of becoming a subject. This is the process Judith Butler (1997) calls 'subjectification'. From the point of view of psychoanalysis, loss is central to the originating split between self and other which occurs through birth and which enables the self to understand itself as a *distinct but nevertheless interdependent* object in the world; as an object related to but differentiated from others, *as a subject* in relation to others. This loss is re-enacted repeatedly through the ongoing tensions of human relationality and the fundamental interdependence to which relationality attests. As soon as you become one thing, you are no longer in any clear sense the other that you were. Your belongings shift and you change. The subject is constantly being recreated through difference, metamorphosing, changing. This changing involves a constant process of differentiation from significant others, losing connections with them; losing relationship, but at the same time establishing new relations with new others. These new relations position you differently in relation to those other others and so on.

According to Freud in his 1917 paper 'Mourning and Melancholia' (Freud, 2006 [1917]), melancholia is *one way* of responding to the fear and pain of the repeated human experience of change as a form of relationship loss. It is characterised by unbearable ambivalence towards the lost love object which was at some point interdependent with the self. The lost object can be a person like a lover, a mother, a friend, for example, or 'an abstraction taking the place of the person, such as the fatherland, freedom, an ideal and so on' (Freud, 2006, p. 310 [1917]). This unbearable ambivalence towards an object upon which one is dependent for self definition, but from which one also desires autonomy, outs as rage, anger and violence towards that lost aspect of the self. But because that aspect of the self is never fully lost or separated from the self (there is always at the very least a memory, or a trace of it), the loss cannot be processed or 'gotten over'. But because the object itself is gone from the subject's consciousness, in the sense that the relationship is broken and the object's existence has been repressed and denied, the anger, confusion and fury at the loss is rained down on the self. At its most extreme and tragic this melancholia leads to an inclination to self extinction via suicide.

Failing to be able to fully grasp its own interrelationship with the lost object, the grieving subject turns its rage and disappointment in upon itself. Initially it does this via self reproach, subsequently escalating to increasingly violent forms of sadism and self harm. For Freud, '[i]t is this sadism which solves the mystery of the inclination to suicide which makes melancholia so interesting and so danger-ous' (Freud, 2006, pp. 318–319 [1917]). Suicide as per this Freudian analysis is borne out of the inability to contain the ambivalence and uncertainty which comes out of the constant threat of the loss of relationship. This threat *grows into* a problem of the relationship *with the self* in the context of the broader set of complicated and changing relationships in which the subject is embroiled. The source of the subject's persecution is by this point sadly taken to be *the self*. On the occasions that the lost object appears like a ghostly spectre, as it must do from time to time, because repression is never final, it is perceived to be the singular source of the subject's persecution. But outside of these moments of conscious clarity, with no ability to stop its persecution because the cause of it is not under-stood, the fear and pain experienced by the subject is extinguishable only through retroflexed murder. Suicide, from this melancholic position, is a form of displaced or 'mis'placed murder which introjects hate, despair and confusion towards the always paradoxically *absent/present loved/hated* object.

Difference as constitutive

When using melancholia as a heuristic device with which to understand the ostensible failure of Western style liberal democracies to provide the fruits of social equality, the first question to be considered is the nature of the hidden loss being harboured within them. *Power, Politics and the Emotions* contends that the hidden loss being struggled over is the forms of *social difference* – classed, disabled, gendered, generational, sexualised but, especially, ethnoracial – which are ostensibly excluded from Western liberal nation states via the various categorisation processes of citizenship (see Stevens, 2011). Within the contexts of the sociohistorical conditions of Western imperialisms such social difference was imagined through 'an assumption of internalized population homogeneity of ethnoracial sameness and of externalizing difference' (Goldberg, 2002, p. 31). This is an assumption which positions difference as inferior and ostensibly external to the imperial centre. I say social difference is *ostensibly* excluded here because this ethnoracial sameness has always been mythological, constructed through the nation's imaginings of itself. Within the postcolonial context, where this fantasy of ethnoracial sameness is increasingly difficult, if not impossible, to maintain, the approach has been one of 'differential inclusion' (Lewis, 2000) or 'repressive tolerance' (Marcuse, 1965), whereby difference is formally, but unequally included in the enactment of the public realm and institutional life. This means that those subjects (or groups) seen to be representative of difference must conform to certain normative behaviours in public and keep the unmanaged expression of difference outside of formal state practices, confined to the informal; community or the family contexts. Difference is understood to be naturally external to the state, but naturally within civil society. Both aspects, the state bureaucracy and these less formalised contexts for action such as the community and the family, make up the broader 'state's personality' (Goldberg, 2009). But difference is something which can only be *brought into* the formalised operations of the state managerially, in a contained way.

Following this line of argument there is therefore a paradoxical inclusionary/exclusionary dynamic at the heart of the Western liberal democratic state where the loved/hated lost object of social difference remains *impossibly* both internal *and* external to the state. Social difference cannot be *reconciled*, only repressed. But from a psychosocial perspective such a repression is never a clear or straightforward rejection. Social difference is the repressed aspect of the Western liberal state in the sense that when it is recognised to be internal to the state difference is either invisibilised or tamed, it is only positioned as external to the state *through the act of state definition*, the pulling together, unifying of the state itself. Within liberalism then, the idea of the state and difference making practices are co-constitutive. Social difference is always the 'constitutive outside' (Mouffe, 2000, 2005, 2013), but simultaneously inside, of the liberal democratic state. These inside/outside complexities are explored in much more depth in Chapter 2.

It is because of this complicatedly internal/external nature of difference that the vitriol and blame for governmental failure to contain social difference is turned back onto the state itself. The fantasy object of reproach is *mistakenly* identified as the *state itself* as though it is separate and controlling of social difference, rather than defined and enacted through it. This 'mis'location of blame *onto the object of the state* means that it is the model of the state itself which is repeatedly called into question in contemporary Western liberalisms. But this calling into question sidesteps the thorny issue of the liberal state's fundamentally paradoxical relationship to social difference. This *relationship*, the *connection between* the institutions of the state and civil society, community and family, remains unrecognised (repressed) and therefore essentially unrevised. This is a dynamic whereby social difference is consistently positioned as the root of social division which causes the disunity within the polity. This disunity is in turn seen to produce governmental failure. In response a technical shift in governing processes is sought as the means to resolve the disunity produced through social difference. This is where *neo*liberalism comes into the *current* liberal state picture, as a means to produce the required technical shift for the management (in the sense of the containment, movement elsewhere or the attempted eradication altogether) of social difference.

From a melancholic viewpoint, apparently increasingly widespread civil society support for neoliberalism's increasingly aggressive anti-social measures to control difference in the form of community cohesion measures, family interventions, anti-immigration legislation and benefit cutting can be understood as an *investment in neoliberalism's promise to resolve the 'problems' of social division*, fragility and ambivalence which present threats to life. This analysis is *instead of* understanding support for neoliberalism in terms of straightforward support for the priority of economic gain (Brown, 2003; Connolly, 2013; Dean, 2009). Neoliberal techniques and practice such as the managerial ones I consider in more detail below are proffered as a solution to the *liberal governmental failure* to successfully include social difference into institutional life in a way which militates against social division. Thus, the new managerial state is offered as another better form of the *modernised* late liberal state, a state idealised to be *devoid of (supposedly) harmful* social difference, a *neo*liberal *state*.

My argument here has affinities with that of Lisa Duggan (2003) who claims that neoliberalism's 'most successful ruse' has been its ability to represent economic *norms* as non-normative matters of neutral technical expertise. It is through this ruse that neoliberalism gets associated with the realm of 'practical politics', involving supposedly necessary unavoidable forms of policy like strong anti-immigration, benefit cutting for certain groups, perhaps best encapsulated in the English context by the Thatcherite acronym TINA: 'There Is No Alternative' (see also Massey, 2012). This 'practical politics' is pitted in supposed contrast to the realm of social and cultural differences which is positioned as qualitatively different in kind, related to issues of (private) ideological choice and preference *rather than* (general) human necessity. This ruse can be seen as crucial to the production of a contemporary depoliticised neoliberal hegemony, a sort of global neoliberal 'policy-scape' (Clarke, 2012; Rizvi and Lingard, 2010) where nothing but 'what works' matters (Clarke & Newman, 2012).

> This "neo"liberalism is usually presented as a kind of nonpolitics – a way of being reasonable, and of promoting universally desirable forms of economic expansion and democratic government around the globe. Who could be against greater wealth and more democracy?
>
> (Duggan, 2003, p. 10)

Technical necessity becomes allied with the general (social) good, and ideological and cultural choice becomes associated with the private particularised desires and individual benefit.

Yet this pretence to the prioritisation of the general universal technical serves to hide a particular ethnoracial white masculine social ideal (Brown, 1995; Duggan, 2003). This is a particular white masculine ideal naturalised first within liberalism via the public/private state/family split, progressively more entrenched through neoliberalism's increasingly aggressive assaults on social difference. Thus, in a deft reversal of the public/private dichotomy, the fear of social difference in general is actually a fear of particular forms of social difference such as Blackness, femininity, debility and Islam amongst others. All of these differences have been *denaturalised* within liberalism, associated with intimate passion and embodied experience rather than with the general via an association with reason and cognition (see Chapter 2 for more on this split) reserved for the white masculine heterosexual Judaeo-Christian subject. The faith in the supposedly general technical is therefore actually anchored to a particular set of privately enacted behaviours, attributes and abilities associated with a *normative subject*. The denaturalised and thus particularised forms of difference such as Blackness, femininity and queerness, for example, are nevertheless fundamental and *internal* to liberalism's and neoliberalism's emergence as governmental formations. They are just not widely recognised as such.

The ascendency of neoliberal whiteness

Following this line of argument about (certain) social difference as liberalism's constitutive outside, it is possible to see this repressive melancholic dynamic as the means by which Western (neo)liberal democracies come to increasingly know the Other, whilst paradoxically refusing the crucial knowledges as to *how* that Other became known. Imperial histories are left out of the liberal political story which becomes *the* story of the state. In the English context this means that the British and European colonial histories so crucial to understanding the enactment of the British state are split off from the contemporary presence of minoritised citizens in the UK (Fortier, Ferreday and Kuntsman, 2011; Gilroy, 2004; Hesse, 2000). Chapter 4 presents a powerful example of this happening. The relationship between the British/English majority (idealised to be white) and the racialised Other is understood to be severed. (White) knowledge is effectively split from the (racialised) social relations of its production.

From within such a melancholic dynamic, racialisation processes are Manichean and repressively split; polarised, where:

> [r]acialization ... operate[s] through the institutional process of producing a dominant, standard, white national ideal, which is sustained by the exclusion-yet-retention of racialized others. The national topography

of centrality and marginality legitimizes itself by retroactively positing the racial other as always Other and lost to the heart of the nation.

(Cheng, 2000, p. 10)

But this resistance to knowing the racialised Other, this fundamental ambivalence towards the Other's subjectivity, and therefore its humanity, is also a failure to know the *whitened* (neo)liberal self. I use the notion of whitened here specifically to draw attention to the way that whiteness is a fantasy position which comes to be through material, symbolic and affective work (Hunter, 2010). As such, whiteness takes on different meanings in different times and places; it is both elastic, bringing different groups of people (for example, the Irish, Jews, Eastern Europeans) into its purview, and also frustratingly fixed. But within modernity, whiteness operates as *the* metaphor for the dominant liberal norm. It is the unknown empty standardising ideal against which race can be seen. Whiteness is indescribable in its generality, its apparent everythingness; the dominant standard of *humanity* against which the (raced) particular is measured (Dyer, 1997).

This is the point at which liberalism and whiteness become fused in their claims to represent *human generality*. Whiteness becomes the euphemism for the general of humanity defined through liberal universalism. The everythingness of whiteness is the embodiment of liberal values, individualism, universalism, rational progress and equality. Whiteness and state making become synonymous. But, the more abstract whiteness becomes, the more it requires imposition through material, affective and symbolic work (Knowles, 2003). Following Goldberg,

[t]he more ideologically hegemonic liberal values seem and the more open to difference liberal modernity declares itself, the more dismissive of difference it becomes and the more closed it seems to make the circle of acceptability.

(1993, pp. 6–7)

This means that the various ideas of equality, diversity and inclusion and related concepts like community cohesion and human rights operate as powerful euphemisms for attempts to resolve racialised and ethnicised difference within the framework of the liberal nation state. They work to collapse and elide other relations of social disadvantage within their purview such as those of gender and sexuality, and serve to reinstate whiteness as an unmarked general. Following Wiegman neoliberal whiteness is the 'governing ethos of the popular', 'best conceived not as a project, not even as a distinct phenomena, but as *the* cultural condition' of post imperial times (2012, p. 153).

The claim I am making here is much larger than one about whiteness *per se*, it is about a broader *liberalising imperative* which underwrites a range of revisionist political projects addressing ethnicity, gender and sexuality, all of which are intersecting and all of which coalesce in defining the parameters of humanity. In this sense whiteness could be seen as the liberal governing ethos of neoliberal capitalism. And, from the perspective of the continuities between liberalism and neoliberalism, whiteness is the ethos of the impulse to govern, whether it be liberally or neoliberally. According to Goldberg the most recent incarnation of this neoliberal governing ethos is decoupled from 'any conscious modesty or humility, from any finitude', it is the 'reach for the perfect replica and the perfectionism of the momentary' (Goldberg, 2009, p. 263). It is not just that whiteness *is* sameness. It is the generalising universalising impulse, the impulse to have power over life, the ultimate controlling impulse.

The power of whiteness as the euphemism for the modern liberal subject lies in its epistemological power to control the criteria of incorporation and existence into general *human* existence. Because of the relationship between epistemology and ontology from within the performative frame outlined further in Chapter 2, this epistemological power translates to an ontological power. Ethnicising processes, by which I mean the process of producing ethnic difference as a means to differentiate problematic racial homogenisations like the idea of Blackness, can be seen in precisely this way; as the paradoxical production of difference *in order to* enact the generality of the supposedly non-ethnic. Particularisation and generalisation work together to objectify. But this objectification process amasses power for the objectifiers, *the knowers*, positioning them omnipotently, controlling the rhetorical (again in the performative sense outlined in Chapter 2) terms of life itself.

As an *extension* of this epistemic-ontological process *neo*liberal whiteness works biopolitically in the sense that Chow (2002), Koshy (2001) and Puar (2007) have recognised following Foucault (1994). *Neo*liberal whiteness comes to be through its micromanagement of information, bodies; objects in general, via ever more complicated techniques for rendering the world of difference knowable in order to manage the threat to life (material, social and affective) that it presents. It works by the careful management and containment of difference, *bringing difference into sameness*, gathering allies as it does so. Therefore, an important consequence of the ability to define the world is the ability to bring difference inside to create inclusion. Normative (neo)liberal whiteness is extended through its silent *benevolent* outreach; through the very power to reach out and to offer inclusion to its excluded Others (women, older or queer subjects, for example); and thus through the power to make decisions about which groups come into its purview on the basis of which form of inclusionary/exclusionary bargains. Whiteness becomes civilisational and untouchable in its promotion of the general 'good'. Invitations to come into the human race operate as invitations into neoliberal whiteness.

Death by managerial desocialisation

To recapitulate my basic argument at this point: the neo in neoliberal is characterised by aggressively recuperative moves to remove supposedly disruptive social difference associated with personal family or community experience from the institutional spaces of the liberal state in the name of sustaining the collective cohesion, tolerance and equality which are assumed to produce governmental success. From this perspective neoliberalism can be read as a new *methodology* of liberal governance; a desocialising methodology which works more aggressively than traditional liberalism to bring certain particulars into line with the general good. It does this paradoxically by valuing difference and particularity (which turn out on investigation to be certain normative forms of particular). On the basis of this analysis the new public management (NPM) or new managerialism (Osborne and Gaebler, 1992) is the supposedly neutral technical policy apparatus developed to enact this new de-socialised paradigm of governance under the guise of ideas of institutional modernisation and transformation ostensibly more attuned to the particular needs of a range of institutional subjects, including workers and users.

The new managerialism brings in an elaborate apparatus of auditing methods rooted in the tradition of financial risk analysis (Power, 1994, 1999). What John Clarke calls 'the performance evaluation nexus' (2004). This performance evaluation nexus operationalises new managerial governance ideals focused on producing behavioural change within individual selves 'at a distance'. Following Davies and Bansel:

> Audit technologies are a means of governing subjects; of making them more governable by constituting them as the sorts of subjects demanded by the programmatic ambitions of government. In being taken up as one's own ambitions, the ambitions for government become a technology of the self. The operation of these technologies on and in the subject simultaneously secures the subject's variability and subjection. It secures their individuality and their regulation as responsiblised and accountable subjects who support an expanding industrialisation of the [institution] . . .
>
> (2010, p. 9)

The new managerialism is the means by which *subjective* morality, goals and desires become muddled with that of the entrepreneurial *institution*. New managerialism's three Es of economy, efficiency and effectiveness regularise and standardise professional practice into narrowly defined and measurable targets which are potentially *personally* as well as professionally meaningful. In other words audit technologies are generalising technologies which bring the particularities of the individual soul, its passions and its identities into line with the general institutional good. Thus, Lynn Froggett suggests such new managerial shifts make for what is on the whole a depoliticised 'docile and well disciplined work force' (2002, p. 85). Shore and Wright go so far as to label the new professionals as 'parasitical' (Hood, 1991; Shore and Wright, 1999, pp. 567–568, 2000) or 'cloned' (Essed, 2005). As such the performance evaluation nexus operates as a means to construct normative governing subjectivities and, as I discuss in more detail in Chapter 3, it provides a means of bringing subjects into the white masculine governing ideal.

The performance evaluation nexus works *through feelings*, harnessing passion, creativity, commitment and innovation, institutionalising trust in the name of protecting against indeterminacy, (financial) risk and failure (Power, 1999). It operationalises a form of emotion governance or neuroliberalism (Illouz, 2007; Jones, Pykett and Whitehead, 2011, 2013; Pykett, 2012, 2013; Wright, 2008). But it does so in such a way as to instrumentalise feelings of inclusion in the service of organisational change and transformation. It legislates via informal cultures, rather than challenging established institutional structures. These trends away from formalisation are visible in the increasing use of 'soft' law in equalities policies and the rise of human resource management in institutional life. These include measures such as the promotion of 'good relations', statements of intent, diversity and equality impact statements (see Chapter 7) and other forms of institutional training and learning development provision such as racism awareness or equality and diversity training which have been positioned by some critics as anti-democratic 'psycho-cultural' therapeutic interventions (Kyriakides, 2008). Thus, this performance evaluation nexus can work to enact the forms of repressive tolerance which support the unequal differential inclusion of various minoritised subjects.

The persistence of loss

Doom layered on gloom for the liberal state. Little wonder anxiety pervades its governing institutional spaces; but maybe not overwhelmingly so for all of its critics. Indeed, from a melancholic point of view like the one adopted in *Power, Politics and the Emotions* this neoliberal technicalisation of policy may well be its downfall *because of* the internal contradictions it produces. This is precisely because the pretence to wholesale technicalisation denies the terms of its own justification to wider citizen publics. After all, these terms of justification are still framed through calls to the *social* (rather than the bureaucratic) aspect of the state's personality, via discussion around the best ways to deliver what are essentially the *social* (civil community and cultural) projects of citizenship such as equality and inclusion.

It is in understanding this sort of internal contradiction, the desire for, but exclusion of the social and cultural difference it is associated with, that the melancholic point of view becomes so important. To reiterate the psychodynamic argument I outlined up front, this is because from a melancholic point of view the suppression of liberalism's lost object (social difference in this example) *can never be total*. The lost object is nurtured in a perpetual ambivalence where a 'series of individual battles for the object begins in which love and hatred (for difference) struggle with one another' (Freud, 2006, p. 323 [1917]). But these battles become increasingly violent, loosening the fixation on 'the object by devaluing, disparaging and, so to speak, even killing it' (Freud, 2006, p. 324 [1917]). From this point of view *neoliberalism's* attempts at hegemonic foreclosure on the social within the state, achieved via the exclusion of certain forms of social difference and their representation within a universal technical institutional apparatus (like NPM) produce a crisis *internal to* the (neo)liberal state. Such contradictory inclusionary/exclusionary struggles can be understood as risking the *potential* suicide of the *liberal* state. Suicide in the sense that the snuffing out of the social via the economically rational through the imposition of ever stronger, more coercive and controlling managerial mechanisms to make policy 'work better', by removing the risks of unpredictability produced through socially motivated agency, kills the very thing that makes the idea of the state viable in the first place. It kills the social difference which produces the very agency which requires ordering through the state. It kills off the state's purpose and its energy.

From one point of view we might say hurrah! Good riddance to this malevolent coercive, violating and socially exclusionary state! But this would be to buy into the very idea that the form and nature of the state can only be understood in one way, that the (neo)liberal fantasy of the state as hierarchically, coercively ordered and *de-socialised* is its only essential reality and that any struggle over its nature is therefore futile. This would be to read very firmly against the feminist psychosocial perspective developed in *Power, Politics and the Emotions* as well as to represent a form of 'buy in' to that neoliberal fantasy itself. Such a reading would be to ignore internal as well as externally driven resistance to the neoliberal ideal. It would also be to fail to account for the ways in which, given the state's extensive enactment at a distance, *all subjects* are positioned within the state in one way or another. No one subject is ever purely outside, nor anyone purely inside. This insider/outsiderness means that the external imposition of discipline is never possible; even under the most constrained of circumstances there is agency which potentially prevails. It is from this basic position on interdependence of subject/object, internal/external (see Chapter 2) that *Power, Politics and the Emotions* begins its analysis.

This inside/outside interdependence raises a number of questions about that myriad of governing subjects, the range of 'public officials' (Hoggett, 2009), 'new' (Osborne and Gaebler, 1992) or 'bureau' (Lea, 2012) professionals who make up the 'agents of the state' (Du Gay, 2005) that *Power, Politics and the Emotions* seeks to consider. In particular, it invites more thought about how these governing subjects negotiate the 'psychic life of power' (Butler, 1997) and the inevitable personal losses occurring through the exercise of power within the state. This appreciation of the potential losses as well as gains of governing involves considering how governing subjects are formed as much through subordination as those governed subjects, like public service 'users', 'stakeholders', 'clients' and 'citizen consumers' (Barnes and Prior, 2009; Barnes, Newman and Sullivan, 2007; Newman and Clarke, 2009), who are more usually considered to be acted upon by the state, rather than to be acting for it. This is not to suggest that the governing subject does not reproduce and reconstitute the subordinations of both the self and multiple others, nor that these subordinations are not sometimes egregious (see, for example, Tess Lea's work on the Australian Northern Territories (2008b, 2012) or Judith Butler's analysis of Guantanamo Bay in the United States (2004)). But it is to recognise that this governing subject is *multiply positioned* within the relations of *power* and *inequality*, as subject and agent of power within the state (Barnes and Prior, 2009; Cooper, 1994;

Hunter, 2003). Thus, the approach in *Power, Politics and the Emotions* seeks to accord these governing subjects a much fuller personhood, more responsibility and innocence than they are often accorded when they are viewed solely, or even primarily as 'agents of the state'.

The fact that the loss(es) producing internal contradiction, uncertainty and potential failure within the state can never be covered over completely is crucial to understanding the general impossibility of hegemonic *foreclosure* so important to the argument I am formulating in *Power, Politics and the Emotions*. This is because the persistence of loss points to the agency that always exceeds subjective reflexive self-conscious control. It points to the *distributed* and *always unfinished* nature of agency as something that is multiple, persisting *simultaneously* through past, present and future, enacted through the interdependencies between different subject-objects. From this melancholic point of view the state must, therefore, be considered as it is in its everyday form, rather than its Western liberal idealised incarnation. That is to say that the state must be viewed as an open more uncertain entity because of this uncontrollable, but nevertheless constitutive aspect of agency, which is produced through the inevitable loss of social difference. Social difference, even where this is lost, in the sense of unconsciously repressed, is potentially generative. This is what is so crucial to a melancholic analysis. Death, whether it be at the hands of the self or the other, leaves remains; there is always a trace (Butler, 1997, 2004; Eng and Kazanjian, 2003). The ghosts of the past live on in the present (Cheng, 2000; Gordon, 2008).

Relational politics

Rather than abandoning the state to its melancholic suicide via neoliberalism, *Power, Politics and the Emotions* is interested in exploring the possibilities for renewal and reparation which potentially come from *within* the state via its relational politics. Not by its institutional structures and processes, but from its ongoing everyday ethical life. It is this real, messy and uncontrollable *agency* constitutive of the everyday state, rather than the idealised coherent singular abstracted state of (neo)liberal fantasies, that the idea of relational politics seeks to capture. By focusing on relational politics, *Power, Politics and the Emotions* draws attention to the way in which the state comes to be through the ongoing negotiation of subjective loss, which is at its heart, a process of constantly resisting hegemonic foreclosure around difference. There is always (potentially) resistant agency within the state. It is therefore through this focus on relational politics that I am asking a new set of feminist psychosocial questions around power/agency and subjectivity in the enactment of the state itself. My aim is to shift analytic attention away from 'big' politics conceptualised through ideas of institutional structures, social norms and ideologies to what Tess Lea thinks of as 'the normative state of *being* the state' where 'being the state is the self, a self-state which shapes desire and emotional investment, the visceral medium through which the myth of rational state enterprise is vivified' (Lea, 2012, pp. 116–117). From this point of view on relational politics the state is, after all, not that different from other sorts of everyday relations. To abandon it would be to abandon ourselves.

It should be clear by now that my approach should not be taken as straightforward uncomplicated support for the idea of the state, or as a call for a return to a universal, 'pre'-neoliberal and more socially democratic liberal state (as if that were possible anyway). Instead, my aim in *Power, Politics and the Emotions* is to explore as an empirical matter how the state might be done differently; indeed, to offer examples of instances where the state can already be seen to be done differently via an engagement with the losses its everyday orderings inevitably produce. The idea of relational politics taps into the potentially generative nature of engagements with loss and the political possibilities for containing loss's inevitability and redistributing its effects more equally.

Overview of the book

In Chapter 2 I situate the sort of analytic shifts required to think about the state in this more differentiated and less abstract way as enacted through a combination of material, social and affective relations. I frame this through a shift towards relationality where this is conceptualised via psychodynamically informed psychosocial analysis. In particular I focus on the ways in which psychoanalytic thinking poses a particular set of challenges to liberalism's singular logic by enabling an understanding that the state only *appears* as a coherent and pulled together institutional form through a constant process of *relational politics*. I outline how this pulling together is manifest in the temporarily stable institutional forms which make up the policy every day and the ways that these relations are performatively enacted via the day to day inter and intrasubjective interactions I think of as feeling work. As such it accords unconscious emotion a role in the material symbolic relations of the state. These institutional forms might be like the primary health care organisations and the national leadership college considered in the empirically based chapters (Chapters 3–7) in this book, or at higher levels of abstraction like the English National Health Service or the Department of Education and Skills.

The second part of *Power, Politics and the Emotions* 'The relational politics of governance' comprises the rest of the chapters in the book (Chapters 3 to 8). These chapters focus on the analysis and interpretation of empirical material which teases out how this relational politics works in practice. This material comes from two very different research studies. The first study considered in Chapters 3 and 4 was a lone enterprise conducted as part of a PhD project which, because of a second injection of studentship funding from the UK Economic and Social Research Council, spanned five years (2000–2005) (Hunter, 2005a). The second study was a one person sub-project conducted as part of a larger team based effort (Ahmed et al., 2006) commissioned by government, which spanned three years (2003–2006). The first study gave me the time and space needed to develop an expansive in-depth methodology which involved multiple layers of speaking, listening, reading and interpretation inspired by the feminist work of the Harvard Project on Women's Psychology and Girls' Development (Brown, 1998; Brown et al., 1991; Brown and Gilligan, 1992; Gilligan, 1994; Gilligan, Brown and Rogers, 1990; Mclean Taylor, Gilligan and Sullivan, 1996), developments in psychosocial methodologies (Hollway and Jefferson, 2000; Wengraf, 2001) and, in particular, those influenced by critical race and postcolonial theorising (Gunaratnam, 2003, 2004, 2012). Whilst the formal length of engagement on the second project was shorter than on the first, the principles informing data generation and interpretation were similar for both, especially in terms of the intensive and ongoing relationship to the range of participants, collaborators and institutional processes engaged with throughout the research process (the most sustained examination of these entanglements comes in Chapter 7).

The first study focused on the working lives of 15 governors sitting on the boards of regional level health and social care governing bodies responsible for the commissioning and delivery of primary health care in England (see Chapters 3 and 4). The aim of this project was to explore the negotiation of professional and social identifications of high level professional-managers working within the rapidly changing context of English health and social care at a time when issues of equality and diversity were taking on greater significance in that milieu. As such it aimed to look at the experience of governing in general as issues of diversity were being articulated more clearly within the mainstream practices and processes of governing. Its focus was therefore on a normatively enacted phenomenon within a politically, relatively conservative context such as the English health services. It involved observation of a range of management and executive meetings, documentary analysis and a total of 39 serial biographic narrative interviews with 15 board members working across three organisations. Interview participants included four white men, nine white women, one Indian man and one Indian woman, all of whom described themselves as British or English.[3]

The second study, considered in Chapters 5 to 7, focused on governance in the post compulsory learning context, and in particular in adult and community learning (ACL). It involved a similar range of meeting observation, documentary analysis and individual interviews. Interview participants in this study included similarly positioned senior level professional-managers. But, because ACL happens in such a diverse range of institutional settings, participants were located much more variously than in the health care study, from more formalised contexts like further education (FE) and higher education (HE) to the more informal community settings like evening classes, archives, libraries and museums, with some operating at national as well as regional level in quality assurance and other strategic bodies. This second study was focused on exploring the experiences of senior level Black and women staff specifically within the context of an explicit drive to reduce inequalities in institutional governance across post compulsory learning from within a framework of valuing diversity. As such its aims and objectives were already framed in terms of an explicit intention to explore the experiences of people with some sort of expressed commitment to resistant governmental practices in terms of their involvement in processing the diversity agenda, and from within an institutional context like ACL which prides itself on its counter hegemonic heritage. Individual participants totalled eleven, including five women identifying variously as mixed Chinese and British, Asian, Black/Black Caribbean, three men identifying as Asian, Black and mixed Muslim and British, two white English men and one white English woman. Reflecting this study's aims and objectives and the snowballing sampling strategy which proceeded via participants' connections to the largest network of Black practitioners and learners in the community sector at that time, participants in this study were linked by their explicit investment in diversity work. This is rather than as co-workers in day to day institutional contexts like many of the participants in the health care study.

Loss

The first two chapters in Part II of the book concentrate on the complicated relationship between the pervasive feelings of loss framing the institutional and individual unconscious in the context of neoliberalised shifts in the liberal governing order. In particular they focus on the supposed loss of historically normative white liberal paternalist power associated with the mainstreaming of equality via new managerialist institutional transformations. Resistance to such loss operates as a potential break to a straightforward neoliberal closure of the social, but also as a blocker to other forms of change and resistance to liberally enacted inequality. Chapter 3, 'Governing subjectivities: the politics of ontological detachment and relational connection', begins with the experience of the individual governing subject in the context of modernisation. It explores the basic 'constitutive melancholia' (Butler, 1997, p. 23) of governing subjectification which comes about through the white middle class heterosexual masculine subject's confrontation with the recognition of his positioning within power. Chapter 4, 'The circulation and distribution of bad feeling', continues to analyse the anxiety of this sort of confrontation with white masculine power within the shift to modernisation. This time it explores the way affect circulates to enact a modernised ostensibly more equal institutional space through the idea of affective networks (Hinshelwood, 1989). It is particularly interested in how anxieties become collectively owned and enacted to form the institutional topography; and the effects in terms of the continuing reproduction of hegemonic white masculine orderings.

Hope and renewal

Chapters 5, 6 and 7 shift the analysis to more explicitly prioritise the potential for resistance rather than foregrounding loss. They consider what resistance feels like within the apparent limits set by the sorts of neoliberalised governing contexts identified within Chapters 3 and 4, and how such resistance is maintained. They explore the space which remains for resistance in the context of the (neo)liberal state's explicit attempts to include marginality and difference through equality and diversity policy initiatives. Working from within this same melancholic framework as Chapters 3 and 4, these chapters engage with the ideas of diversity, equality and human rights as more than forms of governmental technology. They therefore begin from a starting point which takes seriously the claims that the turn to diversity *potentially* (rather than necessarily) circumscribes spaces for collective resistance because of its domestication of difference as individualised and sociohistorically decontextualised, which works to gloss over the difficulty, pain and loss of systemically reproduced inequality. However, they consider resistance from within a melancholic frame as ambivalent and multiple, challenging the idea of agency in straightforward terms of resistance/empowerment or radical/coopted.

Chapter 5, 'Resisting the happy governmentalities of diversity', focuses on the rise of a new cadre of diversity worker in the context of critiques around diversity's regulatory urge. The chapter asks questions about the sorts of professionals engaged in diversity work which challenge simplified analysis of these people as either coopted or resistant. In practice these professionals capitalise on the space opened up by the shift to diversity to enact the self *relationally* – as a retroactive opening-up to past history and future possibility. The chapter explores how such retroactioning brings the social outside inside of the institutional space – via family, friendship and community; resisting the individualising processes thought to be characteristic of diversity as a neoliberal governmentalising of the soul.

Chapters 6 and 7 follow on from this investigation into the sorts of relational positioning work which is a necessary precursor for resistance, to consider the nature of resistance itself within melancholic governing contexts. Chapter 6, 'Sustaining collective challenges to policy monoliths', presents an alternative to the heroic, direct and intentional forms of resistance usually associated with emotions like anger and resentment, which is more suitable to understanding contexts of perpetually (and potentially increasingly) circumscribed agency. The analysis bounces off the work of Sian Ngai (2005) to consider the role of 'ugly' feelings in the less heroically edifying smaller acts of resistance occurring through everyday relational politics.

Chapter 7, 'Equalities policy as a relational hinterland', follows up on the theme of resistance in melancholically circumscribed institutional space. This time it turns attention to formal policy processes, rethinking the role of documentary practice within the performance evaluation nexus. From a relational perspective policy can be thought of as a relational hinterland, a meeting point where cooperation across difference rather than a singular consensus is achieved. Viewed in this counterintuitive way policy can be a means to resist rather than create closure and certainty around policy ideals so valued within the (neo)liberal governing project. Policy documents operate funnel like, as a container for multiple investments in equalities and as the means to reprocess these and redistribute them in potentially surprising ways which challenge normative (neo)liberal policy orders. However, the chapter ends by exploring the ways in which the neoliberal ascendency of whiteness can be sustained through such redistributions.

The concluding chapter, Chapter 8, 'Conclusions: mobilising hopeful fictions through differentiated uncertainties', brings together the arguments of the other chapters to develop a more in-depth consideration of the cross cutting theme of hope. From a melancholic point of view, hopefulness is not 'blind'. It enacts a 'realistic' engagement with bad feeling and struggle, disappointment and failure in the present. On this basis the chapter rethinks ideas of governmental failure and neoliberal suicidal crisis as essential to governmental renewal. It does this as a starting point from which to think differently about governance in less hierarchically, more reparatively distributed terms.

Notes

1 The target of my argument in *Power, Politics and the Emotions* is the sort of Western liberal nation states produced through modernity and in particular the British one. This is because this is the state form that I know the most about and the state form out of which my empirical material derives. I am not looking to claim for the specificities of other state forms, nor to claim any special purchase that this analysis necessarily has over other state formations. Nevertheless it is worth recognising here that my feelings as to the relevance of the basic philosophical position on life/death dynamics which I present over the coming pages have a broader purchase than this specific case, since the issue of mortality spans epochs and territories (see Stevens, 1999). The sorts of questions to be answered, as I try to here, are: how do these dynamics play out, to whom or what do they attach, and what do they produce?

2 The adjectives 'English' and 'British' are closely related, but not synonymous. The latter is commonly used to refer to matters relating to the UK including the now devolved Northern Ireland, Scotland and Wales. It is more commonly associated with nineteenth-century British Imperial expansion. English describes the legal territorial formation which remains dominant within the UK. My usage in *Power, Politics and the Emotions* reflects this distinction.

3 The ethnic descriptions used throughout the discussion of data are described in participants' own terms. This commitment to following participants' self categorisation means that there are inconsistencies in the use of ethnic categorisations throughout the empirical chapters. These inconsistencies mean that where participants' logics are being traced, ideas of ethnicity are collapsed into and mingled with all manner of national, regional and raced categorisations. I comment on these inconsistencies only where the conflations relate to the specifics of my analysis. Retaining participants' self identifications throws into relief the contradictions within racialising processes, but it also tells us much about participants' meaning frames and identity investments within these contradictions. Where I am writing from my point of view I stick to the terminology 'racialised minority' to highlight the process of racialisation, or to 'Black and racialised minority' or sometimes 'Black and ethnic minority' to recognise the politically constructed nature of Blackness as inclusive of a range of other racialised markers. Whilst this terminology can be extended to include groups often referred to as 'white minorities', this sort of inclusive usage is contested. Because there are no participants in either study who position themselves explicitly in this way, and because I have yet to find a better way of highlighting the sort of politically inclusive experience of racialisation which most participants still find helpful in understanding their lives, I stick with these notions of Black racialised and minority ethnic/ethnic minority. On occasion I use the notion of 'minoritised' to encompass a broader range of unequally positioned subjectivities than only those of a racialised nature.

Chapter 2

Ordering differentiation: reconfiguring governance as relational politics

The problem of subjugation is not the same as the problem of ordering. At the present time we very often see, in the name of consensus, of liberation, of self-expression and all that, an entirely different sort of operation of power field, which is not strictly domination, but which is nevertheless not very attractive.

(Rabinow in Rabinow and Foucault, 1984, p. 379)

This chapter makes a theoretical intervention into debates on governance from a feminist psychosocial perspective. Its key claim is that the distribution of power and emotion are intimately connected in governance. Indeed, emotions are productive of power in the sense that they constitute part of the means by which the state comes to be, they are integral to its gendered and raced orderings and are in turn part of the means by which the state enacts gendered and raced power. They operate as connecting devices, bringing together multiple actors and objects into the reasonably temporarily coherent form we think of as the state. In the chapter I outline how the ideas of intersectionality, relationality and feeling work can, when taken together and connected to understandings of experience and subjectivity, enable an analysis of the everyday practices of policy making and governance which enact this state. I call these everyday practices the 'relational politics' of governance. I argue that it is because they enable us to keep ideas of emotion, experience and subjectivity in play that the idea of relational politics facilitates an understanding of these everyday practices as situated through, but not determined by, the social relations of power. This refusal to collapse experience and power and to think instead in terms of 'relational politics' between the individual and the social order is also crucial to understanding governance as an ethical practice, in the sense that it is always about the ongoing negotiations between ethics and politics. Thus, rather than mutually exclusive, politics and ethics are interdependent in governance.

The chapter offers a feminist psychosocial analysis of governance as a development of anti-rationalist approaches to understanding the modern state. The rise in such approaches drawing on a Foucauldian governmental frame has been an important influence on the shift to seeing the state as a process, fractured and dispersed across a range of sites such as economy, community and family, rather than singular and monolithic (Burchell, Gordon and Miller, 1991; Dean, 1999, 2010; Ferguson and Gupta, 2005; Miller and Rose, 2008; Rose, 1999). A related shift to discourse has not been without tensions. One danger is that the messier, more contradictory human dimensions to an analysis can get lost in an analytic focus on discursive strategies, mechanisms and techniques of power and, more ironically, in a focus on discursively constructed identities. This is because of the way in which Foucauldians' explicit resistance to the *a priori* existence of the thought, mind or subject which engendered it (Foucault, 1991) appears at the very least to downplay (if not reject entirely) the relevance of subjective experience and human relationships to an analysis of the state. This evacuation of the subject and subjectivity from view has tended to create top heavy programmatic analysis where the social can resemble a machine reforming and reconstituting everything it comes into contact with (Craib, 1998). Thus, any space to explore micro-practices, potentially so attractive within Foucauldian analysis, gets lost in a rush to claim the disciplinary power of history. Discursively constructed identities can appear as historical straightjackets from which there is little escape for living subjects. Ironically then, similar to the more positivistic and normative approaches they seek to critique, governmental approaches can serve to collapse, rather than illuminate, the agentic complexities of governance (Hoggett, 2000b; Stephenson and Papadopoulos, 2006a, 2006b).

In contrast a feminist psychosocial approach to analysing the state seeks to make space for more fully considering the human dynamics of the state; experience, agency, identity as they connect to subjectivity and emotion. But it does so in a way which retains the Foucauldian refusal to reduce them to individualised and internalised micro-practices, where individual action in the everyday context is not driven by sovereign consciousness. Instead micro-practices, action as a benefits officer, a welfare claimant or a social worker, for example, are seen as *relational practices* constituted through the daily interaction between client and benefits officer within the benefit office, or the engagement between social worker and foster parents, or looked after children, or with other workers within the context of the social services child protection teams like those considered in Gail Lewis's work discussed in the next section of this chapter. These are contextually and relationally driven in that they are enacted through human relationships. Drawing on a range of psychodynamic feminist material semiotic and critical race theory, a feminist psychosocial approach rethinks the relational as the space *in between* the individual subject and the social order. Indeed, the strength of these perspectives is that they reject the literal distinctions between the two.[1] In this chapter I elaborate this theoretical synthesis as a means to claiming the relational as crucial to understanding the meso level of governance through which the state materialises as a formation of dynamic and shifting yet ordered set of practices. Relationality, from this perspective, rethinks the terms of the micro-macro debate so apparently intransigent within scholarship on the state by refocusing our attention where the *action* is; action which brings personal histories, biographies, structural tendencies and cultural orderings into one frame. Crucially, this action is at the day to day level which is not thought out and motivated in the rationalist sense. It occurs at the affective emotional level. From this I am suggesting that there is a specific aspect of politics to be taken account of in our discussions of the state; the 'relational politics' of policy making. By relational politics I am referring to the dynamic emotional process through which social categories such as gender and ethnicity get *lived out*, resignified and resisted in the everyday policy process and the ways they act back to reconfigure that very process itself. Thus I am claiming that despite its 'under the surface' 'hidden' character, relational politics is a powerful driver for the shape of the state, the distribution of power and inequality in 'it' and through 'it'.

In the chapter I advance this argument in three stages. First I explore how feminist intersectional analysis allows us to theorise a space for complex experience which sits at the meso level between the individual and the collective. I then explore how psychodynamic ideas of a dynamic unconscious can be used to understand this negotiation in terms of the emotional process of managing difference and complexity; connecting power, difference and emotion at the most intimate level. I then use these ideas to outline how 'feeling work' operates through the dynamic interdependent social and cultural struggles for differentiation, distributing feeling one way or another; thus, enacting the social order(s). Finally, I explain how this feeling work is crucial to maintaining social ordering as an ethical process which is about enacting the socially and culturally good and bad.

My aim here is not to displace or to claim 'better' knowledge about what governance is than more traditionally explanatory accounts. I suspect that this sort of work will always have a valuable place in tracing patterns and orders which form at a distance from everyday experience. Instead, it is to suggest that we need to make sure we are also asking a set of different questions about governance and how these orders happen at the level of everyday practices, to explore opportunities for challenge and change at this level. This is what I think a consideration of relational politics offers. It is what is traced in the empirical chapters which follow in the second part of the book.

Governing through differentiation and complexity

The concept of intersectionality developed out of feminist concerns to understand inequalities as multiple and overlapping. Its analytical focus is the lived complexity of these multiple inequalities (Brah and Phoenix, 2004; Cho, Crenshaw and McCall, 2013; Choo and Marx Ferree, 2010; Crenshaw, 1989; Davis, 2008; Grabham et al., 2009; Hill Collins, 2000; Lutz, Herrera Vivar and Supik, 2011; Puar, 2011; Staunaes, 2003; Valentine, 2007) . It is often viewed as overcoming the apparent incompatibilities between Black feminist thought and feminist poststructural theorising by bringing together the former's concerns over interlocking structures of power and inequality and the latter's concern with subjectivities and social processes (Alexander-Floyd, 2012; Davis, 2008; Staunaes, 2003). On the one hand, it has much to offer in terms of investigating how inequalities are produced on the institutional scale, through structures, process and techniques of governance. On the other hand, intersectionality has been well used in investigations of how 'social identities are formed as the congealed effects of power's workings rather than autonomous groups or identities' (Grabham, Herman et al., 2009a, p. 3; Lewis, 2007). So although some versions of intersectional theorising are critiqued for their additive tendencies, the primary aim of other versions is to *connect* structure and agency through attention to lived experience (Mohanty, 2013; Tomlinson, 2013). From this latter perspective intersectionality is concerned with:

> the complex, irreducible, varied, and variable effects which ensue when multiple axes of differentiation – economic, political, cultural, psychic, subjective and experiential – intersect in historically specific contexts. The concept emphasizes that different *dimensions* of social life cannot be separated out into discrete and pure strands.
>
> (Brah and Phoenix, 2004, p. 76; emphasis added)

Such an intersectional approach is less about identifying the level and nature of difference or inequality engendered by compound social divisions; it is more about tracing their dynamic and competing interconnections across multiple dimensions of social life. It is the potential for intersectionality to think through complex agencies along with structural coherence which makes it useful when analysing how governance works as an organising principle (Anthias, 2013; Walby, Armstrong and Strid, 2012).

Gail Lewis's (2000) research on the entry of Black and Asian women into the occupation of social work is an important exception to the dearth of work on governance which adopts an intersectional approach. Her aim is to capture the lived complexities of these workers' experiences in social work as a specific moment in English racial formation where racialised populations of colour are reconstituted through work from unwelcome illegitimate 'immigrants' to excluded illegitimate 'ethnic minorities'. Using an intersectional analysis allows her to ask two key sets of questions which tend to elide other approaches to contemporary governance and the policy process. The first set of questions relate to how a 'simultaneity of discourse' as women, ethnic minorities and social workers works to produce multiple often *competing* and *contradictory* positionings within a discursive field, such as social work. For Lewis's social workers in Children's Services these contradictions worked through simultaneous positioning as women and mothers, as Black people connected to the Black community and as social workers committed to professional ideals and practices. Therefore, intersectionality provides the conceptual tools with which to begin to tackle contradiction and ambiguity in the lived experiences of governing. The second set of questions relate to how these contradictions enable resistance to the normative governmentalities of such a field.

Lewis's approach analyses how categories of race, gender and profession combine to constitute 'ethnic minorities' as a governable population and the targets of contemporary racialised governmentality. She combines analysis of macro-level legislative intervention (in the form of the UK *Hansard* record of public debates, policy documents at the national and local levels) with micro-level analysis of interviews conducted with Black women social workers in the context of English local authority child protection contexts. Through this micro analysis of interview narratives she traces how these workers claim multiple intersecting *experiences* as a valid place from which to speak within their working contexts. Drawing on feminist theorists such as Joan Scott, Chandra Talpade Mohanty and Adrienne Rich, Lewis conceptualises experience as an anchor for social, cultural, economic and political relations. It is multiple and embedded in 'webs of social and cultural relations which are themselves organized around axes of power and which act to constitute subjectivities and identities' (Lewis, 2000, p. 173).

For Lewis's interviewees this multiple experience was produced through their contradictory positioning across numerous axes of differentiation and power, as Black and Asian, women, social work professionals. As Black and Asian people they had experiences of racist oppression within the broader society; as women they had experiences of sexist oppression within the wider society, but also within the Black community as mothers, wives and daughters; they had professional experiences as social workers within social work, with commitments to enforcing professional practices 'in the interests of the child'. It is these multiple and complex experiences that inform their perspective as workers within the contexts of controversial professional debates around 'same race' adoption within child protection. For many of Lewis's participants these commitments created dilemmas between commitments, for example, where a decision to maintain the placement of a Black or mixed race child already brought up within a particular white familial context conflicted with broader Black community commitment to the logic of 'same race' adoptive placement designed to protect Black children from life in a racist society by placing them within Black families. For these workers positive experiences of Black community, along with the realistic appraisal of the generational and gendered problems within those communities, as well as broader understandings of a racist and sexist society *together* bring specific tools to the social work encounter with which to negotiate the complexities of enacting professional commitments to the needs of the child. This is at the same time as producing costs for the worker as a Black professional sometimes apparently positioned against community commitments which may be more obviously enacted through the practice of same race adoption. Thus, it is this *particular positioning* as 'black woman social worker' which provides an intuitive 'connective tissue' (Lewis, 2000, p. 197) binding these workers to various differently positioned others: Black men, white women and other Black women workers, but also to their variously positioned clients.

For Lewis this multiple intersecting experience provides a position from which to resist the over-determining aspects of racialised governmentality. These Black and Asian women workers' multiple intersecting identifications disrupt unitary notions of subjectivity. On the one hand they are positioned as simultaneously *ambiguously dominant* within the discursive field of social work and the racialised gendered state and in particular in their relations to clients, largely Black and white women. On the other hand they are *organisationally subordinate* as Black women workers within their units (Lewis, 2000, p. 201). So whilst the category of social worker forms the basis of these workers' inclusion in governance practices and the racialised governmentality of clients, other workers and themselves, its lived articulation with the categories of race and gender enables them to act back against established institutional formations to resist racialised governmentality. This acting back is present in the ways these Black women professionals resisted the automatic relocation of a range of looked after children into normative two parent 'family formations'; refusing to accept the idealisation of heteronormative family forms because of their experiences of growing up within communities which valued broader extended family forms as much as the normative ideal. Thus, the refusal of normative practices around looked after children happened *at the same time* as resisting Black professional discourses around same race adoption demonstrates lived complexities. Therefore, what it means to be a Black woman social worker is not decided prior to its articulation in raced, gendered and professional discourses. It gets lived out through their *shifting* multiple configurations in professional practices. These 'complex acts of becoming', as Lewis sees them, can constitute a form of resistance in that their ongoing (re)configurations in relation to other categories of worker, including other Black women, Black men, white women or clients, mean that these workers are not straightforwardly or ever once and for all recruited in support of a particular form of racialised governmentality. Though their resistances are in the vein of cautious, modest, post-heroic politics (Larner, 2006), they nevertheless serve to destabilise the Manichean 'either or' Black/white oppositions of contemporary racial formations which, despite all their claims to 'superdiversity' and multicultural complexity (Vertovec, 2007), continue to idealise whiteness over Blackness.

This difference between workers' ambiguous dominance at the categorical level as Black women with Black and white (often women) service users and their less obviously ambiguous subordination at the organisational level as workers is important. This is because it enables Lewis to avoid one of the most common drawbacks in intersectional analysis which can tend to flatten social relations and organisational dynamics (Cooper, 2009) so that categorically subordinate subject positionings are automatically imagined to lead to organisational disempowerment. Instead she works with an analytical distinction between discursive positioning and *lived organisational relations*. Her emphasis on gendered, raced and professional experience as the intuitive connective tissue for governance does not mean other structural and cultural dimensions of social life are ignored. Instead, they are analysed as lived within a particular (organisational) setting, or 'relational site' (Lewis, 2013). The experiential and intuitive dimension is interposed between the individual actor's self perception and the material and cultural categories through which they recognise themselves socially; as part of a group. It is therefore crucial to maintaining the distinction between these ontological and categorical dimensions, holding them together in a loose rather than determined relationship.

Relationality

Fiona Williams (2000) creates a similar interposition to Lewis in her three way ontological-relational-categorical distinction. Developing Williams' work, I first used this three part distinction to understand the ways in which the discursive construction of subject positions is resisted/reproduced/resignified (Hunter, 2003, pp. 327–329). Ontological identity signifies the process of creating coherence from personal experience; its analytical focus is individual uniqueness. Categorical identity refers to the collective level of subject formation, identification of oneself (or others) as belonging to the same social category or subject position, as a woman, for example. Both are different to subjectivity which spans unconscious interiority as well as conscious experience. It is this unconscious-conscious space of relational 'betweeness' (Bondi, 2005) that I am interested in capturing when I think about the relational.

Psychoanalytic perspectives have been viewed with suspicion by some post-structuralists. Following on from a more general social science scepticism as to the biologically and psychologically reductive nature of psychoanalysis (see Craib, 1998 and also Clarke, Hoggett and Thompson, 2006; Pilgrim, 1992a, 1992b), materially inclined poststructural scepticism flows from suspicions around neo-liberal governmental moves to capitalise on humanist ideas of the sovereign individual (Clough, 2007, 2009; Deleuze and Guattari, 2004; Latour, 2005b; Massumi, 2002; Parker, 1992; Rose, 1998). However, I along with a growing number of psychosocial theorists (Clarke, 2003a, 2003b; Crociani-Windland and Hoggett, 2012; Frosh, 1987; Gomez, 1996; Henriques et al., 1998; Hollway and Jefferson, 1996; Redman, 2009; Stenner, 2007, 2008; Stenner and Taylor, 2008; Walkerdine, 2006, 2010) would argue that drawing on psychoanalytic object relations theories (Gomez, 1996; Klein, 1986 [1935]; Winnicott, 1975 [1958]) can help us to think about experience as 'dispersed, continuous and exceeding representation', as 'exceeding discourse' (Stephenson and Papadopoulos, 2006b, p. 22; Wetherell, 2013a, 2013b) but without collapsing back onto a version of the singular originary subject.[2] From this set of psychosocial ideas I want to emphasise the importance of the unconscious as a means of *organising the lived relations of difference and complexity in daily interactions*.[3] The psychoanalyst Donald Winnicott thinks of the relational unconscious as a third or 'transitional space' (Winnicott, 2005 [1971]) between the self and the world of difference and complexity. It is neither wholly internal nor wholly external, but exists in between, only in and through relationships (whether these be material, social or cultural). Premised on the view that all objects external to the self present the promise of connection and the threat of difference, this unconscious is the ongoing and dynamic inter and intrasubjective process which enables meaningful negotiation between the myriad of promising good and threatening bad objects which populate the external world of daily interaction. The coexistence of good and bad within the self (and within the Other) creates internal ambivalence. This is sometimes turbulent and experienced as emotional crisis which manifests in the polarisation of good and bad in perception. More often, however, this dynamic goes unnoticed as good and bad are integrated; worked out in everyday practices. Thus, the transition which occurs through this unconscious dynamic is from the disordered internal experience of multiplicity, to the *appearance* of simplified, less complex and ambiguous externalised practices and knowledges which form the basis of our agency.

The psychoanalytic claim that unconscious fantasy structures all experience of reality, penetrating and giving meaning to 'actual events' in the external world and vice versa, means that anxiety and the emotions, love, hate, envy, for example, are considered to form a central (if unrecognised and not straightforwardly articulated) element of everyday social interaction. From this perspective, the very ability to bring things into thought, to symbolise and imagine, is predicated on the ability to feel; feeling and cognition are *interdependent*. [4] On the other hand, however, this idea of the unconscious also means that some of our own behaviours and motivations as well as those of others will be 'beyond reason', apparently having a 'life of their own' (Roseneil, 2006). This is the paradoxical nature of reality. Our feelings are indispensable for understanding, but simultaneously constitute its limits. Therefore, there is not now and never can be in the future an all knowing rational subject.

Following these psychoanalytic observations the notion of relational identity refers to unconscious subjectivity as constituted through close relationships with others (for example, as a mother, friend or colleague) and through which we gain a particular sense of belonging. In this way it brings the biographical, social, situational and structural into the same frame. It represents the point at which contradictions between being positioned categorically in one way, perhaps subordinately as a woman, and feeling ontologically empowered as a unique individual successful in her own working and personal contexts are negotiated, so the point at which the cognitive, known, understood structural relations and the associated, more obscure emotional resistances are negotiated. Motivation and agency are theorised through the complex interplay between these structural tendencies and biographical factors. This notion of relational identity (Hunter, 2003, pp. 338–339) therefore shifts the analytic focus away from the recognition of sameness and difference considered in categorical and ontological formations to connection and differentiation as the principles of social relationships. Exploring relational identities involves examining the ways in which actors construct relationships and erect boundaries 'within' and between themselves and a variety of others. It focuses on internal and external conflicts 'within' and between actors over time, and how patterns or ruptures in these inform decision making and less strategic social action.[5]

For the purposes of thinking about relational politics rather than relational identification I am suggesting that this notion of the relational can be applied more broadly to shift our analytic focus in governance. This is a shift away from identifying sets of coherent figures and practices and categories driving change and stability to tracing the *intersections;* the dynamic constitutive connections, the relations of interdependence between entities in governance networks including the links, ruptures and disjunctures between actual and imagined practices and individual or collective subjects (see also Pedwell, 2008). It also places the experiential dimension as core to the interactive distribution and allocation of social power in governance. But this relational perspective extends the experiential in two ways: first, in explicitly dynamic terms, as a form of intersectional and interactive, co-produced doing (Staunaes, 2003). Experience is a multiple interactive achievement, not an *a priori* state. Second, it goes 'beyond' the view that either mutual recognition or functional efficiency is the means to connect governance networks. Instead, a relational perspective suggests that experience constitutes a 'normative cognitive framework' that empowers actors and gives direction to their joint and separate actions (Torfing, in Carver et al., 2002, p. 56). Following my claims about relationality, this normative cognitive framework is as much about less well articulated feeling as it is about knowledge, it is not static, but built up over time and through the close relations by which we learn about 'proper' 'appropriate' ways to engage with one another as practitioners, users, friends, etc. Thus, it is rooted in unconscious practice as much as considered action (Gould, 2009, 2012).

Feeling work

It is through its connection between feeling and judgements that object relations is suggestive of the broader *psychosocial* connections between politics and the emotions; how fantasy fuels politics and politics fuels fantasy. Feelings and, especially, our anxieties about who we are frame our judgements of value and our investments in ideas such as equality, or a social category such as race or a set of ideas and practices, such as an institution like the National Health Service (NHS). Thus, this 'feeling work' (Gunaratnam and Lewis, 2001) is relational, the means by which the individual and the social are connected (Harding and Pribram, 2002, p. 424) and culture is enacted. Following Sara Ahmed (2004, pp. 44–47), one way of conceptualising this feeling work in more dynamic terms is as an affective economy where emotion works as a form of capital in the Marxist sense, gathering value as a function of its circulation. Affect is understood as the means by which this circulation occurs. Therefore, affect, such as hate, does not reside in an object or a sign such as race or the NHS, but is produced as *an effect* of the circulation between objects (like particular bodies) and signs (like the idea of whiteness or Blackness). Signs increase in affective value as an effect of the movement between signs: the more signs circulate, the more affective they become. Affect produces more affect. Thus, supportive attachment to the sign of the NHS, for example, we might say love, is an effect of its movement across objects, professions such as nurses, doctors, physiotherapists, users (as mother, child, grandparent, for example), politicians, civil servants, pharmaceutical companies, etc. Attachments intensify through love's circulation, generating their own proximities whereby this range of subjects are brought into relationship through their attachment to the symbol of the NHS. Thus, the various attachments to an idea generate it as an object, creating its topography. In this way then the emotions are productive of social relations as well as produced through them. Therefore, the emotions do not inhabit anybody or any one thing, 'the subject' is just one nodal point in the economy, rather than an origin or destination. This means that emotions are not cut off from the body, but nor are they reducible to it. They constitute a connective medium between bodies (see also Bondi, 2005, p. 442).

As a connective medium the emotions do the work of alignment, and orientation, they create proximities and distances between subjects (Fortier, 2008). They circulate between bodies, but also get stuck to certain bodies, the 'angry Black man', the 'caring white woman'. As such, they are integral to creating hierarchies of power. They *bind* people within a social order, but at the same time because they also *move* people, they expose the fragility of these orders, highlighting their shifting dynamic nature. If we look at the emotions in this way then feeling work can be viewed as ongoing, continuous, *co-ordinating, cohering, ordering* activity. Therefore, as well as feelings circulating within governance networks, they are *constitutive* of those very networks. It is the erasure of this feeling work as part of the processes of governing which means that feelings become fetishes – as though they reside within an object, rather than connecting multiple objects through governance practices. This is not to say that feelings are not taken on and taken in by subjects in imperceptible ways. But, it is to recognise that any internalisation is only possible *because* of its enactment through material-social relations. Therefore, feeling work is a way of thinking about affect and emotion together, where affect is the more amorphous moving about in the interstices between subject-objects which is then enacted subjectively appearing *as though* this is something owned only by the subject.

In this way *Power, Politics and the Emotions* works against the dualist impulse to view affect, feeling or emotion as different *in kind*.[6] The notion of the relational dimension encompasses affect, feeling and emotion all as part of the irrational, unconscious and pre-discursive. However, it does recognise a difference in quality in terms of the level of connection and articulation between the feeling and its object, or target. In so far as there are differences between affect and emotion they come down to differences in the level of discursive anchoring for feelings (Wetherell, 2013a, 2013b). The notion of affect enables us to think about the less obviously articulated feelings. This is important for the analysis in *Power, Politics and the Emotions* because one of the key points of interest is the repressive resistance to articulating the relation between feeling and its object within contemporary governance. The notion of affect provides a way of thinking about these weaker points of emotional articulation, which form the focus for much of the book, what Sianne Ngai (2005) calls 'ugly feelings', like anxiety, concern, worry (Chapters 3 and 4 especially), patience, impatience (Chapter 6) and disappointment (Chapter 8).

Melanie Klein's work on defence mechanisms lends itself to exploring the complex dynamics of internalisation/externalisation through the sort of more radical historicisation of feeling developed in other feminist cultural approaches like Ahmed's work (Flax, 2004; Hoggett, 2000a; Mama, 1995; Menzies Lyth, 1960; Rustin, 1991). The basic concepts of splitting, projection and introjection refer to the unconscious mechanisms through which boundaries are constructed between self and other in order to resist the disintegration threatened by external social difference and multiplicity. These concepts can be used as *heuristic devices* to understand the ongoing process of differentiation and connection through which ideas of difference and sameness are constructed and equality and inequality are often articulated. Klein's view of separation and difference experienced as a form of violent attack means that individual prejudices, social exclusion and institutional discriminations can be understood as 'rational' responses to the threats posed by difference. It also highlights the dangers of idealisation and overinvestment as potentially producing the annihilation of the other and/or the self as manifest in the reification of difference. Returning to the example of racial formation introduced earlier through Lewis's work, we can see how such splitting processes characterise the 'repressive tolerance' underpinning the Manichean construction of white self and Black other so characteristic of current English multiculturalism, whereby the dominant white self by turns excludes, annihilates (projection) or manically over-identifies with (introjection) the racialised other (Cheng, 2000; Clarke, 2003b; Rustin, 1991).

Klein's later work (1986 [1952]) on the concept of projective identification not only explains how illusion fuels discrimination, but how illusion *produces* discrimination as a form of external 'reality'. It provides a way of thinking about how the introjection of the good and projection of the bad persists into our everyday lives as a form of *intersubjective communication* where we rid unpalatable parts of the self '*into*', rather than *onto*, the other (Clarke, 2001; Walkerdine, Lucey and Melody, 2001). Frantz Fanon's (1986) work provides one such powerful analysis of how this operates in relation to racism, where minoritised subjects are forced to see and *experience* themselves through a dominant white gaze, and thus introject feelings of hatred towards Blackness and the Black body, a process he refers to as the '*epidermalisation* of inferiority'. In this way psychoanalytic thinking provides a 'powerful vocabulary for addressing that component of racial identification that is imaginatively supported' (Cheng, 2000, p. 28), but also taken into the body and practically experienced. Thus, overall object relations is not useful for diagnosis, nor universal analysis of psychological or familial development, nor even only for the way its later incarnations view meaning as multiply contested. Rather, it is useful for the way that it can elucidate 'private' desires as (materially) *enmeshed* in social relations, constituted through and constitutive of them (see also Flax, 1990). It reminds us of the specificity of human subjectivity relationally enacted through material and social practices and processes.

Lynne Layton (2008, pp. 66–68) claims that social processes such as gendering and racialisation with their constructions of 'proper' masculinities, femininities, whitenesses and Blacknesses are at the very heart of subjectivity and subjective trauma, not accidental additions. This is because our interrelations and depend-encies are, from the very start, *lived through* the normative hierarchical cultural discourses of classism, racism, sexism and heterosexism that structure recognition through the idealisation of certain subject positions. This idealisation is achieved by splitting off human capacities such as vulnerability, assertion, connection and dependence, associating culturally desirable attributes with the dominant and these more devalued capacities with the subordinate. This is what Anne Cheng means when she insists that the 'politics of race has always spoken in the language of psychology' (2000, p. 28). For Layton this means that the subject is defined through the unceasing conflict between processes maintaining the splits and those resisting them. 'Normative unconscious processes' refer to the pull for sub-jects to repeat those affective/behaviour/cognition patterns that uphold the very social norms that cause psychic distress in the first place. 'Repetition compulsions' are the place where struggles between these coercive normative unconscious processes and counter-normative unconscious processes are enacted.

This sort of approach means that emotions such as the notion of anger, for example, are experienced through the dynamics of social difference. It helps elaborate Ahmed's observations about the stickiness of the emotions already con-stituted through normative unconscious processes. Taking the example of anger: 'the angriness of oppressed groups could easily be read as "too emotional" – and in the case of feminism typically feminine' precisely because these groups are already constructed as the locus for emotionality (Holmes, 2004, pp. 223–224). Thus, the meaning and legitimacy of anger gets read through gendered construc-tions, reinforcing gendered hierarchies where women's emotionality constitutes a sign of weakness. Anger binds people within an already established gendered order, within which they are normatively invested from the outset.

On the other hand, women's anger can also subvert gendered patterns of domination to enact new relations. Following Audre Lorde (1984), Yasmin Gunaratnam and Gail Lewis (2001) explore how expressions of anger can propel action for change. Both white and Black women experience anger because of racialised oppressions, but these experiences are different because of their respec-tive positioning, indeed processes of racialisation and gendering can produce anger and division between Black and white women. But this anger between Black and white women can also become 'an emotion of ownership, responsibil-ity and transformation rather than one of denial and expulsion' (Gunaratnam and Lewis 2001, p. 15). Rather than bad feeling being emptied unprocessed from white to Black women and vice versa, creating crushing paralysis in the face of the guilt and pain produced through racism, white women's ownership of their own anger at racism and what it does to themselves and others can enable them to discriminate between Black anger and Black hatred. The expression of anger within the context of a relationship can constitute a 'corrective surgery' for violating histories of racialisation and racism (Hunter, 2010).[7] Crucially, whether anger brings about subversive shifts in power relations depends on the ways in which it gets taken up, by whom and at what point. Thus, feeling work is not an individual act, but an act of intersubjective achievement, which is lived through and reconstructs the intersection between multiple dynamics of difference to enact the topography of an institutional space, like the contours of the primary care organisation discussed in Chapter 4, or the collective forms of resistance played out by the diversity workers in Chapter 6.

Ethically enacting multiplicity

In this chapter I am claiming that understanding feeling work is crucial to fulfilling the promise of a broader performative turn in the social sciences as a turn which can maintain rather than collapse the necessary hiatus between ethics and politics. It views the performative frame *as* ethical, refusing to forget the ethical dimensions to the processes of social ordering. This is because it is feeling work which goes on 'in between' the worlds of ethics and politics, connecting, but simultaneously holding them apart. This may appear to fly in the face of much critical social and political analysis which looks to close the gap between ethics and politics, analysing the sureties of categorical group politics as preventing the recognition of complex ethics of experience. However, inspired by object relations, critical feminist and psychoanalytic approaches to the emotions and affect outlined above I am claiming that this hiatus is not necessarily a problem to be overcome, but a matter of existence which means that there will always be a tension between subject-object, individual-group, agency-structure; a tension which cannot be negotiated away. Following this line of argument I want to suggest that it is this feeling work, the struggles to negotiate between individual and group, which constitutes the ethical 'moment' in governance.

This final component of my argument turns on the important distinction between multiplicity and pluralism that is implied, but not explicitly drawn out in the theories of emotion and affect considered above. Whilst pluralism has many ways of conceptualising subjective multiplicity, it continues to imply that only one object can ever exist at once. In perspectivalism, for example, there are numerous 'mutually exclusive perspectives, discrete, existing side by side, in a transparent space, whilst in the centre the object of the many gazes and glances remains singular, intangible, untouched' (Mol, 1999, p. 76). Constructionism's historical contingency works on the premise that numerous alternative realities may have been possible, but now they are gone. In contrast, from the perspective of multiplicity it is *objects* as well as subjects which are multiple.

From this point of view subjects and objects are not things in themselves, but more fluid temporary effects of multiple relations, more like a network of relations. *All things* (including, for example, social structures, people, ideas, body parts, books, door handles) only exist in terms of their attachments, which means that *all* realities, whether they are material or social, are *performed* simultaneously and in continuous process, *through* their multiple relations. The more attachments things have, the more and the better they exist (Latour, 2005b). Thus, they come into being together through multiple network relations. Annemarie Mol thinks of this process of network creation as 'enactment', a process of attuning to, interacting with and shaping objects/structures, bringing them into being, through varied and various practices (Mol, 2002, p. xii) which include, but are not confined to, language. Network realities are always here and there, present and future. We can therefore think of them in terms of projections in the psychodynamic sense in that they are always fantasmic at the same time as materially experienced.

From this network perspective, all networks exist within other networks. This means that it may be better to think in terms of subject-objects as, whilst any one object is inevitably at the margin of one or more networks, they will also be central to another(s). Subject-objects are always *partially* but multiply *connected* (Haraway, 1991; Law, 2004; Strathern, 1991). Because of this, actors' identities are partly defined through their relationship to one network whilst forged in or even forging another (Singleton, 1996). We can see this in Lewis's work above with Black women social workers; marginal to professional networks, but central to users' experiences of the social services network. Following this line of argument as to the multiple, but partial connectedness of subjects, the decision-making subject so valued in liberal democratic politics is not sovereign, it is in 'fact':

> *rendered* singular – turned into a specific location [for decision]. But at the same time it is distributed across time and space into future bodies, future conversations, and into past points of choice or procedure. There is, as it were, continual slippage between presence and absence .... The subject is both centred and decentred. And the possibility of a centred, informed, consenting subject *depends* upon this slippage. It is constituted and made possible by virtue of the fact that decisions have been or will be taken elsewhere, and that these are inserted within, or produce different logics.
>
> (Dugdale, 1999, p. 130; emphasis added)

Thus, the view of politics as a practical performative activity which brings things (including the decision-making subject) into being through the various practices by which relations are made is dependent on seeing the world as multiple. Decisions, then, are distributed through participants within networks, they are practical collective enactments.

However, as I argued above, the emotions as theorised in object relations draw our attention to 'internal' unconscious multiplicity, 'externalised' in a more unified, simplified and cognitively known form. From this perspective the emotions enable us to conceive of multiplicity which appears representationally as objective singularity. My argument is that it is on this basis that we can understand the emotions as enabling the simplifications *apparently* required for political decision making in contexts of multiplicity. Thus, they constitute an essential component of the process of enactment. The feeling work I describe above is the work which brings the illusion of a continuous singular reality into being; it is what drives the congealing and solidifying of experience. But, bringing these two lines of argument together (the feminist material semiotic and the psychodynamic) means that we can understand this ordering as not only cognitive, but as ethical too; a process of creating 'good' and 'bad' orders.

Making politics multiple

This logic of multiplicity also implies that it is the 'outcomes' as well as the inputs of politics which are multiple. The partial, but multiply connected nature of subject-objects means that politics is actually about the negotiation of multiple interconnected options, it is actually about the continuous *oscillation* between singularity and multiplicity (Dugdale, 1999). It is this process of oscillation between emotional multiplicity and cognitive simplification/singularity, between ethics and politics, which I analyse in terms of relational politics.

Politics then is *ontological* (Mol, 1999, 2002; see also Cussins, 1996) in the sense that it is not about the sort of singular, completed and closed decisions imagined in more mainstream policy-making literature, but it continually creates difference and different conditions of possibility. Decisions constitute *multiple* actions, a form of practice which brings about difference in the world. The point is not that the moment of action dissolves the multiplicity that produces it as the notion of decision implies; it only *hides* it, producing the illusion of singularity required in decisions conceived of in either/or terms.

This multiple nature of reality means that the good, such as equality, is also inevitably multiple, always open and contestable (Mol, 2002, p. 177). This in turn means that the aims, objectives and practices of politics also shift *away from* consensus to cooperation, coalition, connection, maintaining difference. Donna Haraway (1997, p. 268) likens this sort of politics to a game of 'cat's cradle' because it is about making patterns and knots, rather than amassing allies and feats of strength. In this game one person can build up a larger repertoire of string figures on a single pair of hands, but the figures can be passed back and forth between several players, all adding new moves, building ever more complex patterns. As such cat's cradle is the product of collective work of interdependent subjects, with no one move repeatable and no one person able to make patterns alone. The goal is not to win, but to create new, more interesting, more adequate patterns, which can contain what will always be contested aims.

This cat's cradle politics should not be confused with politics thought of only as a technical matter of reaching a benignly negotiated compromise between different interests. Nor as endlessly contingent, 'anything goes'. Relations and practices are always more or less power saturated. But the cat's cradle relies on a more open-ended and contestable view of power which, whilst ordered, and often apparently strongly or hegemonically so, can be broken precisely because such *orderings* are always temporary. Domination, according to John Law, is often *not* a system effect, the consequence of a single coherent order, quite the contrary.

> It is a result of non-coherence. Of elements of structuring, ordering, that only partially hang together. Of relations of subordination that are relatively invulnerable precisely because they are not tightly connected. Invulnerable because when one is undone the others are not pulled down with it.
>
> (Law, 2008, p. 641)

Thus, the continually enacted nature of 'reality' does not mean that there is no durability to social relations. Susan Leigh Star (1991) uses the example of the use of red as the colour which denotes 'stop' for traffic lights as a choice which, whilst arbitrary in the first instance, has become such a widespread convention, with such a range of investments and links to other infrastructures and symbol systems, that it is functionally almost irreversible. Systems of social categorisation can be viewed in a similar way, as arbitrary, but supported by such vast and varied discursive-material systems of practices and meanings that they endure despite their arbitrary nature. 'Power is about whose metaphor brings worlds together and what holds them there' (Star, 1991, p. 52).

Conclusions

This process of simplification, this enactment of difference, constitutes the ethical moment which characterises the impossible move from the ethical to the political. The argument I am making here relies on the view that there is *a necessary and unavoidable hiatus* between ethics and politics which means that not all forms of agency constitute politics and resistance. My use of the term 'relational politics' is precisely not to collapse this, it is to recognise a particular aspect of politics which is to do with subjectivity, identification and recognition. It highlights what is political about intersubjective emotional dynamics. Therefore the gap between ethics and politics is the place of political re-examination. Keeping this space in play in our understandings of governance is crucial to resisting the tribal us and them of traditional liberal politics.

What I am interested in highlighting is the emotional dimension to this process of enactment, thinking of it relationally in the sense that I have been advocating so far in this chapter, understanding how the emotions block certain practices and enable others; in short how they enable different versions of reality to be performed. The emotions are what hold multiple identifications together in one way or another as an identity. So the emotions make politics possible because they enable the simplification of multiplicity, but they do not attempt to collapse one into the other as in consensus, they enable coalition.

It is in the relational space that politics must remain as multiple as possible, precisely in order not to collapse notions of the 'good' prematurely. Refusing to reduce this hiatus ensures politics is not reducible to a rational moral calculus, but that it is understood as enacted through power and value laden material, discursive psychic relations, which enact in their turn multiple, partially connected and interdependent goods. State making is therefore an ethical practice in as much as it is a cultural and material one. Nothing within the state is ever only technical or ever only sociocultural, it is always relational in that it materialises at the negotiation of ethics and politics, by subjects in their worlds.

Notes

1 As I argue later in the chapter this does not prevent analytic distinction.
2 *Power, Politics and the Emotions* takes the view that there can be a rapprochement between the humanist inclinations of psychoanalysis and the more poststructural materialist perspectives of affect theory through the notion of the object. From both perspectives objects are central to thought and action, but complex and ambiguous in nature. This complexity is related to their relational nature, whereby all objects are relationally enacted, but are at the same time relationally enacting other objects. Therefore all objects are in fact subject-objects, both the product of and produced through relational practices. The singularity of any one object, like the state or the unconscious, is therefore the outcome of multiple practices which render it coherent and stable (for a time) rather than a property that inheres in it *sui generis*. Objects as multiple, intersectional, do the work of connecting the material, psychological, social and cultural. Therefore, as I explore further below, they are interesting as connectors and coordinators rather than as sources of agency in the traditional sense of cause and effect.
3 As a form of multiply enacted object in the terms I use in the final section on enacting multiplicity.
4 As I go on to explore below this leads me down a very different route to some post-Lacanian theorising on the unconscious as the sole source of radical agency. In what follows I am interested in elaborating the emotions as one form of a range of more or less strategic intentional conscious agencies. As I discuss further below I am viewing emotion as part of a continuum where affect and feeling constitute the more amorphous, unruly and beyond consciousness (Ngai, 2005). See also Chapter 6. This sort of view has more sympathy with critics like McNay, for example (Husso and Hirvonen, 2009), who positions her approach as a relational phenomenology.
5 The issue of whether it is helpful to talk in terms of an internal/external world is a vexed one even in psychosocial studies (Clarke, Hoggett and Thompson, 2006; Gill, 2008). My use of inverted commas when referring to 'inner' states is intended to flag up the difficulty of radically challenging the internal/external dualism in language. The use of inverted commas should not be taken to mean that I am suggesting that ideas do not get internalised, in the sense that we make them our own, mixing them up with feelings about other things, most obvious in the process of dreaming. In fact this very process points to the way in which feelings about things are never entirely our own. As I explore below, my point about thinking relationally is precisely about recognising the space in which things get positioned as either internal or external, as owned by either individuals or society. Neither of which is ever entirely the case.
6 This dualism is undergoing growing criticism (Greco and Stenner, 2008; Probyn,

2005; Wetherell, 2013a, 2013b). Feminists have been especially critical of the way that drawing hard and fast distinctions between emotion and affect can continue or even advance the denigration of the personal lived experience. Deborah Thien, for example, suggests that an overemphasis on affect in transhuman geography 're-draw[s] yet again the demarcation between masculinist reason and feminized emotion, and the false distinction between "personal" and "political"' (Thien, 2005, p. 542). This sort of critique views the turn to affect as another version of the more general cultural denigration of women via their constructed association with emotion (Holmes, 2012; Illouz, 2007; Lutz, 2008; Pedwell and Whitehead, 2012; Swan, 2008).

7 There are, of course, dangers here of false empathising between white and Black subjects which I discuss in this 2010 paper and also Chapters 3 and 6 of this volume.

Part II

The relational politics of governance

Reparative knowing

[T]o read from a reparative position is to surrender the knowing, anxious paranoid determination that no horror, however apparently unthinkable, shall ever come to the reader as new; to a reparatively positioned reader, it can seem realistic and necessary to experience surprise. Because there can be terrible surprises, however, there can also be good ones. Hope, often fracturing, even a traumatic thing to experience is among the energies by which the reparatively positioned reader tries to organize the fragments and part objects she creates.

(Sedgwick, 2003, p. 146)

Following the voice centred relational methodology employed to generate the empirical research discussed in this second part of *Power, Politics and the Emotions*, my analysis presents a multiple layered interpretation of the data. This means that different readings of the same data butt up against one another, add depth to my analysis or take it in a different direction. This is a deliberately hopeful analytic strategy which emphasises the importance of the contestability of meaning for social transformation and which works explicitly against fixing the positionings of research participants, myself as writer or you as readers of this text.

Chapter 3

Governing subjectivities: the politics of ontological detachment and relational connection

> To be an effective member of a modern welfare organization demands subordination to its universal rules, and in so doing requires the repression of desire and the renunciation of forms of subjective identification which might interfere with the necessary objectifications of the clients of the organization.
>
> (Leonard, 1997, p. 93)

> The day will come again . . . when you will see a "successful" person you love who has completely erased the very essence you thought so precious. This will send you into the depths of grief and loss. It is a tragedy that deeply wounds our common psyche. And yet, we must constantly struggle to understand, to be compassionate, to see how we ourselves may have contributed to our abandonment.
>
> (Walker, 1997, p. 98)

Living up to a benevolent professional ideal has always been a basic anxiety underpinning human service work. Whether the aim of such work is fixing bodies, protecting families or finding housing, the desire to do good; a 'public service' ethic or 'welfarist commitment' (Hoggett, 2009) to improve the lot of clients, users, patients or people, has always been in tension with bureaucratically driven professional codes which frame the human aspects of professional practice and service provision in terms of procedurally driven universal standards (Lea, 2008a). Much important analysis has been done on the sorts of collective social resources drawn on in order to carry out this public service work and in particular around the ways in which categorical experiences of systemic inequality rooted in gender, race, class and other forms of social difference underpin radical or progressive intent within governing subjectivities (Bonnett, 1993; Hoggett et al., 2006a; Newman, 2012, 2013a, 2013b; West, 2004). But within institutional contexts where diversity and difference are ostensibly lauded, promoted as institutional 'goods', such as the new managerial ones considered in *Power, Politics and the Emotions*, categorical positionings are recognised as multiple, intersecting and, potentially, competing and contradictory. It is therefore not clear how categorical experience can be harnessed for the purposes of collective resistance.

From the point of view of the governing subject this more explicit commitment to the valuing of difference is not straightforward. It potentially brings about an increasingly complicated 'recurrent, and disconcertingly unpredictable, encounter with self' (Gunaratnam and Lewis, 2001; Husband, 1996, p. 46) because of the way it highlights the socially uneven distribution of professional power within supposedly universal frameworks for service delivery and professional standards. This encounter with self can challenge as well as support the idea of the equality minded, socially progressive public servant, forcing a recognition with personal positioning through social as well as professional power. This encounter can therefore be especially anxiety provoking for those most obviously positioned through social as well as professional *power* as well as for those governing subjects more obviously positioned through social disadvantage.

In this chapter I explore the complex tensions of personal power within institutional contexts by teasing out the relationships between the ontological, categorical and relational levels of experience introduced in Chapter 2, where the relational connects a sense of self (the 'I') to broader collective categorisations (the 'we'). This tripartite analytic structure enables me to untangle a key tension played out in the negotiation of the universal ('we') and the particular ('I') as socially situated, enacted through what I call the 'recognition denial paradox' (see also Hunter, 2009a). This tension manifests in the coupling of an increasingly public formal recognition in policy that the social relations of gender, 'race', generation, age, sexuality and disability are unequally distributed at the categorical level, with ongoing denials of personal (ontological) involvement in these unequal distributions and their institutional reproductions. I think of this denial in terms of an 'abdication of voice'. By this I mean the ways in which governing subjects working within formally pro equality contexts can talk about gender and race as unequal social relations at the categorical level, *even claiming a position within this categorical ordering*, but where they do not situate themselves *biographically* – at the ontological level – in relation to these social categories. Indeed, the claiming of a categorical position through which to speak, relying as it does on at least one, often multiple forms of social recognition, can actually serve to prevent more biographically, *affectively engaged* recognition. It is for this reasons that I argue elsewhere (Hunter, 2005a, 2009a) for an *analytic* distinction to be made between *speaking about* sexism and racism (or other relations of social inequality) and *speaking through* the social relations of difference, gender and race. In other words, a distinction must be made *analytically* between knowing and feeling where *speaking about* racism and sexism implies a cognitive recognition of these relations. *Speaking through* gender and race, however, implies the ongoing affective relational integration of gender and race into personal biographies. It is this less overtly recognised, unconscious relational integration which complicates stated perspectives on social inclusion, creating contradictory feelings around the particular ideas of equality, justice and diversity which frame institutional life.

Substantively the chapter focuses on a case study analysis from interviews and observation with Bill, a white male chief executive officer (CEO) in primary health care. The case study explores how class, race, gender and generation interact in his biography to enact his ambivalent proud yet simultaneously shameful positioning as a 'new man', part of a growing public sector managerial elite who are ostensibly for equality, whilst in practice they continue to play important parts in the reproduction of inequalities. Following the less cynical take on professional power and institutional investment outlined in Chapter 1 this analysis explores the complicated individual enactments of NPM where the reproduction of difference is an inevitable by-product of resistance to professional normativities. Through Bill's case the chapter explores the 'constitutive melancholia' of governing subjectivity whereby following Butler (1997) subjectification (the ongoing process of becoming a subject) always produces alterity.

Subjectification always enacts the loss of something of the self via the self's encounter with its otherness to its self. In this chapter I am interested in how this encounter plays out for those governing subjects positioned through social power and specifically through white middle classed heterosexual masculinities, whereby the subjectification process highlights a relationship to power as well as to vulnerability. Therefore, I focus on the losses as well as the gains of positioning within such categorically normative relations. For Bill inhabiting such a positioning via his role as CEO within a neoliberalised health context is clearly difficult. As somebody who prides himself on his political difference to the norm via his explicit commitment to the idea of social justice, he is able to ally himself with newer, apparently more equal gendered and raced ideals associated with new managerial institutional shifts. In this sense NPM has prospects for him. For as long as classed positioning remains coded through the idea of politics, Bill can apparently resist certain anachronistic white masculine excesses associated with the reproduction of gendered and raced inequality, whilst remaining within normative middle classed masculine institutional hierarchies. Yet, any clear gains associated with white hetronormative middle classed positioning are undercut by his relational positioning through class which situates him within unreconstructed versions of shamefully sexist and racist white working class masculinities. Working classed identification is only a strength for Bill when it is codified relationally through politics. It becomes his weakness when recognised categorically; a vulnerability in the face of institutional power and a vulnerability related to participation in the wielding of racialised and gendered power over others. Positioning himself *to himself* (perhaps even more than to others) as a straightforwardly, singularly heroic advocate for the underdog is not possible where Bill's classed identification is made overt. Within new managerially driven institutional demands for ontological complicity Bill's classed identifications remain repressed, unable to develop and grow, providing a tense and conflicting ground for politically resisting agency.

Through this discussion I am considering the importance of emotional investments in policy ideas at the *ontological* level. Policy ideas, like equality or diversity, do not either eclipse or directly coincide with social investments in a particular subject position. They might not even enter into the day to day conversation, activities or self understanding of governing subjects at work. Instead they come to life, *relationally* as part of a broader enactment of *multiple* intersecting subject positionings within the working context. The enactment of an identity connects governing subjects to any one idea in complex ways, and it is this set of complex and potentially contradictory affective connections which are constitutive of the idea's variable and contested meanings. Therefore, rather than assuming a direct relationship between identity (thought of as *categorical* subject position), motivation and agency, the chapter unpicks how emotional investments in a *range* of categorical subject positions biographically/relationally connect governing subjects to the policy idea of equality in complex and contradictory ways. This means that these subjects can express categorical support but ontological ambivalence (rather than straightforward denial). It develops the notion of *relational identification* as a way of understanding how governing subjects negotiate and translate multiple categorical and ontological commitments; professional, organisational, personal and sociocultural in order to become a 'good' governing subject within their working context, and how this relates to ideas of equality in new managerial contexts. This suggests another way of reading Bill's codification of class through politics. Rather than killing off or erasing the more problematic aspects of Bill's classed self as the notion of ontological denial may suggest, Bill is engaged in a process of dynamic self enactment via a melancholic relational choreography. This choreography works whereby aspects of governing subjectivity shift in and out of voice, intersecting categorical subject positions are abdicated or engaged in different more or less resistant ways, depending on context.

Out with the 'old' and in with the 'new' NHS

The interviews discussed in this chapter and in the next (Chapter 4) were conducted with governing subjects – professional-manager-leaders – working in a local primary health care administration context (see Chapter 1 for more detail). Unsurprisingly, given the ceaseless hyperactive level of managerial organisational reform between the 1970s and the 2010s (Pollitt, 2013) the structure and function of English primary health care administration has undergone multiple technical iterations. At the time that the interviews discussed here were conducted the key organisational innovation which provided the working context for participants in the study were primary care trusts (PCTs). These were administrative bodies undertaking the multidisciplinary operational planning and commissioning of integrated local primary health and social care services for geographically defined populations of 100,000–200,000 people.[1] Whilst there are changes in the organisational composition and roles within this hyperactive context of new managerial reform, many of which are contradictory and lacking in coherence (Newman, 2012, 2013a, 2013b), the overall thrust in its commissioning and regulatory role along with the ethos of 'buyer dominance' within a health care market have been upheld and extended (BMA, 2010; Buckman, 2010; Leys and Players, 2011; Pollock and Price, 2011; Speed and Gabe, 2013).

Within the context of new managerial shifts and continuities the advent of PCTs is important and interesting because of the way in which they were very explicitly positioned at the forefront of new managerial cultural change towards modernisation in the NHS (Ruane, 2012). PCTs were lauded as an example of what managerial means can achieve in equality's terms through the fusion of (service) quality and (social) equality. The sort of professionals taking forward this work, the *new* professionals, would be influenced by more dynamic, transformative and less overtly masculinist working styles (Davies, 1995; Newman, 1995), more flexible, communicative and facilitative of holistic patient led care, and used to working in multidisciplinary, horizontally rather than hierarchically structured teams.

The shift towards equality coalesced with the new managerial challenges to the sorts of professional dominance associated with liberal welfare provision and, in particular, to the rigid professional and social hierarchies characteristic of 'medical dominance' (Fitzpatrick, 2001; Friedson, 1970; Stacey, 1988; Willis, 1989; Witz, 1992) so engrained in health care settings (see also Chapter 4). As the archetypal liberal profession, medicine was a white masculine and middle class project (Stacey, 1988). As such it was structured culturally through a hegemonic white middle class masculine ideal. This ideal is characterised symbolically by rationality, hierarchical authority, objectivity, decisiveness, physical and mental strength, competitiveness and individualism (Davies, 1995; K. Davies, 2003; Hunter, 2010; Pringle, 1998), and materially through a particularly rigid hierarchical division of labour. It is reflective of heteronormative family life where the professional autonomy of largely male doctors was enabled through the institutionally subordinated labour of a range of 'adjunct', usually women, professional others, such as nurses (hospital, community and practice based), health care assistants, psychologists and physiotherapists.

Cloning cultures

The social politics of NPM is complex because of the way in which managerial change is presented as a positive challenge to the traditional gender dynamics of health care, by valuing the sorts of soft skills associated with femininity and presenting an opportunity for the overt questioning of hegemonic masculinity and its practices. A further complication arises because of the way in which it pits newer cultural forms against traditional liberal public service cultures (see also Chapter 4). Its focus on long-term strength, building commitment through organisational culture and value base, the communication of vision, mission and staff empowerment play to a set of feminised norms (Newman, 1995, 2005b, 2012, 2013a). Yet, on the other hand, NPM's push towards building corporate consensus tends to militate against the recognition of social difference, gendered or otherwise. It produces highly conformist cloning cultures (Essed, 2005, pp. 234–235; see also Essed, 2002, 2004) intolerant of anything deemed to detract from broader organisational success and which value a particular generationally narrow hetronormative gendered and racialised ideal. So whilst NPM presents itself as a challenge to institutional isomorphism, in this social sense it bears remarkable similarity to the cloning basis of medicine.

It is this cloning culture which ensures the skewed embodiment of high powered institutional positions within a very narrow section of populations, generally with those positioned as white middle classed men. Nirmal Puwar describes this in terms of the production of a 'somatic norm', 'the white male figure, of a changing habitus, who is taken as the central point of reference' (Puwar, 2004, p. 141) for a range of professions. For her,

> [s]ocial cloning not only occurs at the level of somatics, ways of carrying the body, gestures and mannerisms, as well as a likeness in social background and social networks. It is also manifested in ideas, opinions, political perspective and social taste in general. Anyone too different and radical can very easily be labelled a maverick or someone who is out of bounds for support and endorsement.
>
> (Puwar, 2004, p. 123)

This cloning culture is as much about investments, ideas and taste as it is about the material aspects of embodiment. For those who don't fit the white middle class male somatic norm, stepping into any of the professions still means achieving some level of what Puwar describes as 'ontological complicity' and the concomitant ontological denial of 'race', gender and class difference. Understood in this way this cloning culture enacts the repression of difference so crucial to the melancholic dynamic outlined in Chapter 1.

In the following sections of this chapter I want to emphasise how the relationally shifting, complex and dynamic nature of ontological complicity works so that *all* governing subjects, no matter how they are positioned categorically, are potentially, though *differentially* vulnerable to its challenge. I explore the interconnections between differentially positioned subjects in Chapter 4 and also in Chapter 6. But, in this chapter I am interested in focusing on the demands of ontological complicity for those governing subjects positioned through dominance; those who, like Bill in his appearance as someone very obviously positioned through white middle class heterosexual masculinity, seem to very comfortably embody the somatic norm within primary care. What makes my approach slightly different from Puwar's insightful work is my interest in the way that embodiment and investment interact. From within a feminist psychosocial approach they are not collapsible but are enacted through the relational. This allows for a more dynamic analysis than one like Puwar's which still seems to rest on the idea of complicity via degrees of fit within a category, and therefore has the same additive problems as some of the intersectional analysis considered in Chapter 2. Within such an analysis there is limited room for considering the sorts of internal ontological multiplicity which makes for a shifting sense of self over time within and between categories. Whereas, from the feminist psychosocial perspective I develop in the rest of the chapter, I consider the dynamic contradictions of relationally enacting *one subject* within shifting categorically ordered relations of dominance and loss. From this point of view, I argue that relational identification can be understood as a form of relational choreography: a continuous pulling together and reordering of these relations of dominance and loss, dynamised through emotion, in this case shame and pride. It is this *combination* of multiple shifting positionings that makes investments in power so difficult to confront, and impossible to shift once and for all. However, it is also the tensions and contradictions opened up through this multiplicity which enable change. Therefore, it also means that even those governing subjects appearing to uncomplicatedly embody liberalism's white heteronormative masculine ideal *must* be read as *potential* agents of change. Change is social, but not in terms of a straightforwardly, categorically conceived and enacted social.

Bill's story: enacting professional pride and shame in classed difference

Bill, whose account forms the focus of my discussion in the rest of this chapter, was 50 years old at the time we met, a white male CEO of Babbling Brook PCT.[2] When I first met him he had just taken up post as the CEO of Babbling Brook. As CEO of a PCT he was at the forefront of bringing NPM into a health care context. Despite his busy schedule we met on a number of occasions over two years; twice to discuss the research before taking this forward with the PCT, three times for interview and a number of other times at board and executive meetings. Bill appeared to be an enthusiastic and confident interviewee, humming, singing and becoming visibly excited, clapping his hands during interviews. Considering Bill's elevated position within what he characterised as the 'less conservative' but nevertheless 'risk averse' organisational culture of the 'new' NHS, I admired the level of candour he displayed in interview even from the beginning of our first meeting. Whilst I deemed our first interview a success on these terms, the second was more difficult, with Bill apparently reluctant to discuss elements of his life other than work. In fact when I looked back over the transcripts of our interviews, his account, whilst fluid, is constituted largely by report and argumentation, rather than the sort of narrative flow which tends to bring talk closer to experience (Hunter, 2005a, 2005b, 2009b).

The lone hero: refusing to 'fit in'

Given Bill's categorical positioning within white heterosexual masculinity he already has a certain level of ontological complicity. It could therefore be reasonable to assume that he would occupy his position of professional power in health service management (HSM) with relative ease. But, throughout his account Bill positions himself as different: a loner, an 'odd ball', a 'one off'. 'I'm a simple man,' he says, 'never mind the bollocks.' 'I don't like bollocks, I don't like pretence.' Being British is not something Bill feels passionate about, in fact, 'to be perfectly honest', 'it's embarrassing' and similarly he's never been into the 'ooh cor blimey governor attitude' that forms the basis for a lot of the male bonding that goes on from where he comes from in the north east of England,[3] '*certainly*' not at work anyway. He likes sport, cycling, walking and being outside. 'I hate being in offices. Social justice is my bag.'

Bill also sees himself as different within his childhood context. He did not fit with the strong Catholicism of his upbringing in the north east: it 'spoilt me Sundays', 'I could have been off doing sport or pulling girls'. He was 'a lazy bastard at school', with a 'limited perspective on what I wanted to do'; 'mad keen on sport', 'it was either sport; sport or women, I'm afraid'. Although his rejection of Catholicism positions him as different, it is not presented as a dramatic rebellion, rather the 'normal' response of a young boy more concerned with 'girls' and sport than the 'larger' social issues of the time. Bill's early memories around his Labour Party membership are an interesting contrast to this positioning as socially disinterested teenager in that they hint at a broader perspective even at the age of 16. So too, his consciousness of resistance to the white apartheid regime in South Africa and the ecological movement pose an interesting challenge to common images of growing up in the strongly working class Catholic religious community of the English north east, the quintessential parochial 'white highlands' (Nayak, 2003a, 2003b).

It is within this context that Bill's professional life, culminating in his move into higher levels of HSM via the PCT, is presented as a considerable accomplishment. This is rather than the sort of natural progression associated with the ontological complicity of white middle class masculine positioning. He overcame an unremarkable school career and general academic disinterest to gain a first class degree and three masters qualifications. Notwithstanding these academic achievements, he still 'struggled to get into' general management which he puts down to his difference in the form of his 'odd views'. Despite this struggle, the reading Bill offers of his professional life is of a positive and rapid perspective '*transformation*'. Whilst his difference presents challenges in terms of professional progression there is also a sense that it is a force of pride and comfort. This transformation is prompted through a range of politically framed engagements facilitated via an early shift from teaching physical education in secondary schools into the field of health promotion. The first significant engagement Bill recollects was via Geoff, a '*very, very, very strong social democrat*, with a very *non-medical model of psychiatry*', with whom Bill worked on developing what he claims was one of the first health inequalities strategies in the country.[4] A further important shift for Bill came through undertaking an MA supervised by a 'really radical feminist'. Overall, this transformation is presented almost like a politically informed coming of age which broadened and complicated Bill's outlook on the world and positions him as different to his professional peers as well as to the context in which he grew up.

For Bill his political difference has two key components within a professional context: a commitment to left wing socialist politics and a concomitant concern for structural inequalities and social justice; and a different way of being as a manager, 'conciliatory' and 'empowering', 'entrusting', 'facilitative', 'a light steerer'. It is through this difference Bill pits himself against the traditional HSM onto which a number of characteristics are projected: 'right-wing', 'macho', 'didactic', 'arrogant', powerful and 'inflexible'. The advent of PCTs provided a critical turning point for Bill, where he finally 'got a break in primary care general management' whilst 'I've kept my integrity'. This fit with HSM after Bill's shift into the PCT is unsurprising given the affinity between his commitments to a conciliatory, facilitative and empowering style and NPM's favoured transformational leadership approach (Newman, 2004, 2005a; Newman and Clarke, 2009). Yet, unsurprising too perhaps in the context of his construction of his political perspective transformation, he continues to characterise his working life in terms of an 'inevitable compromise', 'because of the environment in which I work'.

Excavating connection: a classed heart

There is a tension within Bill's account around a kind of heroic, pioneering and resistant uniqueness built up around his commitment to social justice and his sense of himself as a 'simple man', straightforward, ordinary and uncomplicated: 'never mind the bollocks'. Even the 'constant tension' between his left wing politics and the organisational culture in which he works tends to be downplayed as an 'inevitable compromise', just a fact of life, rather than as a form of heroic counter hegemonic resistance. In our final interview Bill offers important information about his class background which facilitates a richer interpretation of elements of his political transformation through the 'structuring absence' of class (Skeggs, 1997). This helps to clarify the complicated significance and operation of such a counter hegemonic positioning for Bill.

Throughout the first two interviews there is not one direct reference to Bill's *own* classed experience. Picking up on this absence throughout our encounters in the final interview, I ask directly about where Bill would position himself in terms of class. He is visibly uncomfortable with the question, shifting around on his chair. When Bill eventually moves to reluctantly position himself, 'I suppose I'd be social class A nowadays, because of my job wouldn't I?', he points to the apparently unassailable coupling of management and the middle class (see Hughes, 2004). However, his quick move to refocus on his father's '*very* working class, non-skilled' background challenges this unassailability as quickly as it is established. It also serves to situate Bill's classed identifications relationally and at the very least ambiguously through this family relation. This move opens up the following exchange in Extract 3.1:

Extract 3.1

[BILL] So I'm upwardly mobile as the term {pause} but I think that background actually is, *still important* it still informs a lot of my *beliefs*.

[SHONA] Do you want to expand on that?

[BILL] Well {sighs} {pause} *always* fascinated to see that *my father, became* increasingly conservative as he moved *through the* [ranks], *conservative* with a large *and a* small *c*. Increasingly *right wing*.

[SHONA] Mmm.

[BILL] *uuer*, as he {pause} *developed*.

[SHONA] Right.

[BILL] And it was something that *my*, uncles, always used to comment on that he'd left his roots behind, or whatever, well his roots were *the working class*,[5] and um, it was something that, I was always at *odds* with *my father* about {pause} *his politics*, and that wasn't because {moves on chair} he'd *sold out*, moved *on*, {very quiet} easy to acc. its far easier to acc., actually *accept*, right wing {laughing} views.

This discussion around class produced a more emotionally alive encounter between Bill and myself where he reflects on other parts of his life rather than moving to situate his difference *only* in terms of his political beliefs. Bill continues on from Extract 3.1:

> I think one of the things I alluded to in the interviews we've had, was about always being a bit different to other people ... and I think {pause} *having* different political views, was perhaps, a component of my difference.

His perspective transformation is re-presented not as a change as such, rather 'it was a transformation, in that I actually, a, almost in a sense I understood, where I came from'. This positive and enabling link between a professional transformation and his personal history subverts the liberally established and neoliberally enforced public/private binary. It facilitates an interpretation of Bill's investment in left wing politics as a means by which he can maintain a link with an important element of his *personal identity* rooted in working classed *social difference* which sustains his *professional uniqueness*. On this basis Bill's 'inevitable compromise' at work can now be read not only in terms of a compromise in his political beliefs, but also in terms of having to compromise a part of *himself*, 'his roots', 'where he came from', his working classed identifications. Professional success and personal loss are intertwined.

The ambivalence suggested by Bill's previous silence on this issue of class is continued through the family story he tells in Extract 3.1. This story links his previously working classed background and his currently middle classed professional position as a manager. Bill's father's story can be read as a foil to Bill's life trajectory in the sense that Bill sees himself as having maintained and kept his personal integrity and a commitment to social justice through a consistently held commitment to his left wing political views. But Bill's uncle's reaction to Bill's father's shift from left to right can also be read as a warning about the fragility of maintaining such left wing commitments throughout instances of institutional (and therefore classed) upward mobility like Bill's movement up into HSM. This is an upward mobility which Bill appears to accept begrudgingly rather than wholeheartedly. Bill's political transformation can now be read as important for a number of reasons. It sediments Bill's link with 'where [he] came from', providing a contested continuity with his working class childhood and local community context, a context defined through the strong interconnection between class and heterosexual masculinity. But it also enables a public 're-branding' of his working classed identifications which is potentially more palatable within the context of new managerialist institutional norms. Politics works for Bill as a euphemism for class.

On the basis of this information about the importance of class for Bill his performance of the ordinary 'simple man' can now be read as obliquely working classed. His demeanour in interview, his use of direct language and frequent swearing, including his catchphrase 'never mind the bollocks' and his caricatured self positioning as a 'short fat bloke' all contradict the diplomacy, objectivity and detachment of middle class masculinity (Hughes, 2004), emphasising Bill's difference to traditional middle classed managerial masculinities. Class is the means by which Bill positions himself as different and therefore *counter hegemonically*, as external to the powerful macho normativities of HSM culture. Working classed identification is the means by which he maintains his ontological integrity within what is for him a morally problematic white *middle class* masculine institutional context, but where he might otherwise appear to fit by dint of his categorical positioning through white masculinity. Class therefore becomes important because it is an obvious badge of difference from a problematic *status quo*, whilst its codification via the euphemism of politics goes some way to avoiding an explicit challenge to the enduringly middle class context of HSM.

Speaking about being a 'new man'

There is some support from within the above analysis for the claim that Bill's categorical identification with working classed *inequality*, his experience as categorically *unequal* (even as these experiences are largely vicarious, reported via family memory (Scott and Scott, 2000; Walkerdine, 2006) underpins an ontologically driven resistance to the inequalities produced through mainstream HSM. From this point of view working class identification is potentially something to be proud of. It plays a key part in Bill's commitment to social justice and as such it is the basis of anti-normative agency. It is therefore something which makes him unique within the higher echelons of HSM as well as, from his point of view, *better equipped* for effective management in terms of style (i.e. integrity) and substance (i.e. commitment to social justice, resistance to professional dominance, reduction of inequality). As such working classed identification positions

Bill outside of the narrow parameters of institutionalised neoliberal use value, and within more local circuits of relationally defined value (Skeggs, 2011, pp. 107–108). It is a form of resistance to neoliberalism's hostility to the social.

But, it is important to emphasise that Bill's classed identifications do not work in one way here. Indeed, class is also something to be hidden, or at least coded via politics, as its literal absence from most of our first and second interviews suggests. One way of reading this coding is in terms of what it suggests about Bill's desire for institutional power; for getting on and fitting in institutionally via the modernising (but potentially personally compromising) erasure of class through a more (albeit not entirely) institutionally acceptable idea of politics. Euphemising class as politics within this institutional context implies a form of co-option and complicity. However, I want to suggest another way of reading this coding of class through politics which works against an analysis of Bill as purely self interested but which does not fall back into the romanticisation of working classed identifications as automatically for the collective social good. Thus another reading of this coding can also be made in terms of Bill's desire as a socially transformed 'new' man, to resist becoming implicated in the sorts of racist and sexist forms of domination he associates with traditional HSM but which are also supposedly manifest within working class culture.

Extract 3.2 is what follows my shift to ask directly about Bill's *self* positioning in terms of the social relations of power and thus, in Bill's case, in terms of white masculinity. Because of the dominant systemic orderings of whiteness and masculinity within the racialised-gendered institutional order, this request can be read as Bill's response to being asked explicitly to position himself through the social relations of power.[6] It is in potential contrast to my probing of class through which Bill is positioned as more obviously disadvantaged.

Extract 3.2

[BILL] I mean OPCS,[7] definitions often say *white*, they then don't break it down to British areas, you go white Pakistani, did I, which well, white isn't an ethnic group, I mean I have, I worry about that, um, but there was just this arrogant assumption that there was white people and then there were other people, and you could break the other people down, into Swahilis and Pakistanis and whatever, which is incredibly arrogant. Um, what does bei. What is it about being {pause} . . . what it means to be male, um, well, depends where you come from, I think, cos from where I come from [in the English north east] *men are men*, and men do menly things like going to work, going down the pub, and women stay at home, have lots of babies um, and pander to their man. And my, my parents are exactly that stereotype, my mum's never worked, only when she was single, and then men, not *new people* hey? . . . um, having said that you know, maybe it's not just a socialised thing in my view . . . when we had my daughter that um we were very *non gender specific* . . . [but] there's something in *women* and there's something *in men*, that that's there is a differe. There is *something different*, and you know, and you can talk about the nature nurture argument, whatever, but, simple thing, men are far more task orientated whereas, women are far more process orientated, and that's you know from education and the child development stuff, you know and um, so there is something that is fundamentally well not maybe, but there certainly is different, but I'm never quite sure whether I mean what's the balance between nature and nurture.

[SHONA] I don't think anybody is.

[BILL] Well, no you know, far be it from me to, um, being male, *yea there's still* an element of breadwinner and all that sort of thing. Um but again, to an extent that's because of the inequalities in the structure within work, men do earn more than women {pause} more than women generally, although in the professions they don't.

[SHONA] Mmm.

[BILL] So there's still that sort of element of culture {pause} being British? It's embarrassing isn't it?

[SHONA] Well {laughing} I don't know.

[BILL] I'd say to be perfectly honest.

[SHONA] In what sense?

[BILL] Um, because of this {pause} what do people from other places think of the British, well they think you know, shaven heads, bare chests, lots of beer, and I've been round, you know, I've been round, I've been to a lot of countries and you know I'd rather go on holiday where people there aren't British people, quite embarrassing at times . . . I don't feel particularly passionate about being British {pause} the British reason, or I don't know what it is, but um, um, it's, it's. I identify with much smaller groups rather than with being British . . . cos the, the stereotype with it . . . Although it's amazing how, you do see people abroad, people who, wouldn't necessarily behave in a certain way at home, when they're on holiday, they're influenced by other people and they almost live out the stereotype.

As a response to a question about self positioning, Bill's starting point discussing the arrogance of (white) institutions' inappropriate use of ethnic categorisations seems a bit off beat, unsure or evasive. Early on in his response he establishes race, gender and ethnicity as all in some senses socially constructed. But, from the beginning he is also very quick to establish a distance between himself and *certain forms* of whiteness and masculinity. From a professional point of view as a manager his starting point with a critique of OPCS definitions makes sense given the high profile and controversial debates around the merits and problematic of ethnic categorisation within public services (Burton, Nandi and Platt, 2008). However, his meaning is ambiguous and confused by revision and unfinished phrases. The statement simultaneously serves to evade a focus on Bill's positioning as white, whilst constructing him as a 'worried' *onlooker* over the institutional politics of ethnicised differentiation. Whilst he does not name racism specifically, the 'arrogance' Bill highlights can be read as a euphemism for racism (Moon,

1999). Much later in this exchange Bill can be read as making a similar move to evade association with racism in relation to rejecting the notion of Britishness, describing his unwillingness to be identified with a stereotype he finds embarrassing, preferring to position himself as identifying with 'smaller groupings'. At that later point, Bill invokes a common stereotype of backward looking parochial masculine shaven head 'lager lout' Britishness, a caricature which has racist (and sexist) connotations (Mann, 2012; Nayak, 1999).

This caricature of the working *classed* racist subject is often used to locate racism elsewhere (Garner, 2012; Garner, Clarke and Gilmour, 2009; Haylett, 2001; Hunter, 2010; Lawler, 2012; Pitcher, 2009; Reay, 2008; Reay et al., 2007; Skeggs and Wood, 2008; Tyler, 2008) away from the (middle class) speaking subject. One reading of the shift in Bill's comments in Extract 3.2 is that this working classed subject is offered as a contrast to Bill's self construction as a (middle classed) professional subject. Thus, middle class positioning conferred through professional status is used as a means to distance the self from racist practices. This is the interpretation drawn by Lawler (2012) in relation to my own (Hunter, 2010) earlier analysis of Bill's positioning as part of a left liberal middle class professional group. Through this sort of analysis the construction of whiteness is positioned as a moral project differentiated symbolically (and materially) through ideals of good and bad. Working classed whiteness is associated with the latter, enacted through a narrowness of perspective and particular type of machismo and racism related to a possessive investment in whiteness (Lipsitz, 1995).

This possessive investment arises in postcolonial contexts out of the legacies of the positive relationship between claiming whiteness and the benefits and advantages of waged labour for groups which without that racialised advantage might be positioned 'outside' of normative social relations. It builds on ideas that 'in-between' people like those southern and eastern European migrants who moved to America in the early nineteenth century claimed whiteness in order to gain privileged access to resources, psychological and social capital (Allen, 1975; Allen, 1994; Roediger, 1991; Saxton, 1991), what Du Bois (1935) called the 'wages of whiteness'. Entrance into whiteness is *earned* through conforming to a range of white *bourgeois* norms and moralities, including entrance into the labour market, appropriate patterns of production and consumption and social contribution such as the payment of income tax (Garner, 2012; Thandeka, 1999) and of everyday comportment and manners (Moon, 1999). The inability to embody this set of behaviours and practices marks the working classes out as shameful, inappropriate, bad or failed embodiments of ideal whiteness. Thus, it is in contemporary ideals of whiteness where neoliberal modernisation and multiculturalism coincide in 'multicultural modernisation' to produce particularly pernicious constructions of outsiderness where working class others become the 'dumping ground' for the 'heavy contradictions of a multicultural welfare society articulated within a neoliberal and middle class imaginary' which seeks to reconstruct the working class poor (Haylett, 2001, p. 357). It is this sort of failed working class whiteness which is associated with negative practices of domination and oppression; a violently 'racist and sexist detritus' (Haylett, 2001, p. 358) which appears more prominently and vividly in Bill's response to my request for him to self position through gender and ethnicity, and which he uses to position himself as outside of bad whiteness.

Whilst Bill's move to consider gender might appear to be in tension, or at least an abrupt shift away from the uncomfortable topic of whiteness, his comments on what it means to be a man facilitate an understanding as to why this image of the working class 'lager lout' is so significant for him. Between these two discussions around ethnicity, where Bill moves to consider gender there is another significant hesitation, and more confused fumbling for words after which he makes a different move to confidently foreground his gendered positioning. In making this move he draws on a particular construction of traditional white working class patriarchal masculinity recognisably rooted within his own background growing up in the north east where: 'my parents are exactly that stereotype . . . where *men are men* and do menly things like going to work, going down the pub and women stay at home, have lots of babies and pander to their man' and he does this as a means to position himself in direct contrast to this as '*non gender specific*'. In doing so, he repeats the move to establish a clear distance between his own more progressive positioning and the worrisome and embarrassing unreconstructed *working class* white masculinities he associates with parochial and racist *negative* embodiments of Britishness.

After doing this distancing work, Bill then vacillates between a biologically essentialist difference based evaluation of gender and socially constructed ones. At this point he becomes unsure again. On the one hand struggling with potential contradictions within his argument where he demonstrates the desire to resist the reproduction of gendered binaries, but on the other hand he seems to be faced with examples of relatively fixed (whether biologically or socially) gendered differences which tally with more traditional views on gender with which he does not want to be associated. My reply is interesting as it could be read as offering Bill reassurance around his comments relating to gendered difference, or, at least, around his difficulty in conceptualising this without retreating to some form of essentialism. More importantly it enables him to abdicate responsibility for his analysis altogether, 'far be it from me' he says, on the basis of his positioning 'being male'. Implicitly he passes this responsibility to interpret gendered relations over to me as his woman interlocutor. This passing over to me then enables Bill to make a return to more confident analysis in relation to the structures of work as creating gendered inequality. Thus, this abdication reproduces a binary split in different ways of knowing gender. Bill as a man knows and pronounces on the public domain, about work and unequal systems. At the same time, despite my positioning as interviewer in this exchange, my expertise is reduced to my personal experience as a woman, minimising my professional and analytic knowledge. This minimisation is potentially reinforced by my taking up a position alongside Bill as part of the unsure 'anybody'. Finally, and perhaps most significantly, Bill moves to place professionals outside his analysis of unequal gender relations. The significance being that by implication, Bill then confidently places himself outside of the reproduction of these structures of gendered inequality as one such professional. Given Bill's stated knowledge around the patterning of social inequality, the significance of this move to position professionals outside of the relations of gendered inequality is compounded by the surprising inaccuracy of this analysis of professionals, and particularly professionals within managerial fields. In fact in contrast to Bill's claims of pay equality within professions, the gender pay gap remains persistently stubborn at more senior professional levels. It is in fact *widest* in working contexts like the one he oversees at 24.4 per cent for 'managers and senior officials' and tends to be *wider still* across this category in health services contexts (see Perfect, 2011).

Enacting classed difference through pride and shame

Overall, this exchange in Extract 3.2 enables Bill to explore his categorical positioning through power, *as a white man*, without explicitly positioning himself *biographically at work* and without making explicit reference to either sexism or racism. Therefore, it works to enable Bill to abdicate white masculine positioning through a superficial acknowledgement of its material significance. Where he does allude to racism and sexism he positions this as elsewhere. This elsewhere is either in the holiday maker 'lager louts' and the stereotypical north eastern heterosexual family unit symbolic of the working classes (the not, or at least the no longer (working classed) him), or in the 'arrogant' (middle classed) managerial institutions like the OPCS where he can never clearly be positioned for as long as he is ambiguously classed.

As I have previously considered (Hunter, 2005a, 2009a), this strategy of positioning the self outside of the discursive reproduction of categorically unequal social relations is common. It relates to the defensive intersubjective polarisation of good and bad as a way to avoid the melancholic anxiety which derives from their interdependence (see Chapter 2). This is an interdependence which positions the self within good as well as bad. Polarised defensive responses manifest in various ways (see Chapter 2). Bill engages a number of these throughout Extract 3.2. These include the recognition of gendered and raced experience as relevant to others in the same social category (here as white middle class managers), but not for the speaker because of some form of exceptionality by luck or design (Bill's difference); by recognising their relevance in the past (when Bill was a boy, interested in pulling girls and sport), overcome in the present (as an adult man disapproving of sexist banter); by claiming their relevance to the personal (within the family and community) but not to the professional (as a health services manager).

There are two interrelated aspects of Bill's abdication of gendered and raced positioning that I want to consider further here in order to extend this analysis of abdication taking it in a more dynamic direction than the one suggested by my analysis thus far where, as I explore below, the only way to resist implication in the reproduction of domination appears to be the complete rejection of the collective enactment of the social. First, I am interested in what this abdication of white masculine voice suggests about the contradictory love/hate nature of class within the broader neoliberal governing project. Class is not always something positive for Bill because the recognition of the way this categorical investment intersects with other forms of identification calls into question Bill's vision of himself as uncomplicatedly resistant and consistently committed to supporting social equality. As well as valued for its enabling quality, class as a source of pride is therefore also to be resisted as a source of shame because of its association with social harms like racism and sexism. Second, Bill's positioning through 'perspective transformation' and the related commitment to cultivating a 'broad outlook' enables him to negotiate this classed ambivalence in a way which troubles his positioning within white masculine dominance, at the same time as it potentially re-secures its social power (and Bill's position in this). Finally, I consider the importance of the continually shifting nature of these positionings.

The melancholy of the beneficiary

At the same time as class, and other forms of social difference (like gender, age, sexuality and ethnicity) produce important differentiation within whiteness, they highlight its subjective instabilities which mean that it has to be continually worked for and actively invested in materially, socially and affectively. They expose its fictional fantasy character. This enables an understanding as to why it would be shame in particular which enacts whiteness. Shame is manifest in the feeling that there is something fundamentally wrong *with the self*, which has had to be hidden, repressed and forgotten. It is communicated in covert or overt forms through the expression of doubts, concerns or worries *about the self* (Lewis, 1990), we can see these in Bill's halting tone, his implicit resistances and revisions and occasional explicit expressions of concern, worry and doubt. Working classed identifications are problematic for the white self because they are a reminder of the fundamentally flawed nature of whiteness, flaws *internal* to the enactment of whiteness itself. Exposing working classed identifications within whiteness produces shame at the reality of not being quite white enough. That is, not quite white enough in the sense of not being able to live up to the material, symbolic and affective ideals of good well mannered polite benevolent kind civilised bourgeois whiteness, the sort of comportment and behaviours that are viewed as underpinning the right to govern within the liberal institutional space. But this exposure of differently classed identifications lurking within this ideal also hints at the *sorts* of material, symbolic and affective work involved in maintaining whiteness. It exposes the fact that the performative work of reproducing whiteness, the wages and investments as I referred to them above, is rooted in the denigration and denial of various others. It is not work to be proud of, but shameful, *racialising* work. Such a highlighting of class therefore demonstrates the fantasy nature of white bourgeois identification *in general*, thus exposing the truth of the white subject, and *not only the white working classed subject*, as never really quite white enough. Nor, from this perspective, is whiteness ever really quite *good* (caring, kind, benevolent) enough in the first place. This is because it is always established through the infliction of pain and the experience of loss, of the Other, but also the pain and loss of the self. There is therefore *always* a melancholic shame at the heart of whiteness (Cheng, 2000; Eng and Han, 2003; Harris, 2013; Straker, 2011; Thandeka, 1999).

At the categorical level whiteness catches Bill in a shameful Gordian knot. Resisting racist and sexist forms of domination associated with whiteness, particularly, but crucially not always *only* associated with working class violent excess and domination, means resisting classed identification. But this resistance to classed identification means buying into whiteness as an oppressive normative cultural orientation which denigrates classed identifications, and working classed identifications in particular, as the bearers of a particular source of overtly and violently oppressive whiteness. Bill's worries are never over. He is either locked into the domination of the Other via association with working classed racism and sexism or locked into self domination via association with middle classed bourgeois whiteness dependent on the denial of important ontologically nourishing working classed identifications. Categorical domination and ontological loss are interdependent. Bill's fleeting expressions of working classed identification risk positioning him at odds with the ideal of bourgeois whiteness; as not quite white enough. But more than this, such fleeting acts of self exposure also highlight the necessary ontological denial and categorical class betrayal involved in achieving or desiring this white *middle class* ideal in the first place. Shame here for Bill highlights the inability to live up to *both* working and middle class ideals within contemporary enactments of neoliberal whiteness, coupled with the impossibility of refusing positioning through either. Bill is always inadequately both. A further difficulty for Bill is that these two interdependent forms of whiteness are involved in a self referential critique which means that neither offers a straightforwardly anxiety free, good enactment of white subjectivity. The only progressive option which appears open to the white subject from within this tightly spun Gordian knot is the recognition of its failure.

Bill's self construction as someone defined through a 'perspective transformation' and the development of a 'broad outlook' takes on an additional significance here in the context of the need to reconstruct a more liveable form of whiteness outside this shameful Gordian knot of failed white subjectivity. In Bill's particular case this must be a form of whiteness which can take account of the central contradiction between the incomplete and ambivalent shifts between working classed and middle classed positioning. Bill's 'broad outlook' achieves such a reconciliation through its relationship to a range of left liberal practices of self development and improvement directed towards amassing knowledge of and therefore power over the self as well as the social and material environment. These practices include the accrual of formal educational qualifications and informal cultural experiences through extensive independently organised travel, sporting and leisure activities and voracious consumption of literatures, all of which are a means to enact particular forms of white liberal capital which position Bill outside of *unreconstructed* whiteness. Through these practices of self control, social cultivation and *knowledge* accrual Bill (re)constructs himself as a 'darker shade of pale' (Reay et al., 2007); a different sort of white allied with a broader less parochial anachronistic set of ideals than his working and straightforwardly traditional middle classed counterparts, like Bill's manager colleagues in the context of the PCT. A forward looking progressive sort of white subject who could even be seen to be positioned against whiteness allied with liberal cosmopolitan progress, acceptance of diversity, even a commitment to anti-racism. Such a personal reconstruction enables Bill to position himself as reflexively knowing; an *onlooker* critical of certain unreconstructed bourgeois conservative or working classed whitenesses. However, this self reflexivity, supposed access to and control over his own interior life, also positions Bill neatly in terms of the rationality and self mastery so fundamental to the performance of white liberal masculinity and which might be expected of him as a white masculine subject. These are attributes which remain central to the extension of *neo*liberal self practices. As such they position Bill as a person of a particular power and value (Skeggs, 2011); via the ultimate *epistemological* (ontological) power crucial to neoliberalism considered in Chapter 1 and as one of the *self* reconstructed civilised whites.

From this point of view knowingness, reflexivity, the ability to civilise the self becomes a, if not the, key marker of certain forms of more progressive left liberal middle classed *sanitised* whiteness (Hunter, 2010; Lawler, 2012). This is because self knowledge is viewed as a means to achieve personal transformation and social progress away from unreconstructed failed liberal enactments of whiteness which are perceived to be the root of racism within this context. Self conscious expressions of shame work as a means to sanitise the self, to absolve the self of guilt to communicate sorrow or regret and to demonstrate the desire to change. In the case of such expressions of white shame as a turn away from (unreconstructed) whiteness they work to reinstate socially progressive good whiteness as separate from a materially, socially and affectively demarcated regressive bad whiteness. They are the means through which whiteness reinstates itself as omnipotent and benevolent. This ability is predicated in forms of education and training where a reflexive relationship to one's own whiteness is endorsed, or even cultivated as a source of capital and *pride* (Hunter, 2010). I can't be racist because I know I am (Ahmed, 2004a). Thus reflexivity, self knowledge as the ultimate form of knowledge, becomes the means to extricating the self from perpetuating domination. However, the danger here is for an 'odd, anxious, hand wringing guiltiness' (Harris, 2013, p. 203) which remains at the superficial level of categorical confession rather than remorse, reintegration and reparation. The left liberal becomes fixed within the same sort of endlessly paradoxical inside/outside recognition/denial complex they are looking to escape from (Hunter, 2010; Lea, 2008a, 2008b).

This reading of Bill's 'perspective transformation' in defended terms as a means to abdicate positioning *through* a particular form of unreconstructed white masculine power is supported by other aspects of this second interview. Later on, after our exchange in Extract 3.2, I move to reintroduce the subject of Bill's gendered and raced positioning *at work*, in an attempt to bring him back to consider the relational context of the PCT which was so underdeveloped in that earlier exchange. Bill's reply to my probing is unusual in its obviously defensive nature. He begins by explicitly denying any masculine advantage: 'my credibility as a Chief Exec {firmly and louder} *isn't based* on my gender!' But he wraps up with a gentler assessment as to the inability of '*short fat blokes*' (his emphasis again) and 'not only women', to get to the top of organisational hierarchies. This shift in his reply serves to temper his earlier resistance to recognising gendered inequality within the *professional* sphere. This time he recognises this issue of organisational progression in terms of categorically ordered gendered advantage/disadvantage, albeit begrudgingly in response to being pressed again by me. But, he does so from a position where *he himself is not being presented as advantaged* via his gender.

One way of reading Bill's shift in response to recognise gendered disadvantage *at work*, but to continue to position himself as clearly outside is interesting in terms of the way it potentially moves towards understanding the complexities of inequality's intersections in a working context via the image of the 'short fat bloke'. This intersection is implied through coupling of 'bloke' with images of masculine excess fatness and physical limitation which together allude to the impact of class on masculine advantage in that context. However, the comparison between women and 'short fat blokes' can also be read as compounding the refusal to recognise Bill's gendered advantage in terms of the way it builds on his earlier refusal to consider any advantage accruing to him *within the professional sphere* by focusing attention on his positioning on the *outside* to power *within that context* via classed disadvantage. It creates equivalence between experiences of class and gender discrimination, bringing Bill into these social relations of inequality as someone who is potentially suffering too as a (white) working classed man and who is therefore outside of the benefits of gendered inequality in the *workplace*. One way to read what appears to be a move to recognise more complex categorical intersections is through the 'politics of empathy' (Rosenberg, 1997) as a politics which serves to obscure the disproportionate impact of racialised or, in this case, specifically gendered social relations on *certain* raced and gendered subjects. From this point of view the overall thrust of Bill's response continues to maintain his positioning *outside* of responsibility for the reproduction of *inequality within the context of the workplace*. The relational positioning through class as the 'short fat bloke' this time becomes the means for him to defensively self position as the working class 'underdog' rather than the beneficiary of white masculinity.

Relationally resisting domination

In this final section of this chapter's discussion I want to consider a more nuanced reading of what Bill's positioning as the underdog suggests about how his classed identifications may still operate to enable a less defended, relationally enacted positioning *within* power. This relational positioning works to produce Bill as a good *enough* governing subject, one who sits *somewhere in between the failed and the infallible* options presented by the (neo)liberal governing ideal.

Despite the range of substantive contradictions, tonal vacillations and stylistic shifts which I am suggesting can be read into Bill's account and which indicate something of the melancholic vacillation between pride and shame within his biography, there are relatively few *explicit* expressions of doubt. Given that expressions of doubt and discomfort rarely straightforwardly identify the shameful object (Lewis, 1990), explicit admissions of discomfort become interesting in terms of the way they can support an interpretation of what it is within the self that is producing shame, and what it is that is being *avoided* through a projection elsewhere. Within this context the turn in the conversation after Extract 3.2, but just before Bill's other statements of begrudging recognition of institutionalised gender inequality at work that I analyse above, is important. At this point Bill identifies situations at work in which he *'really does feel'* very clearly 'uncomfortable' in relation to the reproduction of gendered inequality. These are situations 'when males exhibit true, or you know classic male behaviours'; the 'cor blimey governor' attitude which Bill has claimed to never want to be part of. This admission is interesting because it goes much more explicitly against the grain of Bill's previously defended responses. Whereas these responses tend to minimise gendered inequality within his immediate working contexts, this time he makes a potentially more realistic analysis of institutionalised gendered inequality but he does so by projecting this behaviour onto those positioned through intersecting *heterosexualised* working classed masculine identifications. In what follows I want to suggest that this admission is interesting because these relational intersections between heterosexuality, *as well* as working class masculinity position Bill *outside* of the current neoliberal white middle class masculine governing ideal. But this also positions him *outside* of the left liberal positioning which potentially enables him to differentiate himself from this more *neo*liberalised positioning.

Returning to the figure Bill positioned himself *against* at work through the phrase 'cor blimey governor'. As I noted early on in my analysis above this phrase evokes a specific set of (hetero)sexualised relations (see note 3 below), which are *additional to* the gendered, raced and classed ones implied in the symbol of the 'short fat bloke'. As such this image is more explicitly evocative of the sort of unreconstructed white working classed heterosexual masculinity characterised through Bill's earlier recollections of his boyhood and youth (we could even read these relations as extending into early manhood if we take into account his first professional role prior to his perspective transformation as a teacher of physical and sports education). This is a time where Bill was more interested in 'chasing' or 'pulling' girls, the private world of jest and play, rather than preparation for the rational public world of schooling and work, and especially the sort of serious 'proper' responsible work currently undertaken in his role as CEO of a PCT. It was this pre-perspective transformation positioning as a young man through which Bill is recognisably operating within a specifically working classed imaginary which attaches him to a specific set of heterosexual, hierarchically gendered familial and community relations more representative of the 'cor blimey governor' attitude. The 'cor blimey governor' figure is recognisable through the exercise of gendered domination and it is not so far away from Bill's presentation of self as the 'short fat bloke' the underdog; acted upon and excluded from occupying a position of power.

Bill's strongly expressed defensiveness against recognising any sort of masculine advantage *in the workplace* can be interpreted in the context of the links between, on the one hand, this sort of problematic white hyper masculine heterosexual 'cor blimey' attitude so much more obviously like the working class 'lager louts' Bill is so keen to distance himself from in Extract 3.2, and, on the other hand, his self empowering performance of the 'ordinary man', the 'short fat bloke', just getting on with things in the face of structured advantage. Bill's strong defensiveness is potentially related to the fact that the *link between the two* figures puts him in the frame for racist and sexist *domination* associated with working classed identification. Making a link between the two figures undercuts any *claims to suffering* which Bill could make on the basis of his 'ordinary bloke' persona and risks positioning him through white heterosexual masculine *domination* in the sense of the 'cor blimey' governor attitude that he himself identifies as the root of gendered inequality, *at work*. The resistance to social classed identification works specifically here to protect the disruption of the liberal public realm within which Bill is enmeshed as a professional, as a specifically left liberal governing subject who sees himself as resisting neoliberal manifestations of structured institutional power. What is important to understanding Bill's shifts and defences, their particular form and expression is the relational context of work for the enactment of the multiple intersecting categorical relations through which he is positioned.

Bill's story points to the heavy contradictions within broader late liberal/neoliberal institutional cultures where equality is supposed to be paramount, but where social relations themselves are airbrushed out of institutional life. Bill's difficulty here relates to his positioning through the heavy contradictions of the neoliberal multicultural modernising projects such as the new managerialised NHS where as I outlined in Chapter 1 the fantasy of progress and inclusion relies on a range of *necessary* exclusions. Bill's example points to the ways in which this project is articulated within a 'neoliberal and middle class imaginary' where the attainment of inclusion and progression rests on 'the reconstruction of the white working class poor' (Haylett, 2001, p. 357).

> In these circumstances a representative middle class is positioned at the vanguard of 'the modern' which becomes a moral category referring to liberal, cosmopolitan work and consumption based on lifestyles and values, and 'the unmodern' on which this category depends is the white working-class dependency on working-class 'other', emblematically a throwback to other times and places. This middle-class 'backwardness' for its own claim to

modern multicultural citizenship is an unspoken interest within the discourse
of illegitimacy around the white working-class poor.

(Haylett, 2001, p. 365)

Within such a polarising construction social class can only represent one of two
either or positions, progressive or regressive. Within a new managerial institutional context framed through this sort of polarisation claiming working classed
identification as a strength, something to be proud of becomes extremely difficult, if not almost impossible. Bill's struggle to position himself as positively connected to and enabled by familial and community ties, but not defined through
sexist and racist anachronism, can be understood as a struggle with this broader
discursive polarisation. His refusal to admit personal history into an institutional
space where he sees himself as counter hegemonic becomes necessary, *not* for his
individual professional advancement, he is after all already CEO of a large health
care organisation, but more to support this counter hegemonic positioning.

Overall then the idea of class is a contradictory melancholic hinge for Bill. It
connects him (ontologically) to history, 'his background', through which he is
able to position himself as a subject, 'who he is' in the present. This history works
holistically via (intersectional) classed identification bringing together multiple
categorical identifications: masculinity, sexuality and ethnicity. But it works melancholically bringing issues of vulnerability and power with it. It brings classed
vulnerability and inequality, but also power and domination as a white man working in an institutional context where white middle classed masculinities remain
hegemonic, if somewhat changed within a contemporary postcolonial context.
It is therefore *history as it is relationally enacted* which more explicitly introduces
uncertainty, multiplicity and ambivalence into Bill's story and which means he can
never only be *good* in the sense of resistant to discrimination and straightforwardly
for (gender and race) equality. His historically located experience in the world,
through family, friends, locality – biography – positions him as good and bad at the
same time, as a potentially blameworthy and culpable but also potentially *responsible* subject. His resistance to bringing classed identifications into the institutional
sphere is explainable less as a cynical act of self denial, but more as the result of the
troubling ambivalence produced through his personal positioning through power.

Charis Cussins develops the idea of 'ontological choreography' in order to
explore the subjectification process as enacted through multiple interconnected
forms of active objectification involved in achieving a 'long range' identity such
as Bill's aim to be a health policy decision maker. To be understood as working
in this way identity has at least three components: 'a long term orientation to the
good [the ideal], to be essentially in movement and to have an irreducibly narrative character' (Cussins, 1996, p. 578). Certain objectifications and isolations
work as *part of* a broader *in motion* 'coordinated action' 'in the service of a long-
range self' (Cussins, 1996, p. 600). Understood from this point of view Bill's
abdication of white working class masculine positioning cannot be understood
as an entirely oppressive activity because it is *never* part of a zero sum, either

abdication or not abdication. This is especially so when we think of abdication in the sorts of intersectional terms I outlined in Chapter 2. The language of choreography emphasises intersectionality as a dynamic where it is possible to see certain aspects of categorical identification shifting in and out of focus, isolated *for a time* in the service of achieving the desired self in the longer term.

In Bill's example the abdication of voice can be understood as part of this broader longer range choreographed activity of enacting a 'good enough' managerial self within the context of the new managerial somatic norm described earlier in this chapter. The idea of choreography works nicely here because it denotes agency which is more practised than thought out. It captures dynamism without necessarily implying rational intent. My use of the term 'relational' rather than Cussins' 'ontological' to describe this choreography draws attention to the way that affect and emotion like pride and shame are the *means to the coordination* of this long range self. In my terms the ontological is enacted through the *relationally choreographed* categorical. Therefore, this idea of relational choreography can be used to understand the distinction between categorical ordering and categorical domination. Whether or not a categorical ordering constitutes domination depends on the relational choreography through which it is enacted, and thus its configuration *within other sets of categorical relations* and the contextually dependent *interactions* with other multiply categorically positioned subjects.

Returning to look again for a final time at Bill's apparent abdication of white masculine positioning in Extract 3.2, if we look at the *way* in which he uses the white working class masculine 'lager lout' caricature, this is not quite as straightforward as my initial analysis above suggests. Where he invokes this 'lager lout' stereotype Bill makes an important shift to draw on 'what other people think'. Rather than claiming ownership of this analysis of racism as located within this white working classed masculine group, he moves instead to self position himself again as a knowledgeable onlooker, but this time as onlooker to the analysis *as well as* to the phenomenon itself. He has 'been round', and has experienced at least some reality to this 'lager lout' stereotype. But there is a sense in which any easy pronouncements about this stereotype are made by *other* people. Taking this additional shift into account, Bill's comments in Extract 3.2 achieve two things simultaneously. Whilst moving to distance himself from racist notions of Britishness located elsewhere in the (working) classed 'other'; the not him, Bill also abdicates responsibility for locating racism within this group. He is therefore able to distance himself from racist practices, but also to distance himself from the responsibility for locating those racist practices (easily) in the working class masculine subject. Reflecting a similar sort of nuance he moves to close his comments with what seems to be the beginnings of a social constructionist explanation as to why people might behave in racist ways which makes a *contested connection* between analytically separate lived experience and categorical experience. He does this by suggesting that British people 'live out the stereotype' influenced by an unspecified generalised abstract category of 'other people'. This nuance enables Bill to avoid aligning himself with racist practices, whilst at the same time avoiding the complete denigration of the working class figure symbolised in the holiday maker 'lager lout' caricature.

Similarly, where Bill appears to reinforce the (neo)liberal public/private division through his resistance to working classed identification as a disruptive unruly privately located force which brings racist/sexist domination into the workplace, there is additional complexity. As I discussed above in relation to my analysis of Extract 3.1, after initially being very hesitant to position himself in relation to social class, but on the basis of further prompting from me, Bill began to talk about his classed positioning relationally *through* his family relationships and background and in particular *through* his difficult relationship to his father's upward classed mobility. Whilst, as I also noted above, this short discussion led to a more emotionally alive encounter, this was not necessarily more straightforward or emotionally easier.

When I asked for further elaboration about Bill's observations around his father's story that he presents in Extract 3.1, he reverts to a position of strong defence, mounting the following challenge to my request:

Extract 3.3

[BILL] Well you know, people disappear up you know, well let's analyse, 'but why did you?' 'Cos I fell out of my cot'. I'm not a great believer in some of that stuff, um I *don't Shona*, I don't know where all this comes from, because it doesn't, it doesn't come from anything I can identify in my childhood background etc. um, no, *no*, I, I really don't know.

Here, Bill is clearly challenging my move to ask further questions about his background. Whilst he doesn't finish the phrase 'people disappear up' this falls just short of another of Bill's often used phrases which he usually finishes off with 'their own arses'. These comments could be taken to imply that at the very least any analysis derived from my line of questioning would be self absorbed, if not futile. Another related reading is that Bill refutes a psychological determinism that might be read into my mode of questioning, and which potentially goes against his strong antipathy towards individualised forms of politics consistent with his categorically left wing collectivist commitments to the working class. It chimes well with his positioning as a 'simple man', 'never mind the bollocks' that resists tendencies to over analytic 'theraping', as Bill refers to it elsewhere in our conversation. It is easy to read this resistance to my questioning about family as a refusal to reflexivity.

However, this reading as to Bill's lack of reflexivity runs counter to evidence from other parts of his account, especially the sorts of reflexivity underpinning the 'left liberal' perspective transformation which is so strongly associated with his commitment to social justice, including allusions to an understanding of feminist and multicultural perspectives so important to resisting shameful forms of whiteness. Indeed, in our third interview and after all of the extracts presented and

analysed above Bill's attitude towards engaging with this sort of reflexive attempt
to link the personal and professional shifts again. It has mellowed.

Extract 3.4

[BILL] . . . its actually *nice*, it's, it's, it's {pause} you *don't often* get the time to
reflect on {sighs} what's going on, and *you*, what *you do that*, I mean one of
the things that I've found, and again I might have mentioned to you *before*,
but it's that, *it's taken me a long time*, to actually not wear my *heart*, my
political heart on my sleeve.

The point that I am making here is that there is consistency in Bill's inconsistency
in self reflection and examination. This is an inconsistency which relates to the
contradictions within his classed identifications. If we continue to understand
politics as a euphemism for class in Extract 3.4, then it is possible to make another
reading of the shifting level of Bill's openness to self reflection which relates to his
classed positioning. The resistance to let class go coupled with a self consciously
strategic hiding from public discussion can be read as a form of self protection.
This self protection can be read in terms of the contradictions within (neo)liberal
institutional space which have a particular set of consequences for the construction of the working classes as the moral dumping ground for multicultural
contradictions.

On the other hand 'perspective transformation', ostensibly a cognitive political
investment, is actually linked to a set of classed investments which constitute Bill
as an embodied, emotional and *vulnerable* subject. It is his classed positioning
which situates Bill ambivalently and multiply as someone who is disadvantaged
but has integrity (in the face of problematic white middle classed masculinities),
but who also participates in the disadvantage of others. My persistence in pressing
at his biography in interview and his angry reaction to this pressure is important
precisely because it highlights Bill's ambivalence to class. It exposes the incomplete nature of his 'perspective transformation' therefore disrupting the coherent
complete story of himself as *counter hegemonic*.

It is 'perspective transformation' that enables Bill to situate himself counter hegemonically as *professionally* outside of his positioning within white male
middle class macho didactic managerial culture, but also outside of the equally,
but differently traditional working classed culture of his youth. Thus, this relational investment in difference and counter hegemonic perspective transformation enables Bill to create a liveable working identity as a 'good manager', who
is critical of his institutional space and supportive of ideas of equality, shifts in
gender dynamics and the promotion of 'soft skills'. But this identity is only
straightforwardly liveable where he resists positioning within working classed cultural forms. Bill must always lose something. So he is always stuck talking about
class through politics, disavowing the relations that brought him into being. This
is a conundrum that Judith Butler highlights in her analysis of subjectification as
always melancholic. What I am looking to emphasise in terms of my analysis of

relational choreography is that these losses are constantly shifting, not only in one direction, even from interview to interview.

Within the context of an interview with a person like me who expresses similar belongings it makes sense that Bill may talk more openly about classed identifications because categorically driven similarity may produce what appears to be a safer context for classed identification. On deeper reflection in the context of a relational analysis this interpretation of safety to more openly voice the classed dimensions of his politics in terms of a perspective transformation, on the basis of a categorically class based commonality between us, is only partially appropriate. For sure exposing classed identification in interview is different from wearing this openly within the institutional sphere. But, this shift from resistance and defensiveness to more open reflection represents a general pattern in our research interactions which suggests that class surfaces as a mechanism to protect *us both* from the knowledge of positioning within power. This is a pattern whereby I introduce questions around gender and race into the discussion, Bill veers to explore class, politics and social structures and I then *follow his lead* taking the conversation away from relational context. Even where Bill explores his personal background, this is only ever as it relates to classed culture and politics and never in terms of storied relational experience.

Whilst openly classed identification at work is risky for Bill, within the context of *our* interaction this is less risky than discussing gender and race because of our respective positioning, he as an older white man and me as a young white overtly anti-racist feminist woman. Class is the ground where we appear to have most in categorical common. Prioritising the classed and related political connections between us within the research interaction enables us *both* to avoid confronting our gendered difference and racism. This persistent return to class as something to be proud of, to be worn on the sleeve, prioritises our common vulnerabilities, rather than our power as a means to collaborate within the interview.

Yet this resistance to let class go as a structure of disadvantage also suggests something very important about the realities to contemporary classed denigrations within the neoliberal context and their relation to other categorically ordered relations of power and vulnerability. This is a conundrum both Bill and I are caught up in, vacillating between individual and categorical. But if we read class relationally through the idea of shifting choreographed positionings viewed as part of a longer broader interconnected range of actions, working together to produce a longer broader range, changeable goal, we can read action differently from good or bad, responsible or innocent. This shifting of class alerts us to specific realities of class denigration and its consequences not only for classed experience, but for the ability to build resisting coalitions.

Conclusions

In this chapter I have taken the individual governing subject as my starting point for understanding the everyday relational enactments of the state. Through this approach I have aimed to show that governing identity and governing agency is about more than a set of professional and institutional commitments. The social and the professional are interdependent within the lives of governing subjects. The idea of relational identity draws attention to this interdependence and to an examination of the way governing subjects understand themselves through a network of social *as well as* institutional relations. As professionals they are part of a broader relational network of others, families, friends, communities and the variety of others with whom they interact and through which they gain a sense of subjective belonging. These relationships bring with them a set of intersecting absent present back stories which position the governing subject through the social categories of power and inequality such as class, ethnicity, gender, generation and sexuality. It is through this network of categorically ordered intersecting social relations that professional identity and agency are given meaning. Being a manager, as in this example or some other professional role, such as nurse or doctor, is framed through the categories of gender and ethnicity, but *via* the context of understanding created through intimate belongings as a friend or family member, or through other aspects of biography. As such, the *governing* subject comes to be through their multiple relational entanglements. In this sense governing subjects are multiple, rather than singular. They are multiply positioned through their relationships with others and their understanding of themselves as governing subjects are related to these positionings.

Governing subjects' relational multiplicity is experienced as ontological coherence through a relational choreography of these intersecting back stories and governing agency is the product of this choreography. Feelings about their different categorically ordered relational belongings, like emotions of pride and shame for Bill in the example developed in the chapter, are the means by which these negotiations are achieved. These feelings create the patterning to the connections with others in the governing context, whether this be other colleagues, or service users. Individual governing agency is not predictable through an understanding of either professional positioning or more intimately imagined individual interests because relational investments bring these together in complicated ways. These investments are multiple, dynamically interacting and shifting through, within the subject and through its changing relations with others. For Bill this choreography is achieved through his perspective transformation which enables him to hold onto the working classed identifications which give him a sense of continuity and belonging and also a means through which to position himself against the normative positioning within power in the context of the PCT institutional space. He can remain someone who is for equality, despite his apparent positioning through the forms of institutional and social power that reproduce gendered and racialised inequalities.

Because of the way that class is constructed within neoliberal institutional contexts classed identifications pose a specific danger for Bill perhaps less in terms of his blocking professional upward mobility; after all he is already at the head of his current organisation as CEO. Instead class matters more in terms of the way in which admitting working classed positioning would confirm Bill's association with the oppressive reproduction of racist and sexist domination and inequality which is positioned as the limit of the neoliberal institutional propriety. He abdicates association with problematic white heterosexual masculinity through his investment in the positioning as 'new man': a down to earth, but enlightened onlooker over others' embarrassingly discriminatory behaviour. This abdication positions him as someone who understands the subtleties of nature and nurture and the difficulties of ethnic categorisations. But the problem with positioning himself outside of this limit occurs for Bill when his positioning within institutional power is put in question. This is because there is no means with which to differentiate himself from the neoliberal institutional norm, without positioning himself outside of his relational networks of family and community. Perspective transformation provides an important means for Bill to manage this inconvenient problematic.

On the basis of my relationally driven analysis of the shifting nature of these abdications of social positioning, I am arguing that there is something more at play than a straightforwardly cynical resistance to positioning the self through class as a means to relinquish responsibility for the reproduction of inequality associated with the limits of the liberal governing order. Despite his position at the vanguard of new managerial organisational change Bill continues to position his working life as an 'inevitable compromise'. He is sceptical and anxious. He is not straightforwardly invested in new managerial institutional norms and ideals. Indeed, he clearly works hard to position himself outside of these norms too. His abdications can equally be read in terms of Bill's complex relationship between subjective vulnerability and power/domination because *self interest* as a governing subject and *other interest* as someone who is governed through social relations are bound up with one another. Such abdications of social power are melancholic because they constitute much broader abdications of relationship with and knowledge of the *self* via the denial of the (working classed) Other within. Bill's resistance to positioning through white masculinity is as much a sign of his positioning through classed vulnerability as it is about an enactment of straightforward white (middle classed) masculine power.

Thinking about governing subjects as relationally choreographed in this way has methodological implications for the analysis of governing subjectivities which means that they can never only be interpreted and understood in singular terms as responsible or innocent. Nor can subjects be understood in terms of straightforward linear self narration within an uncontested meaning frame. Their choreography must be traced in the sense of plotted through its contradictory as well as its complimentary relationalities. I have taken some time in this chapter therefore to develop a multi stranded relational interpretation of one person's account of their working life as a governing subject. I undertook this sort of detailed analysis with multiple layered readings in order to present the sort of robust and nuanced interpretation necessary to understand the complicated and contested relationship between domination and resistance in institutional space. This sort of multiple relationally driven analysis is important in order to be able to understand the potential for resistance in the most surprising places and with the most supposedly normative governing subjects.

These multiple relationalities cannot be rationalised by the subject themself because they do not have full cognisance of the absent presences, the losses, through which they are constructing the self. To recognise that the subject cannot know and then, following that, cannot fully narrate the self in a straightforward sense is not to question the veracity of participants' accounts. Instead this is to recognise that governing subjectivity must be understood psychosocially putting a self narrative into its worldly context, and understanding its culturally constructed nature; in this example, with the most apparently normative of governing subjects, Bill, a white middle classed heterosexual man. The contestability of meanings and practices which I have drawn out in Bill's ambivalent positionings are important because they suggest the capacity for coalition through difference, rather than on the basis of something in particular, some abstracted sense of categorical sameness which is impossible to achieve. Classed inequality is complicated and shifting because of the difference between Bill's public institutional positioning and his privately lived positionings. It presents opportunities and losses, pride and shame and a basis for resistance to institutional inequality, but also potentially for its reproduction. This ambivalence becomes especially important when trying to understand governing subjects who appear to be positioned straightforwardly through dominance because it points to the ways in which governmental belonging is never straightforwardly inhabited. The resistances produced through struggle can potentially be nurtured for the purpose of resisting the institutional normativities through which institutional inequality is ordered.

In Chapter 1 I argued that the neoliberal ascendency of whiteness works subtly through the careful management of difference, bringing difference into (liberal) sameness. We can see a version of this working in Bill's account where classed difference gets brought into governing sameness via the idea of perspective transformation which serves as a means to position the working classed other as responsible for inappropriate racialising practices because of its failure to move on, to transform. The intersections of class, gender and sexuality work to produce good and bad subjects, where overt expressions of racism and sexism function as the symbolic limits to positioning within the liberal governing norm. Bill's positioning at this limit forces his reconstruction as a 'new man' as a means to differentiate himself from this. Practices of self reflexivity associated with left liberal recuperative whitenesses are a means to positioning outside of this dynamic. In the next chapter I consider how this construction of a similar sort of failure to move on serves to produce the basis of the collective construction of institutional limits within another already marginalised population, this time the 'older Asian male GP'.

Notes

1 PCTs were created under the 1997 New Labour Government (DoH, 1997). They replaced local health authorities as flagships for devolved professionally led primary

health care involving community nurses, physiotherapists, occupational therapists, as well as the numerous and hitherto professionally dominant GPs. The long-term aim was to provide jointly commissioned health and social care services in a more corporate and integrated manner. Funded directly by the Department of Health, and responsible for purchasing as well as providing local health care, in their heyday Trusts held 80 per cent of NHS budgets. In the latest round of health care reform heralded by the 2012 Health and Social Care Act these organisations have morphed into clinical commissioning groups (CCGs).

2 All names and locations have been changed to protect participants' anonymity. In summarising and representing key points in Bill's story for the reader I attempt to remain as true to his original wording as possible. Phrases in quotation marks within the main text are direct from transcripts, and where Bill emphasised words/ phrases I have retained this emphasis in italics. Where emphasis has been added by me I state this in brackets. Larger chunks of conversation are indented with an extract number for ease of identification in analysis. For more on the interviews and process see Chapter 1.

3 This colloquial phrase 'cor blimey governor' has its provenance in cockney slang where it denotes surprise, awe or appreciation commonly thought to derive historically from the religious expression 'God blind me if that is not the truth'. In its more contemporary usage it is also associated with the sort of classed sexual innuendo commonly portrayed in English comedy film between the 1950s and 1970s and in particular with the comic series of Carry On films and with the performer Sidney James. (Indeed, there is a 2000, made for television film about Sidney James which uses this catchphrase as its title 'Cor Blimey'.) With their heyday in the 1960s and 1970s, this series of comic films and the working class music hall and varieties' comic tradition of which they were emblematic are now viewed anachronistically, associated with a pre-equalities era where (hetero)sexual gendered innuendo was considered more socially acceptable, at least within working classed contexts. My reading of Bill's usage of this phrase is in keeping with this sort of humorous innuendo derived from his relational positioning in the north east where '[e]lements of an industrial heritage were embodied in an appreciation of skilled physical labour over mental agility, a collective sharing of heavy, often sexual, adult humour, and an established drinking capability' (Nayak, 2003, p. 13).

4 Health inequalities strategies began life as one of the core initiatives in the 1997 New Labour Government's health reforms, initially as part of the short lived locality based Health Action Zone initiative. By 2003 localised strategies had morphed into a National Programme (Barnes et al., 2005), since carried through in various guises by successive administrations.

5 The north east of England has a strong historical association with the development of formalised left wing politics as part of working class culture via the labour movement, with the establishment of workingmen's clubs; trade union activity and the 1936 Jarrow March against the 74 per cent 'breadline' unemployment (Nayak, 2003).

6 This sort of direct request for participants to position themselves within the social relations of power is heavily contested within qualitative interview methodologies, especially those concerned to subvert relations of power within the research context. Objections cluster around the potential for already socially powerful participants to fail to understand the relevance of social positioning, to say what they think the analyst wants to hear, to clam up or to reinforce the powerlessness of various others in their responses. In this case, as I discuss in much more detail in my 2005 (Hunter, 2005b) paper on the design of this particular research study, this questioning strategy was deliberately developed in order to *explore the response* of

those positioned through power to the highlighting and calling to account of this institutional and social power. This is in contrast to approaches which assume an *a priori* resistance to such highlighting.

7 OPCS stands for the Office for Population Census Surveys which is the UK official body for social classification and statistics. In the health care context it is associated with the collection of social statistics for medical procedural interventions and measures of clinical outcomes as well as the basis for local commissioning and other forms of health population data.

Chapter 4

The circulation and distribution of bad feeling

> It is as though a path can be traced from one person to another . . .
>
> (Hinshelwood, 1989, p. 75)

> In our culture the affective networks of institutions have come to be remarkably efficient at exploiting individual's feeling-states and experiences, reifying bits of human beings and estranging them from the human world.
>
> (Hinshelwood, 1989, p. 82)

Whereas Chapter 3 focused on the complex and dynamic negotiation of multiple emotional commitments at the *ontological* level, this chapter moves the analysis on to consider how multiple *categorical* commitments (such as gendered, raced and professional positioning) coalesce and coordinate relationally, *through emotion,* to create 'the organisation in action' (Callon, 2002). It continues to consider the ways in which anxiety and loss underpin modernisation, but this time at the institutional rather than the individual level. It explores the sorts of anxious collective professional identifications enacted through modernisation discourses that bring the organisation into being. It focuses in particular on the ways in which ideas of equality/quality become discursively associated with ideas of the new professionalism and how this reflects broader cultural idealisation of the new and progressive within neoliberalism. Thus, whilst equality is not necessarily explicitly articulated as a new managerial organisational ideal, it is implicitly articulated as part of this (or mainstreamed within other practices and ideas as I consider more explicitly in Chapter 5) through the idealisation of the 'new' and the simultaneous denigration of the 'old'. Ideas of new and old become associated with different enactments of professionalism allocating differential value, bad and good, a differential allocation of value which supports processes of exclusion/inclusion. In this way the construction of clear lines between the idealised new and the denigrated old welfare professionalism becomes a means to enact institutional inclusions/exclusions. Therefore, this chapter deals even more explicitly than Chapter 3 with the way in which hierarchically ordered ideas of inclusion/exclusion are constitutive of institutional life and the ways in which these inclusions/exclusions are being reconfigured within the context of new managerial change, and the way that this is happening through new managerialism's redrawing of (apparently) long established technical and cultural orderings.

In this way the chapter demonstrates how the emotions 'interfere' with and transform the ways in which policy ideas get taken up and worked through in specific organisational settings. The emotions are, therefore, not only important because of their power to transform the ways in which policy ideas like modernisation get taken up and worked through in specific organisational settings, but also because of the ways in which this working through enacts subjects as socially positioned, in this case as gendered, raced and generationally positioned constituents within the governing process. Thus, emotions can become powerful means of marginalisation and inclusion in governance, blocking and facilitating developments in policy logic, design and implementation.

As I described in Chapter 2 'medical dominance' (Fitzpatrick, 2001; Friedson, 1970; Stacey, 1988; Willis, 1989; Witz, 1992) has always loomed large within the health services as the archetype for hierarchically ordered, role and rule governed 'old' professionalism; where the professionally autonomous doctor dominates the clinical setting and patient care, assisted by other 'adjunct' professionals (such as community and practice based nurses, psychologists and physiotherapists). This situation has been exacerbated in primary care by the historical status of GPs as independent contractors: self employed health care providers contracted to supply an agreed package of general medical services to the NHS who are remunerated in terms of patient list size. This rigidly hierarchical ordering is sustained culturally through a process of reductive social cloning around a white masculine middle class heterosexual somatic norm.

The shifting sands of new managerial change, valorisation of holism, interprofessionalism and flexibility produced a context ripe for culture clashes between a range of professional groups as they came into increasingly closer contact with one another (Davies, 2003; Malin, 2000; A. Williams, 2000, 2003). Some of the most acute tensions have been around the blurring of boundaries between medicine and management (Berman-Brown and McCartney, 2000). However, nursing too has become more assertive relative to medicine, undergoing its own significant reform throughout the 1990s, increasing levels of credentialisation in an effort to gain more clinical responsibility and autonomy (Davies, 1995; Evetts, 2011; Salvage, 1990; Williams, 2003). Others, such as health care assistants, physiotherapists and pharmacists, followed suit (Blenkinsopp and Bond, 2003; Cameron & Masterson, 2003; Thornley, 2003). As a feminised profession nursing has been able to capitalise on its association with more feminised gendered norms valued within NPM. Through ideas of person centred care, holism, responsiveness and communication, it has presented itself as the human face of medicine in order to leverage its own professional autonomy, gaining a place at the health care management table (Richman, 2004; Wyatt & Langridge, 1996).

PCTs' commitment to corporate management and interprofessional working validated these and other professionals' bids for involvement in health care planning and operational development viewed as a potentially positive means to challenge medical dominance. The advent of PCTs also presented a significant challenge to this largely autonomous organisational positioning of GPs via a formal board and committee structure which included representatives from the range of professions, allied to medicine, as well as those in social care and other local authority managed services such as housing and sometimes even prison services, along with lay members and health service managers. As such, these shifts represented a dissipation, but also a redistribution, of professional power which included a set of complex re-stratifications *within* professional groups including general practice, where some members took on managerial responsibilities for others in their professional group (Hunter, 2005a; Pickard, 2009). Kirkpatrick and colleagues (Kirkpatrick, Dent and Jespersen, 2011) suggest that in some health care contexts this has gone as far as the professions colonising management, rather than the other way around as per the initial fears of a range of professionals. This colonisation is occurring through the discursive construction of and negotiation between the 'old' (bureaucratic) and the 'new' (managerial) professionals (Evetts, 2009; Leonard, 2003; Light, 2010; Speed and Gabe, 2013).

My argument in this chapter picks up theoretical ideas raised in Chapter 2 around the distribution of good and bad feeling (Ahmed, 2004b) as constitutive of an institution's topography. Building on the work of Hinshelwood I claim that the organisation can be viewed as an 'affective network' where 'channels of unconscious, non-symbolic communication are separate from, but intertwined with, the verbal and cognitive communication' (Hinshelwood, 1989, pp. 77–78). Bits of experience, effects, emotions, feeling-states, like a sense of blame for example, are moved around, passing from one member of the organisation to the next, stopping when one person is established as a blameworthy culprit – a scapegoat. They allocate blame unevenly through repeated projective dynamics which locate bad feeling in one identifiable boundable object. This happens through a process whereby:

1 Individuals use the context of the social network as a means of passing onto others certain feeling-states, elements of identity, which they wish to disown – a form of psychological *defence by projection*.
2 Personal affects of the individuals come to be possessed by the social network to form the energy for institutional activity.

And as a result of the above two properties:

3 There is a depersonalisation of the individual's experiences and feelings.
4 The individual becomes deeply fused to the group or institution since the social network, to a degree, *is* the individual.

(Hinshelwood, 1989, p. 79; emphasis in original)

As such Hinshelwood's notion of the affective network is a way of understanding the way in which affect travels between people, objects and ideas, and how this travelling process connects them to one another and orders their relations. It is rooted in psychodynamic ideas of transference (Freud, 1959 [1912]) and project communication (Klein, 1986 [1952]) which facilitates an understanding that there is a sort of dynamic collective unconscious being *enacted*, dispersed and distributed across time and space through projective processes (Pile, 2012). Following the performative analysis developed in Chapter 2 my use of Hinshelwood's work emphasises the ways in which it is through such unconscious projective processes that an organisation comes to be, through the contested connection between subject-objects and signs. In this case this unconscious projective process enacts the PCT through the maintenance of the illusion that it is progressive, for systemic equality, where this is far from the way many of its members experience it. This disjunction between the real experience of inequality and the institutional ideal creates the constitutive anxiety of institutional life which surfaces more or less obviously at specific points. These more obvious surfacings undercut the stated desire for more equality. In order to manage these anxious intrusions into institutional life the blame for ongoing institutional inequality is transferred, split off and projected onto one group of supposedly bad practitioners.

In the chapter I use empirical data presented in the form of an imagined dialogue to show how the affective network enacting the PCT's institutional shape functions and how this enactment works to (re)distribute blame within the PCT. While affective networks are real in the performative sense outlined above, the data presented here is used as a representational device. The imagined dialogue shows how the emotions of loss, fear and frustration coalesce around new managerial organisational change to generate blaming dynamics within the process of health policy formation. It represents the symbolic processes of transference and counter transference, the projective communications which work to circulate these blaming dynamics between material subject-objects, in this case person to person between group members, which enacts blame symbolically moving from one set of practitioners to another. This circulation of blame constitutes organisational insiders and outsiders attaching certain unwanted social characteristics and behaviours to professional groups. In this instance these blaming dynamics work through institutional shifts away from general practice to position them problematically and therefore subordinately because of their association with the older hierarchical professional orderings apparently so much more antithetical to the achievement of service quality/equality idealised within the PCT. But this blame is not distributed evenly, it coalesces around one particular group of GPs, 'older Asian male GPs', who are constructed as an especially stubborn blocking point for achieving the sorts of more equal institutional relations idealised in the PCT. Through this analysis we can see more clearly than in Chapter 3 how new managerial ideas of equality are very specifically attached to liberal ideals of gender equality. These splits are therefore related to the ways in which attachment to such liberal ideals of gender equality can produce toxic forms of resistance to achieving 'race' equality. Through this discussion the chapter challenges predictions that the new managerialism would bring more equal ways of working to health and social care governance. Instead it suggests that it can equally be creating more toxic forms of melancholic and self destructive internalised division. The discussion also challenges the coupling of newness and progression with modernisation discourse, suggesting that previous inequalities persist although their specific configuration may have shifted.

An imagined dialogue: 'We'd all be equal if it weren't for those old Asian men GPs'

The key issues of contested interpretation in qualitative research are briefly considered in the preamble to Part II of this book. But, because imagined dialogues take the 'juddering movements of contextualising, de-contextualising and re-contextualising meaning' (Gunaratnam, 2003, p. 142) common in qualitative analysis a step further than more usual forms of interpretation conducted in Chapter 3's narrative analysis it is worth discussing their status in this chapter. Because the more subtle relational dynamics which tend to be exposed through detailed within case analysis, like Bill's story in Chapter 3, are often obscured through traditional means of representing findings across cases (Mauthner and Doucet, 1998), a more powerful method is required to highlight their operation.[1] The construction of these dialogues constitutes a form of interpretive collocation (Mello, 2002) where data around the same theme from different research accounts are placed alongside one another in order to demonstrate similarity and difference, coherence and tension across a data set. Dialogues are not intended to be an unmediated representation of 'fact'; they are contested, and like *all* data they constitute partial insights into social relations. Such analyses are a powerful means of developing a layered understanding of qualitative data and of being more inclusive of multiple perspectives and their interaction in analysis. The value of such an analysis is what it tells us about the nature of group dynamics as they are constituted through emotion, and in the absence of a face to face group discussion, but also in terms of thinking through problems and possibilities for connecting across difference in organisational settings. In the case of this project specifically it enables me to represent some of the dynamics I witnessed whilst observing a range of organisational interactions such as PCT board and executive meetings, which I was not permitted to record or explicitly report in the study, but which inform my understanding and analysis.[2]

The dialogue below includes data from ten of the participants in the NHS study some of whom knew one another and worked together and others who did not. It involves three GPs, two white and one Asian man; two white women nurses; five managers, one white man from a health services background, another Asian woman from a general management background, two white women from nursing backgrounds and one white man social services manager. The eleventh participant is me a white woman academic. All of the data extracts are taken directly from interview transcripts, including my interventions. It is their juxta-position which is imagined, not the actual words. It is worth emphasising again that these juxtapositions are already representing my interpretation of the affec-tive network of the PCT. The discussion explicates this interpretation. It is not representative of the actual affective network itself, but it represents the dynamics at play as I interpreted them within the PCTs I was researching. In this way it also enables me to explore the similarities in collective institutional processes across different organisations. This means that where I talk about the dialogue as though it occurred I am interested in bringing these relational dynamics to life for the reader, I am not claiming any 'truth'/'fact' as such for them.

The dialogue

[SHONA WHITE WOMAN ACADEMIC 25] So tell me about what it's like working in the health service.

[SAM WHITE MAN GP 52] [Well] I did a year in Africa, there the hospital was run by, very much by the doctors, medical directors, a team of about ten doctors, nearly all expatriate, either Indian or British, expatriate doctors, and there was one female doctor and mostly male, but of course the doctors were such a different breed, different training, different background, to everyone else that it was very much one team I think. {pause} The funny thing is com-pared with the National Health Service job satisfaction in Africa seemed to be higher, because it was doctors who were totally in control of the entire system from top to bottom, and things that you can't do here, you could do there. So you ran the whole system top to bottom, and all the rules, which meant you were doing fewer things that you thought were stupid, any rule that affected the way doctors did their jobs in Africa the decision had been made by a group of doctors, quite reasonably. In the health service, there are all kinds of things which are irrational, stupid, for example, if someone needs to stay on medication for a year so they only need checking every six months, but they've got to come back here for me to write the prescription, three, four, five times, now {pause} if the system was controlled by local doctors you could hand that over to the pharmacist. So we've got a feeling of being disempowered if you like, on a professional level.

[IAN WHITE MAN GP 39] But in terms of managing the patients we still have a fairly hierarchical structure don't we, where a GP or the doctor is seen as the important part of the team, and I mean nurses can have their own autonomy, and social services have their role, and whatever, but at the end of the day, we haven't really got that yet.

[SAM] In my job in the surgery, I make very responsible decisions, you see people who are dying, we see lots of serious illness here, so in a sense compared with the managers in terms of making people redundant, closing things, changing jobs, I think that the GPs are probably the hard men.

[NAVNEEN ASIAN MAN GP 42] *Now we do* work in teams, you know, whether we *like it or not*, you know, that all that the disease management a lot is done is by nursing, *we have to work as a team*, always in the past the doctor made the decisions say *we do it this way*, and so I think it is a *change*, and people do find it *quite threatening* and um, particularly with *male doctors, one GP finds it very threatening*, he rang me 'Is this nurse coming? How can she come? Why should she come?' and he's a *single handed older GP*, and he finds it *so threatening*, '*How can she come to a meeting where doctors are discussing to do with medicine?*' so I think the number of those GPs is going *down*, but there are still some that are there.

[IAN] I think things have changed, I mean we're going to be predominantly women in this practice, predominantly part time women, I think that's the way that it's going in many practices, um I think it's a shame to some extent, I think we didn't have the balance right, we needed more women at work, I think it will, probably will end up going too far the other way, there won't be enough men um doing the job, um I think we're a lot more flexible, or trying to be a lot more flexible about the way in which we work, giving people opportunities to work in different ways.

[NAVNEEN] The *old* general practice, the way it's set up, there's no *flexibility*, and a lot of the new doctors want a sandwich service, so I've got a second female doctor now, who's recently qualified, *very good* high quality GP, so we've been *because* of the [reforms], we've been able to accept, *new, young enthusiastic GPs.*

[BILL WHITE MAN CEO 50] In my view, the reality is somewhat different, and you know, to be *perfectly honest* it stems down to the hierarchical control, the hegemony of the medical profession, um, every time change as I see it is required, necessary, desirable, there's often a barrier of vested interests of the medical profession.

[RITA BRITISH ASIAN WOMAN HSM 34] Cos' they're independent contractors and you can't tell them what to do, you never tell a GP what to do otherwise you get hung.

[BILL] I think a lot of it stems back from fund holding and the ethos of fund holding, the macho you know, who, 'we've got the cash we can do what we want'.

[MAUREEN WHITE WOMAN CEO 47] It's very difficult to explain, [as a manager] you have to work very hard to be accepted by GPs.

[SHONA] So that's about not being a clinician is it?

[MAUREEN] I think to begin with if we go back to the days that we started the PCG [Primary Care Group], I think because of the ethnic make-up of the group that I was working with, there was possibly, I was female, they were all Asian males, and I had to work hard to become credible, I just sort of *worked* to gain my credibility um.

[JAYNE WHITE WOMAN NURSE 41] *Oh, yes* and I know it's going on with patients, very much that they don't understand the needs of women patients, and I've often had to fight for women against GPs male GPs. And I think women, have to prove themselves so much before, they'll get respect, probably more so than men. You have to do a lot more for recognition and respect than men do, to be heard. They won't sit back and listen . . . but we, we are there to represent standards and choices for people and I think sometimes they forget it a bit and they're not that good at listening and recognising that we've got equal say in things and a big contribution.

[LUCY WHITE WOMAN NURSE MANAGER 38] Yes, that's right and I think we've still got that hanging on, you can tell that from the, the older consultants can't you? They're still in that sort of mode.

[LYDIA WHITE WOMAN NURSE PRACTITIONER 47] With some of the Asian doctors there is a cultural thing there, the way that doctors are trained mainly in India, is the old British Empire style, *so they are taught* according to the British system, so they're quite hierarchical, and um, you know, they can be quite rigid in their thinking, and those doctors, I think have found that quite difficult. Certainly working with them on the [Primary Care Trust's] board, when we *began*, we had quite a few issues, because they were all Asian doctors, one or two of them, *very, very good*, but the others quite sort of, '*stera*'[3] and um, dictatorial in their approach.

[GEORGE WHITE MAN SOCIAL SERVICES DEPARTMENT MANAGER 52] I've been *quite staggered*, [given the ethnic make-up of the PCG] I remain, really, quite puzzled, by their attitude. Like the attitude of a range of GPs to that whole issue it feels like a real *over hang* from, from the old days, this, this, this *incredible* individualism. The overall *feel* is of a largely *male* organisation, there's some incredibly *rude* behaviour that goes on, it's quite, it's quite staggering, looked at from the outside and I'm just sitting there thinking, {raising voice} '*What the hell's going on?*' You know, it's *just really rude*, you know, and then, not infrequently, people are *directly rude to each other* and will have head on clashes, you know, it's real sort of *testosterone* feel to it.

Breaking with a gendered past

The dialogue begins with a general question from me around life working in the health services to which Sam, one of the GPs, responds. His lengthy response does a lot of framing work for the range of issues developed in the rest of the dialogue. It highlights the structuring of the health care team and the pattern of working relations as a crucial part of this working experience; it sets up a comparison between the present and past; it also sets up a racialised and gendered framework. I consider the racialised dynamics in the following section but first I am interested in the way Sam's comparison between the two health care systems serves to demonstrate the ways in which the new NHS's more recent configurations (where traditional professional hierarchies are contested) disempowers GPs within the health care team. The comparison is then taken up by each of the other participants whose comments both support and challenge Sam's initial observations to construct notions of the old and the new. Within the dialogue as a whole

Table 4.1 The characteristics of the new and the old professionalism

	New professionalism	Old professionalism
Structured by	Equality between professional groups (and women and men)	(Gendered & racialised) hierarchy between professions
Ways of working	In multidisciplinary teams	(Professional) identity, role and rule governed
	Flexible, dynamic, facilitative, communicative	Inflexible, aggressive, didactic or passive
Key concerns	Patients, holistic care, accountability, quality	Exclusively either clinical/technical focus or care/needs focus

there is convergence as to what it is that constitutes the new and the old professionalism respectively, with little recognition of any overlap between the practices of the two. The characteristics of each as they are considered within the dialogue are summarised in Table 4.1 below. The key tension between Sam and the other participants in the dialogue is around the merit or disadvantage in these changes and the impact of these reconfigurations on health care work.

Sam's initial comments also serve to situate the key protagonists (as he sees them) within the story of health service change as managers and GPs. Very early in the dialogue the gendered characteristics of professional relations are made explicit through Sam's positioning of himself and other GPs as 'hard men' in relation to (softer) managers. This theme then gets taken up by the other participants in various ways, through a consideration of the entrance of women into general practice and the relationship of (men) GPs to (women) nurses. Although the gendered dimension of the conversation is not always explicit it can be traced in a number of ways. The slippage between GPs and men, and women and nursing, most obvious in Jayne's comments, is there in other formulations. The repeated juxtaposition of new women doctors (or other women members of the health care team) with flexibility, 'high quality', standards, listening/communication, enthusiasm, and, on the other hand, (old) men GPs, or the practice of general practice as 'macho' 'stera' 'testosterone' filled 'rigid'/inflexible dictatorial self-interested, serves to associate the old and the new with certain gendered discourses. It is through these juxtapositions and slippages that gender equality, quality and certain ways of practising profession become linked. Even where I intervene to attempt to reposition the discussion in terms of professional relations, the discussion continues with reference to the social relations of gender and race as these intersect with profession. Indeed, Maureen's response to this attempt suggests a more emphatic prioritisation of the social. One way of reading this struggle between the old and the new is as a struggle over the changing social and, in particular, the gendered relations of health and social care within the context of the PCT.

This reading of the dialogue supports the observations made around the complex contestations around shifts from the old to the new primary health care system. In particular it supports suggestions that a 'clash of masculinities' (Davies, 1995, pp. 183–184) between the old GPs and the new managers would create space for new alliances to be forged in particular between nurses, 'radical doctors' and 'new-style managers'.

The dialogue suggests that NPM has certainly opened up space for valuing more feminised ways of working within health and social care and also for women health care professionals to enter the more public arena of policy development. The PCT constitutes one key avenue through which this is achieved. It also seems to have created space for traditionally gendered professions (such as nursing and social work) to contribute to the work of the PCG/T precisely because of their assumed expertise in the softer skills valued by NPM such as working with patients, empowerment and (e)quality (in) care. The moves that different professional groups make in order to 'fit' this construction of the new professionals, however, are not the same. New medicine and new management move to construct the self as less hierarchical, more concerned with quality and parity with other professions. New nursing and social work build on histories of practising holistic or social care to move to construct themselves as concerned with linking structure and process (communication in particular), 'standards', as Jayne says, to develop quality care for the needs of users. In this way the empirical findings support predictions that consensus would constitute an important dimension of new managerialist culture, where 'internal conflicts are viewed as divisionary at best and at worse destructive' (Newman, 1995, p. 20; Newman, 2013a).

This move to consensus and the suppression of internal conflict is represented in other ways in the dialogue. As the conversation progresses there is a sense both through the language used and the tone of participants' comments that the new is coming to *displace* the old, in some form of inevitable and natural transition. Navneen presents this change as a simple matter of (older men GP) numbers. Although George comments on the remaining '*over hang* from the old days', that's how 'it will probably end up', says Ian. It is (only) GPs and consultants (doctors who are presented as unable to accept this natural transition), who are, according to Lucy 'still hanging on' to 'that sort of mode'.

Whilst the dialogue is suggestive of new gendered articulations within the PCT there are two significant problems here. Newman (2004) comments on the tendency for change narratives in modernisation discourses to become normative, involving mis-rememberings of the past and over-tidy perspectives on the present; the discussion within the narrative around inequalities is representative of such a simplistic reading. Reading at the literal level the story runs that: gender inequality is diminishing as the health services become more equal through the natural attrition of older men staff. However, when I more closely examine the emotional dynamics within the dialogue in the following section it becomes clear that gendering *and racialisation* are still prevalent; it is only their subject-objects which have been reconfigured. The second issue in this current reading relates to what happens when there is a perceived *rupture* between the past and the present.

Throughout the dialogue the articulation of the old and the new involves the expression of what are on the whole split polarised, rather than reparative, social relations. It is through these splits that the notion of the new becomes idealised and the past denigrated.

The symbolic centrality of medicine

Building on Hinshelwood's observations on the affective network, Hoggett and Miller (2000, p. 357) have highlighted how split 'collective sentiments' such as feelings of despair or apathy can be collectively held, becoming attached to collective discourses, 'permeating the social networks of an area, rather than being individually held feelings'. These sorts of split collective emotions often occur as responses to uncertainty within organisations, asserting a powerful grip on the life of a group. The centrality of medicine, and general practice in particular within the dialogue, points to the construction of such strong collective sentiments directed towards this professional group. The pattern of the dialogue supports this split: the construction of its most heated and confrontational aspects in terms of tone and the language used, for example, the references to 'threat', hanging, fighting, the focus on general practice, and the 'old' general practice in particular. Most of the emotional energy within the dialogue as it is constructed here is focused on GPs, including the emotional energy of the GPs themselves.

This symbolic construction of the *old* general practice performs an emotional function across the dialogue, constituting the focus for the projection of bad feeling and anxiety within the PCT. As I represent it here in the dialogue this happens by way of the following process: Sam begins the dialogue by conveying a sense of disempowerment as a GP which he passes on to Ian, another GP. Ian resists this feeling, passing back an arguably more realistic analysis of GPs at the top of what remains a 'fairly hierarchical structure'. Sam then takes on this more positive assessment, able to take pride in his responsible positioning as one of the 'hard men'. However, Navneen another GP, comes in with a challenge to Sam's more positive repositioning of GPs, more explicitly reintroducing bad feeling through a sense of insecurity and threat. This threat is then taken in by Ian, who shifts his perspective to reflect the shame and regret with which Sam began the dialogue. At this point Navneen resists this regretfulness, adopting the more enthusiastic tone he associates with the flexible new young good high quality GPs. Thus, he positions himself with the 'new' cadre of GP, in opposition to Sam and Ian's desire for the past. There is an emotional ambivalence represented up to this point in the dialogue. This is an emotional ambivalence which is working throughout the group which serves to diffuse bad feeling, shifting it one way and then another between participants. A change happens when Bill offers his perspective as a manager (see Chapter 3). He forcefully and unequivocally challenges this ambivalence, claiming 'the reality is somewhat different' and relocating the origin of bad feeling very clearly within the medical profession and their unwillingness to change. From here, each of the participants successively reinforces this sense of GPs' anachronistic inflexibility which creates the distance and difference between GPs and themselves. After the other CEO, Maureen, introduces ethnicity as a salient issue there is no variation in this emphasis represented in the dialogue. Bad feeling escalates and intensifies as it circulates through the nurses and social workers' comments, increasingly forcefully projected onto GPs.

It is through this emotional process that I have reconstructed relationally in this imagined dialogue that the 'old' GPs are symbolically split off from the rest of the PCT, constructed as obstructive hierarchical rude individualistic self interested sexist and damaging to service accountability and quality. They are, therefore, constructed as the blameworthy culprits who keep the PCT unequal, despite its aspirations to live up to the modernisation ideal. These split projective dynamics serve to maintain the PCT's more equal modernised ideal of itself, whilst recognising the ongoing unequal reality. It enables the other members of the health care team to distance themselves from the ongoing existence of inequalities within the PCT through their rejection of the old professionalism. Thus, the old GPs' continuing presence is symbolically important for the group as a foil for the good practice of the new professionals within the PCT. Figure 4.1 below is a diagram representing the split dynamics of the new PCT.

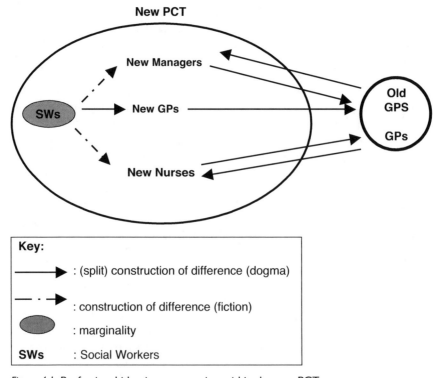

Figure 4.1 Professional identity construction within the new PCT

There are a number of important issues here around the dynamics that this split creates within the PCT. At a general level this projection of bad feeling onto GPs is clearly detrimental to joint working within the PCT. Ironically, it can serve to reinforce rather than challenge the dominance of medical concerns within the day to day work of the PCT. That in itself can place disproportionate pressure on certain members of the health care team traditionally positioned as organisationally subordinate, such as nurses, health care assistants and administrators who take on the 'management' of 'bad behaviour' within the PCT. Maureen and Jayne's comments are suggestive of the ways in which this is often compounded by the uneven gendered distribution of this responsibility within the PCT, with women having to work hard to 'become credible' themselves or support others, like women patients, to gain credibility in the face of discriminatory masculine behaviours. The feminised nature of such emotional labour is then of course reinforced. Finally, this split also perpetuates the sort of blame culture from which PCTs are seeking to distance themselves, only shifting the object of blame. Just as this split between the old GPs and 'the rest' of the new primary health care team feeds off and into the reconstruction of gendered divisions within primary care so it does in relation to racialised divisions within primary care. In fact it is precisely the intersection of gender and race which serves to shift blame for persistent inequality in a further important way as the dialogue progresses.

In the second half of the dialogue at the point where Maureen's comments seem to be challenging the certainty of Bill's perspective with a more thoughtful comment about the difficulties between GPs and managers, I ask for clarification as to what makes it difficult to work with GPs. This is an important interjection in so far as the construction of the imagined dialogue is concerned because it represents my attempts to be clear about the prioritisation of participants' connection between the professional and the social rather than prioritising my own reading. Maureen's response produces another shift in the dialogue whereby ethnicity is foregrounded above both masculinity and profession as the cause of difficulties ('because of the ethnic make-up of the group'). It is after this point that South Asian men GPs come to symbolise the old professionalism, but with its social characteristics more exaggerated to the extent where the problematic past is directly associated with British imperialism (their 'British Empire style', according to Lydia) and difficulties directly framed in terms of these GPs' anachronistic approaches to the (public) role of women, for instance their place on the PCT board and as chief officer of the PCG. Indeed, this image gathers affective momentum as it circulates throughout the group (see Chapter 2). After Maureen's comments, the language used becomes more vivid: 'fighting' 'hanging on', 'rigid', 'stera', 'overhang', 'rude', 'staggering', 'puzzling'; the images are evocative of the dualistic combat occurring within the organisation between the older Asian GPs and 'the rest'. Thus, by the end of the dialogue, this escalation of bad feeling fuels the racialisation of the split between the GPs and 'the rest'. As a result the failure to achieve quality-equality, so important to current constructions of public service modernisation, is projected onto older Asian men GPs.

It is important to be clear about what I am claiming about the social relations of race and racialisation and how they are operating here. First what I am interested in demonstrating here is not that all PCTs would demonstrate the same sort of racialising processes, though, given the stance I outlined in Chapter 1 about contemporary multicultural nationalism and as I go on to argue below, I do claim some basic reality to such a postcolonial discursive framing as a constitutive absent presence (I comment most directly on what this means for the pervasiveness of racialising processes in Chapter 8). What I am more interested in pointing out through my analysis here is that within such postcolonial contexts racialising processes operate as an already present shorthand for enacting exclusion. Racialising discourses are available to enact perceptions of threat which are already constituted as meaningful through particular histories of association and which are further reinforced in different enactments. These histories are surfaced through feeling. The more they are surfaced via emotion the more intensely they are felt. Therefore, my suggestion is not that South Asian GPs are always necessarily positioned as the locus for blame and bad practice because of postcolonial histories, but that in this case they constitute the most obvious and easily available scapegoat for blame because of a particular set of institutional histories which enact this racialising of blame as a possibility.

My second point, and somewhat relatedly, concerns the direct lines between imperialism and medicine which are vividly drawn in Lydia's case here. For Lydia, as I consider elsewhere (Hunter, 2005b), her family and her husband in particular have very direct experience of this imperial medical system and its role in migration because her husband, one of these older Asian men GPs, migrated from India to England in the early 1960s to complete his medical training, before settling here to marry Lydia and establish what was a single handed GP led practice in an area of high socioeconomic deprivation. Sam, similarly, is someone who has very direct experience of colonialism and medical government within colonial contexts. Whilst generational change means the number of GPs with this sort of direct experience is literally reducing, neocolonial relations continue to very strongly frame medical culture and training in the English system. This was particularly the case for one of the PCTs that participated in this research represented within the dialogue. Collective sentiments like the ones I am representing here in this imagined dialogue feed into and off broader discursive trends towards the racialisation of 'poor performance' in the health services (Kyriakides and Virdee, 2010; West, 2001) and more general constructions of hyper-masculine South Asian cultures (Alexander, 2004). Both constructions rely on the image of minority cultures as anachronistic and backward-looking in their commitment to tradition. They are rooted in assumptions as to the particular intersection between gendered and generational relations in South Asian cultures where it is imagined that strong patriarchal norms oppress women within the family context and in public life. It is this image of oppressive anachronism which is constituted as the limit to their inclusion in the modernised national culture (Hunter, 2006; Lewis, 2005).

This racialised and gendered split between the old and the new has serious consequences for health and social care practice. It enables primary care organisations to see themselves as representationally equal and for equality as understood by the liberal definition even when unequal practices are clearly evident within their organisational cultures; so it can work to block organisation wide support for deeper culturally driven systemic institutional change. It can also serve to obscure the appropriate focus for organisational change. The emotional dynamic operating within the dialogue pits white women professionals against Asian men professionals; so it was Lydia and Maureen whose comments were most explicitly directed towards Asian men GPs. This then serves to obscure the role of white men (or indeed minority ethnic women) in perpetuating sexist, or 'bad quality' organisational practice. This occlusion is in spite of the fact that within the dialogue the nearest representation of the caricature of the old medicine comes through the perspective of the oldest white man GP, Sam. Conversely, the nearest to a caricature of new medicine is through the approaching middle age Asian GP Navneen's comments. The way in which this obvious contradiction within the dialogue goes unnoticed suggests that this image of Asian GPs, which enables their scapegoating within the PCT, is much like what Paul Hoggett (2000a, ch. 7) thinks of as a dogma: an illusion which believes itself to be the truth, rather than an illusion which understands the fictitious nature of reality.

The essence of a fiction is that it is self-contradictory, it always operates '*as if*' aware of its own contested relationship to reality. Therefore, the issue with dogma is not that it completely misleads, or misrepresents, but that it is unreflexively held through the tight coupling of particular subject-objects with particular meanings. This tight coupling is achieved through the polarisation between good and bad. The space of ambivalent interdependence between representation and object is collapsed and understanding becomes determinist and narrowed. In the case of Asian men GPs' association with 'poor performance', there is a 'truth' in this, in the sense that this staff group have tended to be employed in unpopular inner urban areas in single handed underresourced practices and faced the twin challenges of low levels of financial investment and infrastructural support in areas with long histories of deprivation and high incidence of ill health (Bornat, Leroi and Raghuram, 2009; Jones and Snow, 2009; Widgery, 1991). The movement of such practitioners into the 'new' NHS has undoubtedly not run smoothly. There are some who do have nostalgic longings for a more traditionally ordered general practice (West, 2001) and they do often also preside over practices which are 'poorly performing' in the terms of the ubiquitous league tables. But, to collapse this complex set of social, cultural and material factors into the image of an undifferentiated older, anachronistic and inflexible Asian GP is to slip into dogmatism.[4] If such dogmatism is used to deny loss as it is from a psychosocial perspective, then the pertinent question is: what loss is it that such dogmatism is hiding here?

Melancholic longings

Returning to the beginning of the dialogue, to focus more explicitly on feeling, a sense of loss is the very clearly overriding emotion at the outset. For Sam and Ian their present experience as GPs is defined through their struggles around the changing meaning of what it is to be a good health care professional in the rapidly shifting organisational contexts of the new NHS. Threats to their understanding of their professional worlds and their positioning within these are expressed in feelings of anxiety, fear, shame and loss which surround the shift from the old to new. For these GPs the loss being mourned is the loss of masculine medical dominance, and their unambiguous positioning as the responsible 'hard men' at the head of the health care team. The blame for this loss is attributed to the rise of women professionals; nurses coming into spaces where 'doctors are discussing to do with medicine', but also women GPs who take gender equality 'too far the other way', to where 'there won't be enough men doing the job'. However, the strong denigration of the past and those associated with it and the desire to *supplant* old practices with a set of new ones, which works *throughout* the dialogue and through *all* of the other participants' comments, is suggestive of the more widespread shared melancholic dynamic underpinning this shift from old to new professionalism.

It is worth presenting a reminder of what is being claimed here in relation to melancholia as it has been outlined until now. Returning to the work of Anne Cheng (2000, pp. 7–14) introduced in Chapter 1 melancholia is *a pathological response* to loss, the counterpart to mourning. Unlike healthy mourning which involves melancholy as a normal process of sadness, melancholia 'is interminable in nature and refuses substitution' (see also Crociani-Windland and Hoggett, 2012; Hook, 2012); the melancholic is psychically stuck, bringing the lost object into the self, feeding on it, as it were. Paradoxically then, this stuckness is both nourishing for the self, but also debilitating, since the melancholic subject experiences resentment and denigration for the lost object they are ingesting.

> The melancholic's relationship to the object is now no longer just love or nostalgia but also profound resentment. The melancholic is not melancholic because he or she has lost something but because he or she has introjected that which he or she now reviles. Thus the melancholic is stuck in more ways than just temporally; he or she is stuck – almost choking on – the hateful and loved thing he or she just devoured.
>
> (Cheng, 2000, p. 9)

At the moment that the subject and object become intrinsically (con)fused, loss becomes violent exclusion. This is because the return of the loved object would jeopardise the fragile 'digestive' process which is so important to maintaining a coherent and positive sense of self, or group identity for the collective. Thus, melancholic ambivalence manifests in *violent* exclusion. Following this logic, the denigration of the old GPs is the PCT's melancholic response to the central paradox of welfare governance experienced to a greater or lesser extent by all welfare professionals; that their professional raison d'être is supposed to be to do good, but they work at the heart of a system which operates unequally, internally for its employees as well as in its relations with users. As we saw in Chapter 3, for Bill the tradition of welfare professionalism is something to be proud of, rooted in notions of service (Hoggett, Mayo and Miller, 2006b), but at the same time something shameful precisely because of its implications in the reproduction of inequality. Thus, the other PCT members' projection of dominance onto the old GPs betrays the desire to rid the self of responsibility for dominating and exclusionary practices.

In Chapter 1 where I first introduced the idea of the melancholic bind, I drew attention to the centrality of the ambivalent exclusion-yet-retention of racialised Others to maintaining the dominant white ideal so important to sustaining contemporary white liberal identity. Through my analysis of Bill's narrative in Chapter 3 I began to explore the ways in which this dominant white ideal is differentiated through multiple social relations and the ways in which such differentiations enable distinctions between good and bad whitenesses to emerge; distinctions which are also crucial to sustaining white liberal identity in postcolonial contexts. The dialogue presented in this chapter builds on both of these threads. It highlights much more explicitly than Bill's narrative how the meaning of being a welfare professional is bound up with this broader postcolonial melancholia and the role that welfare professionalism plays in sustaining this contemporary white liberal identity. Thus, the dialogue provides an insight into the ways colonial histories operate through the emotions as an always present framing absence, something which cannot be clearly articulated because of its association with domination but which interacts with, indeed is constitutive of and must be managed through, contemporary organisational dynamics.

Sam's opening comments are important in locating what is often thought of as the 'golden age' of welfare professionalism (Wilding, 1982) firmly within its colonial context as part of a racially structured patriarchal capitalism enacted through the interdependent development of welfare policy in the metropolitan home and abroad in the colonial peripheries (Williams, 1989). This colonial experience was very clearly, as Sam describes, 'nearly all expatriate, either Indian or British, expatriate doctors, and there was one woman doctor and mostly men, but of course the doctors were such a different breed, different training, different background, to everyone else', presiding over African health care users. As I note above these comments position the contemporary organisation and its members in terms of the material as well as the cultural legacies of the circulation of bodies and practices between these spaces.[5] Through this frame Sam's sense of disempowerment at home is representative of white subjects' complicated feelings of loss associated with the change in status that comes with the shift away from the certainties of Empire through the postcolonial to the supposedly post-racial. However, any feelings of imperial pride are very quickly neutralised within the dialogue by the shift to pride in the changed NHS. This shift in pride serves to associate colonialism and the older Asian men GPs' anachronistic colonial pride onto the 'victims' of colonial enterprise, and away from the systemically dominant white professionals. Through this complex projection, older Asian men GPs are positioned as symbolic of the ongoing 'intrusion' of imperialism's failures into the contemporary moment; it is *they* who cannot move on from colonialism, who cannot relinquish race and *they* who cling to aspirations of dominance manifest in their refusal of gendered equality. It is through this connection between gendered discrimination and the older Asian men GPs that the reproduction of gendered inequality in particular comes to stand in for masculine post imperial excess within the dialogue. As the dialogue progresses the older Asian men GPs come to constitute 'serviceable ghosts' (Cheng, 2000, p. 13), necessary because they provide the foil for contemporary liberal white professionalism which is so keen to avoid guilt for the degradations of its imperial past. The association made by the group between these denigrated professionals and the reproduction of gender inequality serves to explain its ongoing reproduction within the PCT as a whole and simultaneously serves to downplay, or even erase, the issue of racialised discrimination. The use of ideals of gender equity (no matter how limited) to discredit older Asian GPs is particularly important as this shifts responsibility for gender inequality away from normative dominant masculinities, but also provides the justification for ignoring the unequal experiences of Asian GPs. Thus, it is interlocking *multiple* social relations of gender, generation and ethnicity that work together to sustain the melancholic dynamics of the PCT. Reading NPM's modernisation primarily through gendered relations threatens to perpetuate the exclusion of older Asian men GPs. Similarly, reading postcolonial melancholic dynamics through race alone also fails to get at the ways in which racialised denigrations can occur through the ostensible desire to value gendered equality, a dynamic which holds the inequalities experienced by gendered and raced subjects in play.

Conclusions

In Chapter 2 I claimed that the same feelings can have contradictory and paradoxical impacts because of the way they are lived through the intersection of multiple dynamics of difference. This uneven distribution of bad feeling serves to enact organisation and its members in a particular form. In the dialogue,

> angrily blaming oppressors was part of challenging the dominant group's right to exercise power, but it could also limit the possibility of developing new views, of compromising. If not situated, a focus on blame [through anger] could also be used against marginalized groups.
>
> (Holmes, 2004, p. 223)

These complexities are manifest within the dialogue. Fear and shame around the old professionalism serves to challenge both medical dominance and traditional masculine hierarchy within the PCT. However, the split that this creates between the old and the new becomes racialised and can therefore serve to enable the PCT to sustain racialised relations of inequality just as it purports to challenge gendered inequalities. This operates at least in part through the way in which the collective sentiments serve to idealise the new, sustaining the illusion that the reproduction of inequality is related to what is past, and that they will dissipate in time as part of a natural, ostensibly progressive evolution.

My intention in this analysis is not to discredit what participants are saying and feeling. There are a number of 'truths' in what they are claiming about the old versus the new, in terms of the changing nature of professional autonomy within a more performance managed, procedural and economy focused public service context. But what is at stake in this chapter is what these valid anxieties and concerns attach themselves to, how they are distributed and the potential consequences and what this means for joint working and governing processes which can work to challenge the frames of such contexts. These shifts are made more complicated because the past was of course not a panacea for equality. Thus, one of the core difficulties within the dialogue is that the lost object of the good welfare professional was always a fantasy as per the argument laid out in Chapter 1. The more this past is idealised as a means to protect from the threat of more neoliberally inclined institutional change the more problematically this fantasy becomes fetishised to ward off anxiety. The projection of blame onto older Asian men GPs means that the group can revision the imperial past, at the same time as deluding itself that it is 'righting' its wrongs. This redistribution of blame means that it does not have to consider the reproduction of hegemonic white masculinities. The women professionals' support for this redistribution of blame is perhaps more vehement because to question otherwise would also be to put themselves within the frame for 'guilt' as well as innocence. So, just as for Bill in the last chapter, motivations change and shift relationally. Their dynamic nature is part of the difficulty in challenging them because they shift, but they also gather their own momentum. In the next chapter I explore how momentum can be challenged and resistance enabled.

Notes

1 The idea of creating dialogues came from Yasmin Gunaratnam's (2001) study of hospice workers and users where she concocted an imagined dialogue around food within a hospice setting in order to draw out the hidden racialised and gendered dynamics informing multicultural service provision in that setting. I initially produced dialogues between professionals from within the same professional group to demonstrate the construction of collective identifications within PCTs (Hunter, 2005a).

2 I have been successfully using dialogues for teaching purposes with post qualifying professionals working in health and social care settings, and also with undergraduate Social Policy and Sociology students. The success of using these dialogues in this way is at least in part because they are so recognisable to students in terms of their experience of working within health and social care. They are a powerful means to

enable students to begin to identify and grapple with the circulation of racialised and gendered power dynamics within their own organisations and to understand their contradictory now-you-see-it-now-you-don't-nature. See Chapter 2 and the preamble to Part II.

3 Colloquialism, shorthand for sterile.

4 I consider this issue of fiction and dogma in more detail in Chapter 8.

5 Although the increasing entrance of new migrant groups into medicine is changing the ethnic ordering of the NHS, this form of colonial hierarchy white British, Indian, Black African and Black Caribbean is still recognisable in the ethnic origins and stratification of NHS employees; white British and Indian doctors, large numbers of Black African and Black Caribbean nurses, but negligible doctors. This is sustained through the ongoing legacy of colonial education systems (Doyal and Pennell, 1994; Henry, 2007; Kyriakides and Virdee, 2010; Skills for Health, 2003; Smith and Mackintosh, 2007; Smith et al., 2006; Ward, 1993).

Chapter 5

Resisting the happy governmentalities of diversity

> A politics which neglects that moment of identity and identification –
> without, of course, thinking of it as something permanent, fixed or essen-
> tial – is not likely to be able to command New Times.
>
> (Hall, 1996, p. 237)

> The intervention of postcolonial or black critique is aimed at transforming
> the conditions of enunciation at the level of the sign . . . not simply setting
> up new symbols of identity, new 'positive images' that fuel an unreflective
> 'identity politics'. The challenge to modernity comes in redefining the
> signifying relation to a disjunctive 'present'.
>
> (Bhabha, 2004 [1994], p. 354)

In this chapter I begin to situate the discursive 'turn to diversity' as part of what is enacted through the melancholic neoliberal response to the liberal state's prob-lem with social difference that I outlined in Chapter 1; as part of an increasingly aggressive (neo)liberal ordering strategy for the containment of social difference. But my concern here (and in the Chapters 6 and 7 in different ways) is to critically engage with the idea of diversity as one of a number of multiple and overlapping sets of discourses which are enacted by governing subjects who are interested in promoting some form of socially transformative action from within the state. My concern is to explore how this neoliberal governmental strategy is enacted variously and unpredictably in everyday governing practices and how it might produce resistance to normative institutional enactments even as it contains and disciplines difference. This takes me back to a consideration of the importance of identity as a relational enactment which brings together past and present through the connection between sociohistorically located biography (positioning) within the present institutional space.

The influx of diversity consultants, champions and trainers into public and pri-vate sector organisations, part of what Prasad and Mills (1997) call the 'diversity industry' (see also Hamaz, 2008), is one mechanism by which it is argued that the organisational profile of equality, identity and difference have been raised at the same time as it is claimed that attention to issues of structural inequality and discrimination has been diluted. Elaine Swan and Steve Fox (2010) examine this proliferation of diversity workers as an emergent occupational group with varied career trajectories which reflect the mixed experience of the workers whose perspectives are considered in this chapter:

> Many start life as grassroots activists. Some inherit equality and diversity work as part of a wider occupational role as no-one knows where to put it. It sticks to some because they are 'black'. And it comes with the turf in some human resource management (HRM) roles. Regardless of the origins of their work, diversity workers are now being incorporated into professionalised and managerialised practices as part of new public management (NPM) and the 'new equality regimes'.
>
> (Swan and Fox, 2010, p. 568)

As such, diversity workers and diversity work sit at the intersection of a range of competing and contradictory discourses which position diversity workers as 'outsiders within' in the sense that they bring broader concerns of social justice associated with informal 'extra' institutional struggles for equality into formal institutional spaces. From within the current governmental frame diversity's association with managerial ideals and practices, like the softer quasi legal tools used in mainstreaming (guidelines, communications, codes of conduct, parts of the performance evaluation nexus referred to in Chapter 1), have seen it positioned as positive in the sense of being for things, rather than against them; as creating encouraging organisational environments where employees can work to their full potential (Liff, 1997; Zanoni et al., 2010), enhancing overall quality in service provision and delivery (Commission for Racial Equality, 1995). This is in contrast to the way in which from within this governmental frame equal opportunities discourses are associated with more negative 'anti'-politics which involves the sorts of punitive (for the perpetrator) hard legal redress which comes with being against things rather than for them (see, for example, Ahmed, 2012).

In line with some of the broader critiques around the supposed neoliberal co-option of this mainstreaming shift,[1] the assumptions about diversity workers tend to be that on entering formalised organisational spaces they have become cowed; a commercialised and commodified version of the more radical grassroots equality activists infiltrating institutional (and especially public service) spaces in the 1970s and 1980s (Newman, 2013; Squires, 2006). These arguments turn on the assumed tensions between the supposedly binary position of professionals and activists. This supposed binary positions professionals as organisational insiders, disinterested in a broader politics of social justice and more concerned with their own career progression within a context of the broader organisational development. The opposite is assumed to be the case for activist outsiders, apparently more concerned with advancing broader claims for social justice outside of the institutional space. These positions are seen to offer different resistance strategies:

as radical and autonomous but marginalised activists or as reformist assimilated and incorporated professionals.

For the critics of the 1990s turn to diversity (Bagilhole, 2009; Benschop, 2001; Blakemore and Drake, 1996; Kandola, Fullerton and Ahmed, 1995; Konrad, Prasad and Pringle, 2006; Malik, 2013; Prasad and Mills, 1997). The concern is that diversity professionals, operating as 'outsiders within' institutional contexts where space for resistance is limited, quickly become co-opted into governmental languages and practices. This governmental logic assumes that no matter how historically legitimate they may be, collective identity based claims to equality remain disruptive to social cohesion (see, for example, Inter Ministerial Group on Equalities, 2010). As such, the fear is that these workers leave behind 'purer' forms of more radical, politically motivated social justice activism associated with the idea of collective group oriented equality and seek incremental rather than transformative organisational change according to a more individualised diversity model. These sorts of insider/outsider dilemmas become even more complicated where newer forms of identity politics such as queer politics have been co-opted within an understanding of diversity (Duggan, 2003). Individualising processes mean that diversity workers are being called on to embody diversity for their organisations, where their bodies and their subjective positioning as women, Black or queer staff come to literally, as well as symbolically, diversify the organisational space, and the very process of being 'inside' is perceived to set them apart from 'their' communities 'outside' (see Hunter, 2006; Kimura, 2013; Puwar 2004). Yet at the same time as individualising processes risk situating diversity as an essentialised property of individuals, part of the reason for the popularisation of diversity discourse from within a range of activist movements is the possibilities it presents for positively engaging with issues of identity and difference within a politically transformative framework (Sudbury, 1998). Creating a framework more attuned to 'the multitude of characteristics that mark each person as unique' (Bacchi and Eveline, 2009) than one driven by a more categorically inclined, group based politics, diversity can work with more intersectionally inclined forms of analysis where power is more complicatedly distributed, at the same time as it is sedimented. It has therefore proved important to the development of feminist, Black and queer activisms (Duggan, 2003; Newman, 2012; Tomlinson, 2013).

As my analysis in Chapter 3 has already shown, binary insider/outsider understanding underplays the complex, multiple and intersecting relations between institutional and personal positioning involved in the relational process of subjectification through which governance is enacted. One is never simply inside or outside of institutions. Whilst loss (of what you are outside) is core to institutional subjectification processes, it is always incomplete and dynamically shifting. Personal biographical social histories (subjective losses) are always carried into the institutional space as absent presences. Insiders are always outsiders (Hunter, 2006) because temporalities and spatialities are always *out of line*. The institutional present is always disjunctive, to use Bhabha's (2004 [1994]) term.

Histories are always in the present in the sense that they are lived day to day, but they are historical to the institution because they form part of its outside, the not institutional present. The crucial thing about more transformatively inclined, institutionally based social justice work as I represent it in this chapter is that no matter what sign this work is enacted through, equality, diversity or something else (and, as I claimed in Chapter 1 and following the line of analysis in Chapter 2, this work is always enacted multiply anyway), it seeks to surface these absent social presences (the past and potentially the future) in the present. These surfacings come through the multiple affective connections enacted through the subjectification process. Subjectivity is itself a temporality (Mbembe, 2001).

For those involved in governing for diversity and equality specifically, rather than governance in general (which implies governance through diversity and equality, but not necessarily actively for this), there is a sort of reflexive 'intentionality', what I think about in terms of retroflexivity, to this subjectification process though which workers come to see and know themselves as positioned relationally via multiple affective relations with students, colleagues, friends and family. Rather than something to be negotiated around, these affective relations are constitutive, they serve to animate and enliven (Fraser, Kember and Lury, 2005; Lury, 2012), to enact as I claimed in Chapter 2. As Bruno Latour recognises 'attachments are first, actors are second', 'the more attachments one has the more one exists' (Latour, 2005, pp. 216–217). This relational identification process is the means by which diversity workers are brought to life as diversity workers via their attachments and, by implication, in terms of their losses, as from this psychosocial perspective losses are also always a form of attachment.

This discussion builds on Chapter 3's argument as to the importance of relational identification, to more explicitly consider its role in resisting institutionally reproduced racialised and gendered inequality. In particular it situates diversity work as a form of relational work, because of the way it connects self/identity and politics, enacting relational positioning within (sometimes in spite of) a categorically ordered frame. Chapter 6 looks at the nature of resistance itself, but in this chapter I look again at the affective 'encounter with self' between the professional and the social already introduced in Chapter 3. This time I interrogate the role of such an encounter in engendering new knowledges of and commitments to the past on the part of diversity workers, instead of focusing on the losses reproduced. The chapter unpicks the way in which affect and experience is crucial to the ability to resist inequality, because of the way it resists the collapse between politics and subjectivities, by keeping a more multiply engaged ethical space (the relational) in play between the categorical and the ontological. This is the space that Stephenson and Papadopoulos (2006b) think of as the place of continuous everyday experience but which is not self conscious or intentioned in the liberal individualist sense (see Chapter 2). It links knowledge of the self to knowledge of multiple others, since self knowledge is not internal, but other (object-subject) oriented. It is relational in the sense that it is 'an accrued depth of feeling' which 'speaks to the constitution of self and belonging through the tightly woven skeins of social memory, social connections, time, and place' (Degnen, 2013, p. 555). Such a space constitutes a point in time from which to know ethically rather than cognitively, a sort of relational starting point for developing a more relationally inclined kind of expertise important to doing transformative diversity work. Thus, relational knowledge ostensibly about diversity is enacted through diversity. This sort of diversity knowing opens the self out to the possibility of the political as a form of more strategic purposeful action which might be more similar to what is commonly understood as political in the sense of collectively transformative. Becoming a diversity worker as a form of self knowledge practice is therefore like a form of ethical readying, a gathering of the self together, for a more intentioned strategic form of action, but where intent is never singular but multidirectional and past/future oriented.

This consideration of 'ethical readying' brings me on to deeper questions of what is actually at stake in this discursive shift from equality to diversity. When the concerns of those engaged in diversity work are taken into account the core questions are about the ways in which discourses of equality and diversity perpetuate the exclusion of the social and cultural from the institutional space, and the way any such exclusions are a means to supposed institutional depoliticisation, rather than about the substantive content of equality and diversity (whether they are left or right for example). From this point of view diversity's 'feel good factor', the way it privileges positive action to promote diversity in the future, rather than focusing on redress for past discriminations, is what is at stake. This is because it is this 'feel good' factor which fuels, and is in turn fuelled by, the supposed ideological neutrality of new managerialism through its resistance to keeping past harm in play. Relational identification disrupts this refusal to 'look back'. Instead it opens out to the past via multiple affective connections which challenge this feel good aspiration with experiences of social division and antagonism; bad feeling. The first-hand accounts I analyse in this chapter show the retroactive connections between past antagonisms and the present moment to be a central part of diversity workers' knowledge. Thus, emotions, experience and affect can serve to connect ideas of diversity to the political materialities more often associated with inequality and the social politics of resistances to these. From this I argue that participants' desire to keep feeling, and especially social antagonism and bad feeling, in play in their critiques of organisational inequalities can be considered as an important form of political intervention. This is the case whether these feelings are packaged in terms of diversity or equality.

Diversity and feel good governance

Within the English context one of the highest profile and earliest statutory interventions to emphasise the positive dimension to achieving more diverse and inclusive organisations through mainstreaming came via the 2000 Amendment to the 1976 Race Relations Act (Race Relations Amendment Act (or RRAA), 2000). The Amendment's recognition of institutional inequality, along with its introduction of a 'positive duty' for public sector organisations to actively promote 'good race relations', was designed to mainstream race equality across all organisational practices and processes in order to address systemic institutional disadvantage for Black and minority ethnic staff as well as service users and the general public. The controversial notion of institutional racism worked with the notion of 'unwitting' (see also Chapter 7) to relocate responsibility for racialised inequalities away from racist individuals and ethnic cultures to (white) institutions; their practices and processes. Following Macpherson:

> Institutional racism is the process by which people from ethnic minorities are systematically discriminated against by a range of public and private bodies. If the result or outcome of established laws, customs or practices is racially discriminatory, then institutional racism can be said to have occurred. (Macpherson, 1999, paras 21–22)

The resulting introduction of a range of techniques, processes and tools developed to benchmark and demonstrate reflection and action on racialised inequalities, such as 'race equality statements', rankings and league tables, brings issues of diversity and equality more clearly into the new managerialist performance evaluation nexus that I commented on in Chapter 1.

There is no doubt that the advent of these techniques and practices grouped under the 'new equality regimes' (Ahmed and Swan, 2006) opened up opportunities to talk more openly about basic issues of Black and minority ethnic underrepresentation and inequality; conversations which had already been opened up in relation to gender through the establishment of the Women's Unit (WU)[2] and its Policy Appraisal for Equal Treatment Guidelines (Cabinet Office, in Squires, 2006). Together the positive duty and the WU's work on other mainstreaming mechanisms paved the way for recognition that all levels of organisational life, including aspects of the culture, must be considered in order to promote equality. The establishment of the Commission for Equality and Human Rights (CEHR) was the high point of this recognition, bringing a range of other identities into the equalities legislative purview under the banner of 'protected characteristics' (Cooper, 2011, 2012; Fredman, 2011; Ridell and Watson, 2011). This collection of measures has produced an institutional climate in which the development of staff groups and networks for 'underrepresented' staff, as well as other forms of positive action measures including specific staff development opportunities such as mentoring and role model programmes, have been acknowledged as central to successful organisational development in general (Bhavnani, Mirza and Meetoo, 2005), because of the way they focus on the development of potential and especially for their ability to raise the confidence, aspiration and practice of marginalised staff groups. Issues of diversity are formally recognised as being about identity and not just material wealth.

The network participating in the research discussed in the following sections of this chapter is a good example of the sort of positive action initiatives established as part of the new equality regimes.[3] This was the largest national educational network for Black and minority staff and learners operating in the learning and skills sector at that time. It was housed at the key advocacy agency for the promotion of adult and continuing learning (ACL), the National Institute of Adult Continuing Education (NIACE), and comprised about 400 active members.[4] The network's aim at that point was to promote strategic policy issues relating to Black and minority ethnic staff and learners from within a politically driven anti-racist frame where Black, following the network's website, 'includes members of African, African Caribbean, Asian and other communities who are oppressed by racism'. Therefore, as active members of the network all of the staff interviewed were engaged in critical work for diversity and equality across the sector. Interviewees included six women and five men educational professionals from a range of ethnic groups who were working at middle or senior management levels within an ACL context.[5] Two participants were employed solely under a diversity remit, but for most participants this responsibility was rolled into other management or strategic responsibilities.[6] As with all the data presented in this book? all names are pseudonyms and some information which obviously compromises anonymity has been changed. Participants' ethnicity is described in their own terms.[7]

Resisting institutional good feeling

One important aspect to the analysis developed in Chapters 3 and 4 was melancholia's ambivalent temporal inclination towards the past, to what is lost, and how this loss frames institutional life in spite of the desire to move progressively forwards implied in modernisation. Part of what interested me in these chapters is the ways in which institutions and individuals manage the impossibility of moving on from a history which was discursively framed as toxic because of its association with inequality seen as antithetical to modernised progressive efficient effective equal ideals. As I traced it in these chapters, bad feeling is contained institutionally through its projective attachment to groups associated with the past (white working class men in Chapter 3, and in Chapter 4 older white and Asian male GPs). Association with the past becomes problematic because it is positioned as the cause of bad feeling in the present, displacing concern for inequality itself.

This sort of projective attachment works as part of what Bhabha (2004 [1994]) identifies as modernity's 'historical retroversion', whereby racism and colonialism are objectified as the archaic, the repressed ahistorical outside of the progressive myth of liberal modernity, in an attempt to enact a universalising 'homogenous empty time' of the 'People-as-One' (pp. 358–359). This historical retroversion is a core part of the liberal state's repressive spatialising production of its insiders and (constitutive racialised) outsiders that I outlined in Chapter 1. The temporal/spatial collapse achieved through this universalising modernist retroversion attempts to deny agency to those positioned on the temporal outside whether this be of modernity itself, the nation or, as in Chapters 3 to 6, the (neo)liberal institutional space. In what follows I build on this analysis of this repressive past/ present split to be more explicit about how the related temporal spatial collapse works to objectify through ideas of diversity. I look specifically at how this objectifying retroversion is related to the institutionalised compulsion to good feeling and at how this retroversion is challenged by the retroactive processes of 'living history contemporaneously' by moving '*back to the future*' (Bhabha, 2004 [1994], p. 361; emphasis in original) via relational enactments of the self as a diversity worker.

Extract 5.1 comes from my first interview with Anne Senyah, a Black Caribbean woman in her forties working in a strategic policy development role in the archives libraries and museums service. She has been active in socialist politics since her university days and this has included longstanding membership of a Socialist choir. Extract 5.1 is her initial response to my question about how she sees diversity. In it there is a very clear resistance to governmental retroversion of racism as something belonging only to the past. This resistance to historical retroversion means that the past is positioned more positively than the present, but this is positive in the sense of being productive and enabling, rather than happy.

Extract 5.1

I have always found, I mean I am quite happy to use the term 'diversity'. It is something that comes into our everyday work within the sector. But, I do feel that unlike the 1980s when we were actually talking about radical issues of anti-racism and it was quite clear what people were fighting for, diversity neutralises quite a lot of the strength of those arguments. . . . I think that [diversity] is a language that is imposed rather than self-defined. So what I am saying is, if I had the choice I would be talking to people about anti-racism. Government has imposed the term 'diversity' and it comes through in everything that is filtering down from Government in terms of reports and action planning, strategic development, it's all about diversity. So everyone has to almost embrace that terminology and run with it. And to say anything otherwise, if you still talk about anti-racism, you know, and you've got that kind of language you are seen to be at odds with this more positive language of diversity . . . it's almost as if to say in changing the language and trying to steer the discourse along a different track you are trying to argue that somehow you've solved the problem, and that the most overt forms of racism that led to the likes of, you know the outcomes for Stephen Lawrence and his family[8] don't exist anymore you know? . . . Another word that I really really really hate, which is coming through again from government in the main is this notion of tolerance as well. It couples diversity in terms of how more often you are hearing the terms respect, tolerance and diversity as the lexicon of government publications and I find some of it problematic because when you use a word like tolerance it just jars, it makes you feel as though the majority culture is tolerating, putting up with these alternative or contrasting or different cultures. And it's not about embracing and celebrating difference . . . There's been a real resurgence of that kind of terminology now and I find it really problematic . . . there's nothing respectful about tolerance. You can tolerate somebody and at the same time hate them. And tolerate is not a positive term and it is being used as a positive term when coupled with diversity.

Notwithstanding what seems to be a quick qualification in her first sentence here, Anne begins by stating her willingness to use the term 'diversity'. Taking her initial statement at face value it could even be said that diversity can be engaged happily. However, the rest of the passage serves to suggest a superficiality to this happiness, whereby diversity exists rhetorically outside of practice as a form of terminology to be used, rather than as something to be developed in practice as part of a collective engagement 'when we were actually talking' about anti-racism. One reading of this passage could see Anne as constructing a straightforward politicised/depoliticised dichotomy where anti-racism is the former and diversity the latter. Read in this way the language/practice, surface/depth, bad/good, present/past dichotomy supports what seems to be a straightforward historical retroversion which reflects the normative association of anti-racism with a more politically agitating, punitively motivated and unhappy racist past and diversity with a more neutrally even positively framed and less politically agitated post-race present. The only difference is that in this formulation the value judgements have been reversed with Anne positioning diversity as regressive because it is (politically) neutralising of argument and disagreement. Anti-racism is positioned progressively by way of an association with a more radical (politicised) less happy struggle or fight based on a strength and clarity of positioning around collectively achieved social justice. Anti-racism is constructed as radically action oriented, an energetic driving force rather than a more passively, less apparently purposive static idea like diversity which is just 'coming into everyday work'. Diversity is presented in more pedestrian and mundane terms, about a perception of happiness, rather than a practical activity like fight or struggle associated with 'real' emotional engagement.

For Anne, there is a sense in which diversity fuels the superficial nature of good feeling through its re-presentation of the difficult social realities of racism, such as the racist murder of the South London teenager Stephen Lawrence in 1993 (see also Chapter 7). This re-presentation is achieved by positioning such painful experiences as historical in the linear sense, as in the past, 'solved' and over; as not existing anymore. Whilst the articulation of the anti-racist 'we' who is 'at odds' with diversity's good feeling is potentially socially inclusive, it is clear that the unequal outcomes being fought over are related to specifically racialised positioning(s) and in particular that of the Black community living in Britain. Diversity's representation of good feeling therefore enacts specific social exclusions, in this case the exclusion of Black people's experiences of racism and any grief expressed as a result. Through this suggestion Anne's critique is challenging the necessary connection between good feeling and social progress assumed in diversity's supposedly necessary relationship to modernisation, a connection which supports the positioning of Black people outside of the institutional space. It begins to point to diversity's relational economy through which bad feeling for some is interdependent with the good feeling of others. Thus, Anne's analysis in this passage is highlighting the partiality of good feeling in two ways. First, good feeling is partial because it seeks to block out or cover over the bad feeling on which it depends, second, because of the way good feeling is distributed through social positioning. Whether diversity feels good or not, depends on where you are positioned; 'with' the institutional lexicon, or 'at odds with it' as Anne is here. Black people's experience as individuals, within family and within communities, must be re-inserted into institutional space as a form of historical retroactivation which potentially shifts the accepted linear institutional narrative which in turn supports the established relational economy. This is a universalising relational economy where the institution is positioned as happy and Black people are positioned as the unhappy outsiders.

Anne's use of the example of Stephen Lawrence as emblematic of Black people's day to day experience is not incidental.[9] It positions trauma in the form of death and violent death at white people's hands, as a particular form of bad feeling which is very clearly at the heart of the history and experience of Black people in Britain. This explicit situating of trauma is important because, following Jenny Edkins:

> Events of the sort we call traumatic are overwhelming but they are also a revelation. They strip away the commonly accepted meanings by which we lead our lives in our various communities. They reveal the contingency of the social order and in some cases how it conceals its own impossibility. They question our settled assumptions about who we might be as humans and what we might be capable of. Those who survive often feel compelled to bear witness to these discoveries.
>
> (Edkins, 2003, p. 5)

As such the traumatic reveals the pretence of easy solution, the difficulty of establishing certainty and responsibility in any given situation. The Lawrence murder is interesting in this respect as it points explicitly to the connection between overt violent racism supposedly in the past and the bureaucratic processes, murder investigations in that case, designed to provide a form of redress for that violence. But it raises very explicitly the issue of whose responsibility is being denied and hints at the different potentialities being denied as a result. In this regard the Lawrence murder is particularly interesting as it has been owned more or less consistently, since the publication of the MacPherson Report investigating the police response to it, as a national trauma; traumatic for the whole country, whether white or Black. Precisely what was so traumatic about this event and the aftermath was that it placed the responsibility of white liberal institutions in question. The use of this particular example by Anne only compounds diversity's failure in that it can be read as an alert to the chance lost to shift national relations by keeping bad feeling and trauma in play in the institutional present; an opportunity which had been provided by the Lawrence inquiry and its subsequent report, but denied by diversity's subsequent re-imposition of good feeling.

This critique levied by Anne at diversity relates to the way in which it works as part of an institutionalised 'happiness duty' (Ahmed, 2010, 2012). The duty demands that the commitment to diversity be embodied, 'embraced' in Anne's terms, by leaving certain things, like racism and its violent traumatising effects, unspoken. There is a sense in which diversity must be wholeheartedly invested in with no space for half measures. It is a dichotomising and polarising duty. This pressure to be happy, embedded in the idea of a positive duty to promote equality, operates as a negative duty not to speak about racism in the present, but to project an image of institutional happiness and contentedness. Elaine Swan talks about the projection of smiling faces on management literatures and promotional materials as an example of how this duty works (Swan, 2010a). But, it is a duty which is unequally distributed, especially incumbent on Black and minority ethnic staff. The duty works on the assumption that institutional unhappiness is not caused by events themselves, like racist murders, or the more common but related forms of everyday institutional harassments, but by the revelation of those events and their causes, like racism. The author of the revelation of this unhappiness then comes to be situated as the cause of the unhappiness that they reveal. In this way diversity operates to set up a relational economy whereby staff who speak bad feeling, like anti-racism in this case, come to be positioned as to blame for organisational unhappiness precisely at the points at which they reveal the operation of racism and the unequal effects produced by it (Ahmed, 2010, pp. 590–592; see also Ahmed, 2006, 2007, 2010, 2012; Ahmed et al., 2006; Swan, 2010a). This conflation between the feeling of unhappiness and its messenger is important because of what it suggests about the way in which such positive happiness duty works as an attempt to curtail agency, and in particular the agency of Black staff through the objectification of the past which is what I want to turn to explore more specifically now.

The tone of Extract 5.1 is mixed, beginning with a matter of fact reporting of how things just are, giving way to moments of frustration which well up '[what] I really really really hate', as critique is layered on critique, but then appearing to dissipate 'I find some of it problematic'. This welling up of frustration becomes especially obvious at the point at which Anne makes an important link between tolerance (and later respect) and diversity. Her tone and the force of repetition at this point in the extract serve to underline her very strong antipathy around the imposition of the term diversity, as it links to tolerance/respect, as part of the 'lexicon of government'. When Anne points to tolerance as what she 'really really really hate(s)', she is pointing to tolerance/respect as a form of what Wendy Brown identifies as a governmental strategy whereby 'the people are rallied around a certain intolerance of dissent' (Brown, 2008, p. 106) as an extension of an intolerance to difference. The issue for Anne in Extract 5.1 then is not necessarily diversity *per se*, but its coupling with a 'repressive tolerance' (see Chapter 1) operating in contemporary liberal democratic contexts whereby, as Anne says, 'you can tolerate somebody and at the same time hate them'. Tolerance is a way of dissembling; of pretending things are OK when they are not; of hiding the true location of bad feeling, keeping it under the surface, redistributing and fixing its origins in something or someone. Thus, it is through this discursive framing of tolerance and diversity that minorities themselves are positioned as 'these alternative or contrasting or different cultures' at odds with good feeling; as something special to be tolerated, not in the sense of cherished, but as problematically out of the institutional ordinary. The diversity/tolerance coupling is therefore also one means by which Black subjects themselves, like Anne, are made to feel bad, 'it just jars' she says. Furthermore, this coupling is the means by which these subjects are positioned as repositories for institutional bad feeling.

Shirley Tate (2013) points to the way in which tolerance is an objectifying discourse which positions Black staff as the objects of tolerance. Drawing on her work on ugly feelings, Sian Ngai (2005, see also Chapter 6) considers the way in which such objectifying operates through the emptying of disgust and contempt onto Black staff, because tolerance always points to that which is the focus of disgust and contempt. Hate comes into the institutional space via tolerance. What interests me here is the way that tolerance, as another form of good feeling, covers up the nakedness of disgust and contempt in favour of the day to day forms of disattendability which attest to the positioning of Black staff as beyond abjection within the institutional space. From the beginning of Extract 5.1 Anne is clear about diversity's limiting effects on agency; it is about symbolic imposition, the removal of choice. But if this everyday disattendability is taken seriously, then part of what is being resisted here by Anne in her antipathy towards diversity as it is coupled with tolerance is the absolute removal of personhood and any related potential for agency. The point about the everyday disattendability of Black institutional subjects is that they are there within the institutional space, but not there, noticed sufficiently to know that they are not noticeable (Tate, 2013, p. 7). They are there, but not there in the sense that they exist within institutional space as objects, but not as connected enacted subjects. It is this sort of complete denial of subjectivity to the extent that attempts to exercise resistant agency are irrelevant which is at stake in Bhabha's analysis of retroversion as positioning racism, and thus racialised subjects, as temporally outside of universalising (white) time.

The everydayness of this sort of disattendability of Black staff is a means by which the modern (neo)liberal institutional present is pitted in relation to the archaic social external past. The language of diversity and tolerance is about splitting the institutional and the social along two 'different tracks' to use Anne's metaphor and this two trackness means that one cannot impede the other's progress because they are not within the same realities. Anti-racism is associated with the extraordinary uncontrollable socio-cultural (and politicised) outside. It is agitating, demanding of attention and space. Diversity is positioned as a form of control in contrast to the uncontrollable. Thus, the idea of diversity works as a disciplinary mechanism via its association with the mundane ordinary institutional processes: 'reports', 'action planning', 'strategic developments'. Diversity, as it is coupled with tolerance, polices the boundaries between the political outside and depoliticised inside; bringing the outside inside without disrupting institutional boundaries. Anne's use of the verb to 'jar' is interesting because it is suggestive of the way in which bad feeling is located in surprise, in the out of the ordinary. The verb to jar means 'to be not pleasant'. If a sight, sound or experience jars, it is so different or unexpected that it has a strong and unpleasant effect on something or someone. Where the expectation is that you remain unsurprising, unchallenging to the *status quo* and thus disattendable completely, reasserting commitments to the outside can produce a form of surprise. From this point of view retroactively positioning the self within history is a way of creating institutional surprise and re-establishing the self as a subject-object, rather than only an object.

This re-establishment of the self as a subject-object is more like the way in which Anne perceives diversity on her own terms, and in contrast to its governmental turn. She continues in Extract 5.2:

Extract 5.2
It is more about political awareness and a personal sense of identity. It's more about those issues than looking at diversity, difference; its equality in a broad sense. So for me I would say it was more about a political awakening and an exploration of personal identity.

Here Anne's perspective on diversity enables subjective, self conscious engagement positioning in equalities as a broader form of political engagement. Whilst she frames this as a politicising process, diversity is a specific sort of political, which is coupled with a subjective dimension, 'a personal sense of identity'. It implies finding out something new about the self. The notion of 'awakening' is interesting because it can be read in at least two ways. It suggests being alerted to things not previously recognised about the self, but which were maybe there latent, behind your back so to speak, whilst you were sleeping. From a psychosocial perspective sleep is not a state of complete unawareness and detachment, but one where unconscious processing takes over and interacts with consciousness. From this viewpoint 'awakening' can also be read as a process creating the potential for different sorts of broader connection and sensitisation 'awareness'. This process is not individualising. It is about making various gestures outside of the self, a process of extending the self out, opening the self out spatially 'in a broad sense' as well as temporally. Understood in this way the idea of 'awakening' is suggestive of something more relationally retroactive, facing forwards, backwards, outwards.

From this analysis of Anne's account what is at stake for diversity is not so much whether it sits on some sort of traditional left/right spectrum, as its ability to enact a socially transformative politics which enables connections to be made between politics and identity and between the external sociocultural and the institutional inside. Perhaps unsurprisingly for an outsider-insider like Anne who already understands herself as politicised and energised through her engagements with socially transformative politics, the institutional recognition of diversity is not straightforward because the threat of co-option remains substantial. This is precisely because of the way institutional discourses have been so adept at working with socio-cultural discourses of identity via the idea of diversity and its companion's differentiation and individuation. One way in which this happens is through the rewarding of outsider-insiders externally, experientially and dialogically generated knowledge with progression on a career track. For some diversity workers the emotional struggle with diversity is therefore the struggle over the experiential containment deemed necessary to professionalisation processes, between desensitising the self to frame knowledges professionally as forms of civilised accounting or keeping the self sensitised, connected as a resistance to such accounting processes. The concern involved here is that the move into institutions at least potentially contains a more radical outside. Yet what this analysis assumes is that there is a singular external outside. However, from a psychosocial point of view the constitutive outside is not singular. As I highlighted at the beginning of this chapter diversity workers have various trajectories into diversity work. Many of the newer cohorts of people moving into diversity work do not have a background in political activism at all, or they have very different ones to Anne's, situated firmly in 1980s socialist anti-racist activism. This multiplicity begs a number of questions as to what the formalisation of experience via diversity discourses means for these workers. How can these workers be understood through the idea of 'a political awakening'? What does this mean for an understanding of the potential for a socially transformative politics? It is this set of issues that I consider in the rest of this chapter.

Retroactioning diversity

Extract 5.3 comes from one of three interviews conducted with Iopia who, similar to Anne, identifies as a Black British African Caribbean woman. Iopia is in her early thirties, delivering basic skills teaching, but within a challenging private prison context where she has just successfully established the post of race relations officer after a protracted struggle with her employers, the prison management, over institutionally racist practices within the prison. Amongst the outcomes of this institutional struggle were the creation of the post of race equality officer, curriculum change for prisoners, race equality training for staff and an increase in the number of Black staff.[10] In contrast to Anne, Iopia expresses an unreservedly positive view on diversity. Here in Extract 5.3 she is explaining how she became involved in diversity work in the first place:

Extract 5.3
Although I'm African Caribbean I was quite narrow minded in my culture [travelling] showed me how ignorant I was to my own Black culture [and to

my friends and family's cultures] so that's why I wanted to get more involved in diversity so that I could show people that diversity means different in all people; don't assume that because you share the same skin colour you'll have the same attitude or you've had the same experience cause you've not and also the fact that when people say that the um, they're not being racist and all the rest of it, I wanted people to understand that sometimes racism is not intentional but the way you've been brought up and the lack of um, understanding of other people leads to racism you don't have to make a racist comment to be racist but the fact that you don't understand somebody . . . means you're discriminating because you're treating people in accordance to your experience. I mean if you're a white middle class male then you're bound to discriminate against a black, working class female that in itself is discriminatory so that's why I want to get involved in diversity to, so that people can understand that. It's not just a new initiative or just a new buzz word cause it's more than that and if you don't understand it then you're just going to continue the same problems over and over again . . . so it's about identifying your own ignorance.

There are a number of ways in which Iopia's perspective could be read as consistent with a depoliticising individualising diversity discourse. She does not explicitly invoke ideas of politics and the substantive content of the extract conforms to many of the neutralising tendencies critiqued by Anne in Extract 5.1. The key themes in Extract 5.3 of ignorance and culture frame race in individualising, objectifying and dehistoricisng terms. Race is locatable in skin colour and in people, backgrounds and community. Iopia herself uses objectification practices for 'show[ing] people that diversity means different in all people', to demonstrate the inappropriateness of homogenising practices, but without any question about the similarity between her own practices and those she critiques. Furthermore, within this extract whilst racism is important, it is not really clear how. Racism oscillates between disconnection from the individual's agency and/or responsibility, shifting from it is 'not intentional', you don't even 'have to make a racist comment to be racist', to being learned, but also at other points to being innate. Racism too is individualised, located in culture and background. It is something to do with 'the way you've been brought up' and individual gaps in understanding. Then again it is to do with the tendency of the powerful to impose their experience but within a categorically derived meaning frame, as 'a white middle class male'. Iopia simultaneously claims that there is something necessary and inevitable about systemic power imbalances where as a 'white middle class man you are *bound* to discriminate against a black working class woman' (emphasis added) and 'that in itself is discriminatory'. There is a sense of a strong Black/white dichotomy, even as there is the desire to shift this to explore ethnic variation in and specificity to experience, 'my own culture'. The fact that Iopia locates racism within an inclusive group of 'people' could be read as an attempt to resist this Black/white dichotomy for racist responsibility. But this is at the same time as it universalises and fails to name racialising power.

Even where Iopia appears at her most critical, where there is an explicit attempt at a break between phenotype, behaviour and experience, resistance to ideas of intentionality and recognition of the impact of the unspoken, this critique tends to fall neatly within the policy framework enacted through Macpherson, demonstrating many of the same weaknesses. For example, the idea of ignorance is particularly contested within this model because of the way it can serve to detract from more complex understandings of institutionalised power through the reduction of racism to a matter which can be transformed by psychological or cognitive means through the right 're-education' (Anthias, 1999; Kyriakides, 2008). When analysing Bill's self positioning through perspective transformation in Chapter 3 I was also critical of the ways in which ideas of ignorance can be used to position the self outside of an analysis of responsibility for racism, as one of the liberal, enlightened and knowing ones, in contrast to the ignorant other who is the reason for the perpetuation of racist practices. There is some mileage in such analysis here where Iopia positions herself as transformed from naïve ignorant to someone with knowledge and therefore understanding and who now has the right to teach others about diversity in the service of their anti-racist transformation. But any proselytising zeal on Iopia's part must be read in the context of two important aspects of her positioning. First, Iopia is in an educative role professionally within the prison context, and the desire to demonstrate and engage others in self development and learning is central to her professional task within the prison context. Furthermore her desire to promote change in others is framed through the central role of self critique in breaking a cycle of racist repetition which is the issue on which the passage ends. This suggests a collective role for individual positioning work. This emphasis on the importance of actively working on self positioning stands in contrast to the way in which Bill, in Chapter 3, is at the very least ambivalent to such positioning work, if not outright resistant to it at points. Finally, and also in contrast to this comparison with Bill, Iopia's positioning work as a Black woman is more obviously related to self empower-ment, to gains, rather than to the sorts of losses that such positioning work might more obviously imply for Bill as a white male chief executive officer.

Problematic as aspects of this passage in Extract 5.3 are, its oscillations are central rather than incidental to an interpretation. From this point of view it does not make sense to read Iopia and Anne's views as entirely contradictory, one as the product of equality's radicalising moment and the other a product of diver-sity's depoliticising drive. Indeed Iopia begins by very clearly situating herself within a process of self discovery in relation to her cultural positioning as African Caribbean, a process not dissimilar to Anne's ideas of 'political awakening'. For Iopia, this is a journey to address her own as well as others' ignorance about dif-ference, where there is a failure to appreciate that 'diversity means difference in all people'. Whilst she is not explicit about identity, her interest in 'difference' and race in particular is an interest in positioning in relation to people, pasts, experi-ence which is reminiscent of Anne's later reflections in Extract 5.2 on diversity as a form of resistance to its governmentalities. For Iopia diversity is viewed as important because it provides a space for experience in the sense of 'identifying your own ignorance' in relation to your broader social positioning. She directly challenges any assertion that diversity is a superficial rhetorical tool: it is 'not just a new initiative or just a new buzz word'. '[I]t's more than that' because it implies some sort of personal reflexive relational positioning through friendships, family and personal biography in relation to different aspects of culture, family, community, the sort of opening out to 'my [Iopia's] own' situated knowledge of self. Iopia's subsequent comments make it clear that her intention is not to view difference simplistically: 'don't assume that because you share the same skin colour you'll have the same attitude or you've had the same experience cause you've not'. (Racialised) difference is complex and ambivalent precisely because people coming from the same group with the 'same skin colour' do not necessarily share attitudes and experiences. This is in terms of Iopia's experiences as a Black woman, but also at least potentially for those positioned on the 'other side' of complex racialised divides like the figure of the 'white middle class man' she invokes nearer to the end of the extract. There is also an opening to understanding the historicisation of struggle, a desire to break repetition, the 'same problems over and over'.

Given the tensions in Iopia's account it is important to be clear that I am not claiming anything for the 'success' or 'completeness' of her substantive analysis here and it is important to recognise that she makes no such claims herself. Instead what I am suggesting is that diversity for her is providing a useful way to think about the contradictions and complexities that she is grappling with in her day to day professional contexts and particularly in this one where she has been experiencing racist exclusion as well as witnessing the exclusion and objectification of her colleagues and service users, Black prisoners. These struggles focused precisely on surfacing the relationship between externalised social histories (in the specific meaning frame provided here by Iopia: group oriented issues of racism), the political and the personal. More specifically this struggle is about the role of experience within such a historical surfacing. One good example of this is Iopia's effort to introduce a Black history course into the core prison education curriculum as a means to enable the largely Black male prison population she teaches to understand themselves within a historical context of racialisation. This historical surfacing is at least part of diversity's power in this extract. Through such surfacing it can connect abstract objectifying racialising systems and experience in some way, for the purposes of resistance. It is in this sense that Iopia's view is not that dissimilar to what Anne perceives to be important about diversity in her own terms. But Iopia's starting point is very different to Anne's in terms of her skills, knowledge and experiences of working through ideas of diversity or equality. Diversity is her starting point, her entry into analysing inequality and practising resistance to it.[11]

It is important to be clear that I am not trying to claim any developed political analysis for Iopia here. In some senses the part of her account that I have presented in Extract 5.3 is so 'thinly' developed substantively that much can be read into it.

But it is the importance of this 'thinness' that I want to draw out here, proposing it as a potential strength. This 'thinness' creates a space for engagement, a potential openness to all sorts of readings and actions which might not be open to exploration from a more substantively 'filled up' position like the one in Anne's account. Indeed, Anne's awakening could be read as less helpful to such an opening up than Iopia's journey. Although in the context of Anne's view in Extract 5.1 such an awakening appears more obviously historicising, it could suggest an on/off awake/ asleep move rather than the less clearly determined journey Iopia sees herself engaged in. My point here is that no matter how strategically well intentioned any one substantively clear position on diversity (or equality) may be, it must be open to change and development relationally in order to be capable of challenging what are relationally shifting power dynamics. Following this line of argument, whilst Iopia's position may not appear to be as strategically developed as Anne's is here, it provides her with a position from which strategic organisational change, such as the changes in policy and practice for Black led curriculum developments within the prison, can be enacted. It provides a basis for historicising by bringing experience of racism and racialisataion into the formal institutional context of the prison in ways that were potentially transformative for at least some learners and staff as well as for Iopia herself. In this sense an affective connection to the idea of diversity provides a way of enlivening Iopia as a diversity worker, a position in which she did not consider herself to be before her struggles to change prison policy and practice. For her this enlivening as a diversity worker came about through the enactment of outsider experience inside the institutional present of the prison.

Knowing potentialities

In my interpretation of Anne and Iopia's accounts I am suggesting that diversity's promise is the (re)connection it makes possible between history, through positioning as part of the community, family, culture external to the institutional space, and professional/worker identity within that space. Yet, I am claiming that this promise is very different from the simple process of retroversion which prioritises loss as the only form of attachment necessary for politically transformative ends. The dangers in such a collapsed retroversion are manifold (see, for example, Ahmed, 2004b; Berlant, 2008; Cvetkovich, 2012), but the main problem is in the potential for obsessive melancholic return to the site of historical injury which results in the sort of embattled blame culture identified in the health care context analysed in Chapter 4. For those on the wrong side of history's homogenising time this has the additional danger of positioning them as essentially traumatised (and traumatising), defined not in their own terms, but through their subordinated relation to hegemonic power (the problem for Bill in Chapter 3 was the converse, being defined through the exercise of disciplinary power). From this point of view there is an important scepticism around the transformative potential of bad feeling which means that care must be taken over the way remembrance is invoked in politics. For Wendy Brown, for example:

If I am right about the problematic of pain installed at the heart of many contemporary contradictory demands for political recognition, all that such pain may long for – more than revenge – is the chance to be heard into a certain release, recognized into self-overcoming, incited into possibilities for triumphing over, and hence losing, itself. Our challenge, then, would be to configure a radically democratic political culture that can sustain such a project in its midst without being taken over by it, a challenge that includes guarding against abetting the steady slide of political into therapeutic discourse, even as we acknowledge the elements of suffering and healing we might be negotiating.

(Brown, 1995, pp. 74–75)

As I read it, the problem for Brown, as she states it in this passage and in the essay from which it comes, is the danger of reinstating and reinforcing linear homogenous time through the formal political recognition of identity as a release; a release from identity and the pain through which this identity is enacted. Within this formulation the sociohistorically situated self is dehistoricised, desocialised though the collapse of identity into pain. The only way to engage with the world from within such a formulation is through the pain induced through the historical loss which is central to any process of subjectification.

From a feminist psychosocial point of view the difference is that loss is central to but not sufficient for subjectification. The aim of engaging with loss is not to subvert or overcome identity, but to gather the self differently. The question these observations pose for my analysis at this point in this chapter (and this is something I return to again in Chapter 7 and the concluding chapter) is how is the process of retroactioning different from the liberal governmental retroversions of such an essentialising 'wound culture'? What sort of expertise and experience is enacted retroactively? To explore this point further I turn now to consider the perspective offered by Madonna, a woman of mixed Asian Caribbean heritage in her early forties who lectures on information communication technologies in a higher education (HE) continuing learning context and has a developing educational consultancy which specialises in work with ethnic minority women learners.[12] Extract 5.4 comes from a much longer discussion with Madonna around her experiences in educational consultancy. This consultancy role has developed over recent years in addition to Madonna's formal lecturing employment. This aspect of her work has generated momentum in relation to her deepening analysis of the unequal experiences of the minority ethnic women learners she teaches and of her own experiences of professional discrimination within the HE context. As part of this consultancy work she had recently, at the time of interview, taken on one of the regional chair posts in the same education network to which the other participants, Anne and Iopia and those in the following chapters, belong.

The passage presented in Extract 5.4 is embedded in Madonna's longer description of attending a public consultation session for proposed changes to the English national equalities infrastructure from a multi-strand separate commission model to one creating a single Commission for Equality and Human Rights (Department for Trade and Industry, 2003). Her attendance at this event was in her position as regional chair of the Black education network. This shift to a single commission model is arguably the most significant change to English equalities infrastructure since the establishment of the first formal piece of legislation, the 1968 Race Relations Act. This shift was framed in terms of the idea of diversity as an official response to the increasing importance of the politics of identity and experience within civil society struggles for equality (Department for Trade and Industry, 2002, 2003). One especially relevant aspect of the rationale around the shift to a single commission for my analysis of Madonna's extract was the aim to encompass a greater appreciation of the intersectional complexities of identities which until that point were not recognisable in terms of formal legal redress. Complaints needed to be brought on the basis of one facet of identity. The idea of diversity was seen to facilitate an appreciation of this lived complexity in policy and as a means to argue for legal statute on multiple discrimination (Fredman, 2011; Mabbett, 2008; Niven, 2008; Solanke, 2011). The consultation was being run by a longstanding, nationally high profile, largely (and exclusively at the event) white women's activist group initially established in the 1970s. In Madonna's own words, 'they were the ones that were pushing forward for consultation and they put a lot of information out'. The purpose of the event was to ensure the inclusion of a range of informal third sector organisations in the consultative process. Whilst there was a variety of representation across a range of equalities strands involved in the broader consultation process and also present at this particular meeting, Madonna's view was that the discussion at the event that she attended was largely dominated by the concerns of a West Indian community group exclusively represented by men. Similar to Anne's concerns in Extract 5.1 about the shift to diversity as moving away from recognition of historical struggle around racism this community group was worried that specifically Black 'histories of struggles around immigration would be subsumed and lost' in the shift to a mainstream single commission model. Expressing concern over what such a potential loss within the move to a single, but multi-stranded equalities framework might mean Madonna begins:

Extract 5.4

I am in two minds about this but if, it's just been striking me more and more that I go to some events and you have people who I think they are very well intentioned. They have a lot of knowledge, they have worked in the area for a long time, and they were probably trailblazers because at the time there weren't people around who were doing [equalities work] and they were able to get on in there and get some things done and move things forward, which is absolutely fantastic, but I suppose I just feel now that there are a lot more [minority ethnic] people in their thirties, forties and older who have gone through the education system and have actually got a lot to say. And it's now looking slightly odd when you see people who are speaking for groups of people and they can be well intentioned and they can have an understanding, but they are not that group of people, and I feel you do have to have that voice that actually comes from the people. I don't live in an inner-city area. I don't live in a community that is. I suppose my community, if you like, is West Indian or Caribbean but I'm not Afro-Caribbean, so there isn't an obvious sort of community I mix with and am actually part of. I am Asian Caribbean {long pause}, I don't fit in with people from the Indian subcontinent. I have nothing in common with them. I know nothing of their lifestyles or their religion. Religion wise I'm vaguely Christian. I am half Chinese but I have nothing in common with Chinese people. I know nothing again of their religion, they are Buddhists. I know nothing about China. I happen to have, you know, these two ancestral sort of links. So, I mean, I'm not saying that I am yet a person to actually represent views of any particular minority group and the only thing or the main thing, I suppose, I have in common with any ethnic minority group is obviously I am visibly from an ethnic minority group, and my family and myself have been through forms of discrimination and whatnot so, so we know what it's like and you know that's something that a white person cannot know, in-depth, because they've never been through it.

This passage is interesting from the outset because of the critical perspective adopted on historical struggle. From the start Madonna is 'in two minds' about equality's 'trailblazers'. From the extract's context these trailblazers include both the white women event organisers and also the West Indian community group represented by the men present. Part of what Madonna is 'in two minds about' is the debate between these two constituencies over the respective merits of claiming specifically racialised or more generalised histories of struggle where there will be some form of 'speaking for'. Similar to Anne's representation of an earlier anti-racist politics Madonna positions these trailblazers as actively challenging, getting in(side), getting things done and moving things forward; filling a gap, establishing equality as a matter for concern. Madonna has a sort of admiration and certainly a respect for this activity, for the longstanding nature of historical challenges, for the knowledge that this brings into institutional debates around equality and, potentially, although less clearly stated here, for the space that this has created to do equalities work in the present. Nevertheless she has reservations.

Madonna positions her critique of equalities trailblazers in tentative terms, but it is focused on the thorny issue of representation; who has the right to represent on behalf of whom? As such, it begins to raise questions which point to diversity's most contentious essentialising and dehistoricising impulse. She frames her specific concern as about the issue of 'speaking for' a community or 'groups of people' when you are 'not that group of people'. Her critique of the tendency to assume a speaking position on behalf of others when you are 'not that group of people' must be read as at least in part directed at the white women consultation organisers as the more institutionally and socially empowered consultation organisers (more institutionally and socially empowered in this instance through their whiteness, rather than their gender). Yet her reticence potentially extends to the dominance of the West Indian male community group too. Madonna's comments do not fall neatly into a Black/white dualism commonly invoked in representational critiques where Black people are positioned as experientially qualified to represent on issues of racialised equality and white people are not. Her position does not suggest this issue of representation can be resolved with better or more precise social matching. Her use of the general collective noun 'people' reinforces this ambivalence because it confounds specific positioning through gender, ethnicity or other social categories. This sort of generalised framing is problematic in the way that it underplays the categorical power dynamics of the two key racialised/gendered constituencies. But this generalising move is counteracted later in the extract when she becomes much more explicit about the importance of racialised positioning and in particular marginalised racialised positioning.[13] What Madonna is challenging here at least as much as the link between the right to speak and categorical identification is the potential for the domination of dialogue on the basis of past experience of working for equality or on the basis of good intention for the future. Madonna's support for 'that voice that actually comes from the people' is most readily interpreted as support for the West Indian community group whose explicit community status could suggest a location nearer to the people and in contrast to the women's groups closer alliance to the formal institutionalised consultation process. This reference to 'the people' could also be read as a claim to include the culturally enacted histories attached to the social injury of discrimination on the basis of ethnicity which Madonna is flagging through ideas of ancestry, nationality, religion and lifestyle.

Seemingly in tension with this support for the inclusion of culturally enacted community history the clearest aspect of Madonna's critique could be interpreted as generational in the sense that 'that voice that actually comes from the people' relates to newer experiences of 'people in their thirties and forties' who like Madonna 'have gone through the education system'. The sense here is that there is a different sort of analysis to that of the trailblazers which is coming from a newer generation of people, including ethnic minorities themselves, who have engaged differently with formal institutions as they have come up through them. There is a sense of historical progression and intergenerational development which shifts the relations between informal and formal institutional engagement (in this example via the institutional consultation process around the Equality and Human Rights Commission). That Madonna checks herself to include 'older' people as well as those in 'their thirties and forties' suggests that it is this more insiderly institutional experience more than any essential aspect to the notion of generation which is important to these 'newer' people. One reading of this analysis is that it conforms to a straightforward historical retroversion which positions sociocultural as informally enacted through the people and histories as useful in the past, but less relevant in the present. Formal institutions become associated with progression for equality. Madonna situates her analysis clearly within historical struggles around the politics of equality, but projects a sense that change is necessary and happening. This change relates at least in part to what she sees as a helpful shift in representative politics as not only sociohistorically culturally enacted but also institutionally enacted.

There is a growth in confidence in Madonna's tone and critique as the extract progresses, a sense of gathering momentum, 'it's just been striking me more and more', which supports the substantive theme of change. This gathering momentum reflects Madonna's growing experience and expertise and that of other people like her who have 'gone through' formal institutional contexts and the related claiming of a right to be included in the debate on equalities. Such a grasping of the momentum is represented in the second half of the extract where Madonna talks confidently from her own perspective. This confidence is rooted in a strong refusal of any clear sort of racialising ontology: 'I'm not saying that I am yet a person to actually represent views of any particular minority group', because for Madonna 'there isn't an obvious sort of community I mix with and am actually part of'. The specific points on which she refuses to 'speak for', including differences in religion, lifestyle, geography, nationality and common ancestry, clarify that what she is refusing are normative assumptions as to any automatic link between ethnicity and the right to represent which could be read into her position as 'an ethnic minority'. Her specific refusal to be identified as Afro-Caribbean is important here because of its association within the English context of problematic state categorisations promulgated through the collection of official statistics (see also Bill's comments around the Office for Population Census statistics in Chapter 3). The refusal is suggestive of Madonna's clear resistance to state racialising processes as well as the resistance to more 'bottom up' sociohistorically configured categorisations. This resistance to all sorts of racial ontologising could be read as Madonna supporting the impossibility of historical return and a clear break with histories of racialisation. But Madonna's ambivalence is not a clear refusal to position the self through racialised social relations altogether. Indeed, 'the only . . . or the main thing' that Madonna is sure connects her to 'the people' is her visible ethnicity which positions her alongside family and minority group and provides her with a position from which to know the pain of discrimination provides historically situated pain for the increased momentum. But that is not all, as part of a collective: 'we know what it's like and . . . that's something that a white person cannot know'. On the basis of this analysis it would be wrong to read Madonna as seeking to deny the racialised relations of power and positioning. It would be more apt to understand her as refusing to be objectified completely and absolutely through a certain relation to pain and disadvantage within these sociohistorically situated relations.

Overall, this extract suggests a much more complicated relationship between subjectivity and history than the obsessive returns produced through wound culture or straightforwardly progressive historical repression of universalising time. Madonna is challenging the progressive gathering of knowledge for representational work via experience in the present. What she is describing instead is a much more retroactive process; backwards, forwards, backwards shifting-in-relation production of the self as someone who knows in relation to diversity. The shift Madonna makes towards the very end of the extract is from representative knowledges rooted in voice and speech and emphasised in the first part of the extract to a more experientially, feeling based register of going through. This shift is a clear example of the shift between speaking categorically about and speaking relationally through considered in more detail in Chapter 3. This is a shift from the cognitive to the affective which connotes the process of sociohistorically positioning the self as connected to socioculturally positioned others. From my analysis of this passage I want to suggest that there is an explicit connection between relational identification and knowledge production which needs to be brought out in order to understand the role of diversity work. Catherine Degnen develops a compatible relational perspective on knowledge in her work on community life:

> Knowing is used to refer to places (both present and erased) and to people (both alive and dead). It can also evoke an individual 'being known' to others or by others. However . . . is about more than a familiarity with, information acquired, or social networks . . . This is because knowing is often evoked by people when seeking to explain what it is *that matters* in the webs of relations binding them to others . . . [I]t is often an accrued depth of feeling over time that is connoted in its use. It is for these reasons that . . . knowing speaks to the constitution of self and belonging through the tightly woven skeins of social memory, social connections, time, and place. (Degnen, 2013, p. 555; emphasis in original)

There are two especially important points made by Degnen here. First, knowing in this affective relational sense does not refer to anything, but to particular matters of concern (see Chapter 7). This suggests that in this case it is race equality that is of particular concern to Madonna. Second, Degnen's perspective makes explicit the distributed temporality through which the self is enacted. The self is understood at the same time as the world is discovered/remembered, enacted, pulled together through feeling; as for Mbembe (2001) the self is in some sense a temporality. As such knowing intersects with 'great social stakes of rupture, transformation, erasure, absence, belonging and exclusion' (Degnen, 2013, p. 557) and it can be contradictory and sometimes nonsensical. It interacts dynamically with not wanting to be known. We can see these contradictory movements in Madonna's account whereby people come to be known and understood as having a role in diversity, but this coming to be known does not have to be through histories of activism; it can be through the surfacing of the less obviously strategic, the everyday activities of going through institutions. This history of equalities enlivens Madonna, but it is not a received linear history, nor necessarily a strategically enacted history; it involves all forms of action, experience in institutions, stories passed down, family stories, community stories. It is a history lived (at least potentially) differently, not repetitively in the present. This sort of knowing is not individualising and internalising, on the contrary it could be viewed as enlivening across time and space via imagination.

It is imagination and its fantasies which are a gateway between the body and society, they not only connect individuals, but they are also 'fundamental to *why*, *whether* and *what* we are ready to experience, perceive and know in the first place' (Yuval-Davis and Stoetzler, 2002, p. 325; emphasis in original). They foreground the potential rather than the actual. The notion of not 'yet' being able to represent highlights an ambivalence for Madonna. It is a reminder that she occupies a space of possibility. On the one hand the idea of not 'yet' could be taken to suggest a progressive analysis where in the future, as Madonna gets to know more, issues of representation will become less problematic. But knowing is a practice, stopping to think is precisely 'to begin to develop an architecture for apprehending a perturbed world which all of the kinds of knowing to which one has access, from the neuro-affective to the rationally processed' (Berlant, 2010, p. 232). How do we live something new in the historically defined present? This desire not to return to the same present is what joins Madonna to Iopia and to Anne.

What these three very different extracts suggest when interpreted together is that the reason that diversity tends to fall short as a governmental enactment is because it fails to account for positioning in the sense that I have been framing it in *Power, Politics and the Emotions*, where positioning within social relations for these participants is relational; about historically situated relations of power and experience, politics and feeling, multiple shifting identificatory practices rather than identities *per se*. Diversity is not depoliticising *per se*, though it can be so where the link between identity and history is split and the affective space in between the two is collapsed, which means the denial of the pain, suffering and loss on which identification is predicated. Thus, from these interview passages the political has a necessary affective experiential, as well as a cognitive dimension. This means two things for diversity. Diversity does not only involve garnering substantive knowledge about equalities or inequalities, it involves self-in-relation reflection on those inequalities as a professionally culturally socially ethnically positioned subject. This sort of self-in-relation work is what I suggested in Chapter 2 forms the intuitive 'connective tissue' of governance. This self-in-relation reflective work is about tracing and making explicit the relationship between the categorical dimensions of the self (the social categories within which we are positioned) and the ontological aspects of the self (as a unique and apparently self directing individual). But this tracing challenges this idea of sovereign self directing singularity. It is productive in the sense that it brings the participant into being, it enacts them as someone who knows about diversity work. But it does this from multiple different directions via family, community and professionally and institutionally, and it is the bringing the self together, the relational enactment of the self through these knowledges which produces participants as diversity workers. The temporal instincts of such a tracing are not necessarily progressive, they too are retroactive in the sense that the past and present shift in relation to different actions and identifications, coexisting as resources for the future. This recognition of lack of sovereignty always brings pain as it did for Bill in Chapter 3, but for these already racialised diversity workers this is a particular form of pain. I am not claiming anything for actions produced through this diversity work by the participants. Indeed, the point is that the work does not necessarily create an obvious direction for action, one way or another; as either socially just and progressive or inequality reproducing and regressive. But I am claiming something about the way the self-in-relation work creates potential for socially transformative action in the form of a readiness for more strategic political action.

Conclusion

In this chapter I have explored the ways in which diversity workers seek to bring the past into the institutional present as a practice which pushes against individualising pressures in contemporary neoliberal space. This retroactioning seeks to multiply relationalities through connection to the past, creating a space for possibility, rather than creating specific directions for action. It seeks to emphasise the inbetweeness of diversity workers as neither collective nor individualised and, through this, it challenges the idea of a radical outsider/reformist insider.

It is important to remember that understood discursively diversity is a term which is nestled within multiple overlapping ideas, investments and practices which face in a number of directions socially and institutionally, a point sometimes easily forgotten in the rush to condemn it as a social and politically narrowing form of neoliberal management practice. Participants' critique of diversity is critique of a 'governmental lexicon' which stifles dialogue and imposes meaning, rather than critique of the idea of diversity itself. It is a critique of the way governmental power currently works through the idea of diversity as a means to the containment of collective difference (just as it previously worked through ideas of equal opportunity). In some senses then these critiques work as a claim to maintain multiple ideas and practices under the banner of diversity. The workers in this chapter negotiate between these various ideas and practices. This negotiation does not detract from work for social justice. Instead, in this chapter I have argued that this negotiation is a crucial and ongoing aspect of this work. From this point of view it does not really make sense to think of diversity workers as co-opted or not. A better way to think of them is as more or less prepared for engaging in more strategically focused social justice struggles within formal institutional spaces. This means that the opportunity to shift between more or less strategic positions is not closed down to these workers and they can potentially shift in and out of more strategically inclined social justice work. Just because an approach appears to be problematic at one point in time in relation to one set of issues, it can at the same time produce a different, enabling effect. This shifting multiple nature of everyday diversity practice also means that diversity workers' ability to enact such strategic work is not their only institutional use value.

From my analysis of these accounts I am claiming that diversity takes hold as an idea as much because of its ability to bring difference, identity and subjectivity into more traditionally politically framed ideas of structural inequalities (see also Sudbury, 1998) as because of its connections to the sorts of managerialist ideas favoured in contemporary neoliberal organisations. From this point of view critiques of diversity can be read as critiques of the way in which this idea can still be enacted governmentally to circumscribe politics in its widest sense through the sidelining of particular forms of affect and experience from the life of the group or organisation. In turn participants' resistances to the depoliticisation of equalities can be read as a resistance to the erasure of particular forms of affect and emotion from organisational life. Thus, the depoliticisation of diversity occurs through its association with some forms of feeling to the exclusion of others, with good rather than bad feeling. It is this erasure of bad feeling which leaves diversity narrowed and ineffective, not anything inherent in the idea of diversity *per se*. What this also suggests is that social justice work as a form of materially rooted politics can still have a place in organisational life framed in terms of diversity. Part of this work for social justice is resisting the emotional closures against which these diversity workers are themselves constantly struggling. Thus, what was important for the diversity workers represented in this chapter was that effective approaches to diversity were couched within a broader, historically situated social critique which was attuned to power and injustice in educational and broader social settings and which could account for antagonisms as still existing in the present.

In so far as diversity does have specificity, it is in its relationship to subjectification process and self-in-relation work. It is a different orientation to institutional life which troubles clear, temporal and spatial boundaries by bringing the social and cultural inside. So it works as a demand to bring in the community, the family; the informal private dimensions of life that Bill so wanted to keep out of the institutional space in Chapter 3. This shift in temporalities implies the bringing of the outside inside the institutional space.

The broader point this chapter brings home relates to the way in which its argument invites a reconsideration of resistance as produced through the relationship between the affective and material dimensions of politics. There is a sense, clearest in Anne's comments, in which it is being claimed that emotions bring clarity to the political project of social justice in terms of what is at stake, what is to be fought over in material terms. At the same time as emotionality brings clarity to the material object of its resistance, it also introduces complexity and ideas of the reproduction of intentionality and responsibility for this. As we see for Iopia, knowledge gained through relational positioning brings as much uncertainty as certainty to her understandings of being part of the collective African Caribbean or her analysis of being a white middle class man. Positioning, which works to bring together the affective and abstract systemic aspects of inequality, does not enable a clear cut resolution. Instead it opens diversity and equality workers up to uncertainty and paradox; questioning as well as solidifying their own sense of self and agency. In the next chapter I consider the role of ambivalence further and build on my analysis of relational temporalities. I do this by exploring suspended agency as a means of resistant action which, like retroactioning, disrupts progressive linear time. As such it potentially forms the sort of resistance which challenges a bad past, good progressive future dichotomy, on which the supposed equality/diversity distinction relies.

Notes

1 See for example McRobbie's (2009) scathing critique of gender mainstreaming as feminist activism made over and undone; Richardson's (2005) critique of gay and lesbian activism as the 'politics of normalisation'; and Shukra's (1998) analysis of the institutionalisation of Black power values.

2 In 2001 this became the Women and Equality Unit (WEU), moving from the Cabinet Office into the Department for Trade and Industry in 2002.

3 As I explained in Chapter 1, this study focused on ACL as part of a broader research project, 'Integrating Diversity? Gender, Race and Leadership in the learning and Skills Sector' (2003–2006). The findings of this broader study have been widely reported on elsewhere in Ahmed (2007), Ahmed et al. (2006), Hunter and Swan (2007), Turner (2006). I discuss aspects of the ACL study in Hunter (2006) and also in Hunter (2008) and Hunter and Swan (2007). See also Ahmed (2012) and Swan (2010b) for other related discussion.

4 Having grown out of the neighbourhood renewal portfolio and undergoing numerous incarnations, the network was given fresh impetus by the work of the Commission for Black Staff in FE (CBSFE) discussed in more detail in Chapter 7. Like most of the specific race equality and diversity initiatives that I also discuss in that chapter it has since been disbanded.

5 The notion of ACL is contested, with a vast range of adult learning provision coming under this label spanning such diverse institutional forms as university continuing education, the Workers' Educational Association, Women's Institutes, local authority provision, prison education and voluntary and community providers. Because of this variety and the fact that this type of provision includes a range of unrecorded informal non-vocational learning, there is no agreement as to the size of the sector. Nor is there conclusive data indicating the social characteristics of the learner or staff base in ACL. Nevertheless, estimates suggest that roughly 19 per cent of all adult learning takes place in ACL contexts (see Hunter, 2005b) and that learners from a variety of disadvantaged groups tend to disproportionately take up this form of learning (Dadzie, 1997). Anecdotal evidence based on high rates of casualisation in the ACL labour force suggests that women and minority ethnic staff tend to be disproportionately concentrated in this type of adult learning provision (Hunter, 2005a).

6 The sorts of roles included equality and diversity coordinator, diversity champion, equalities officer. Very few continued to be framed in terms of equal opportunities.

7 As I noted in Chapter 1 this practice of participant self categorisation has ramifications for inconsistencies in the use of ethnic categorisation in the text of *Power, Politics and the Emotions*. These ramifications are particularly pronounced in this chapter, and also in Chapter 6. For a more detailed consideration of the implications of this issue refer back to note 3 in Chapter 1.

8 Here Anne is referring to the murder of the London teenager which prompted the Macpherson Report leading to the RRAA 2000. See also Chapter 7.

9 Between the year of Lawrence's death in 1993 and 2013 there have been 105 such murders. Racist incidents recorded by the police in England and Wales stand on average at 130 per day, 47,678 in the year 2011/2012 (Burnett, 2013).

10 More details of this struggle for race equality in the prison and Iopia's role in this can be found in Hunter and Swan (2007). I refer to some aspects of this broader analysis in my discussion below. See also Hunter (2006) for more on Iopia as outsider/insider.

11 Indeed, in some ways Iopia's account in Extract 5.3 has more of a feel of the nascent equal opportunities discourses of the late 1980s. This is at least in part because of the relatively underdeveloped equalities agenda within the English prison context. At the time of interview the prison service was only just beginning to get to grips with a race equality agenda as the result of one of the last formal investigations conducted by the Commission for Racial Equality before it was merged into the Commission for Equality and Human Rights. The post of relations officer which Iopia has just successfully established is associated more with the Race Equality Council's model of regional race equality governance established in the wake of the 1976 Race Relations Act (see Chapter 6). In addition, Iopia is working in a private prison context not subject to race equality law in the same way as other public service bodies are, even under the more extensive provision of the 2010 Equalities Act.

12 An earlier analysis of this data extract appears in Hunter (2006).

13 Madonna shifts between ideas of race and ethnicity. In doing so she tends to reinforce a white de-ethnicised and black ethnicised dualism. I use both ideas of race and ethnicity to refer to my analysis of her position in this passage in an attempt to follow as closely as possible her own usage. This relative interchangeability is part of how racialisation works.

Chapter 6

Sustaining collective challenges to policy monoliths

A demon haunts politics but it might not be so much the demon of division – this is what is so devilish about it – but the demon of unity, totality, transparency and immediacy.

(Latour, 2005, p. 26)

I know the anger that lies inside of me like I know the beat of my own heart and the taste of my spit. It is easier to be angry than to be hurt. Anger is what I do best. It is easier to be furious than to be yearning.

(Lorde, 1984, p. 153)

It is traditionally emotions such as fear and anger that are thought to be driving radically transformative political resistance (Holmes, 2004; Ost, 2004). From this point of view emotions provide an energy and momentum which is crucial to any radically transformative reordering of the established relations of power they enact, a critique of injustice and a sense of what needs to change. But, as Audre Lorde recognises here anger can also act as a blocker to change, as a quick but overall unsatisfactory release of pain. Anger is a useful means of clarifying difference 'but *in the long run*, strength that is bred by anger *alone* is a blind force that *cannot create the future*' (Lorde, 1984, p. 152; emphasis added). Part of the problem with anger is that it enacts a clear judgement as to what it is for and what it is against. But from within melancholic neoliberal institutional contexts identifying what to be for and what to be against is a complex, if not impossible business. Therefore, the focus in this chapter is on the role of less obviously radicalising feeling states in transformative politics under conditions of the sorts of melancholic uncertainty characterising neoliberal institutional contexts. This chapter therefore questions the assumed primacy of more obviously agitating feelings like anger in achieving institutional transformation. Instead it offers an analysis of the role of more ambiguous 'sentiments of disenchantment' or 'ugly feelings' (Ngai, 2005) as a supplement to anger. Their ugliness relates to the 'unpleasurablity' (Khanna, 2012) of the states of betweenness and undecidability to which they refer.

The issue of the relationship between emotion and resistance is linked to a consideration of positioning. In Chapter 5 I considered how the institutional push to diversity can provide a space for generating the sort of retroactioning self knowledge which is important to resisting the neoliberal depoliticising social/professional split. This retroactive relational positioning within collective experience of pain and struggle enables a sociohistorically, relationally situated gathering together of the self which enacts a critique of universalising liberal institutional time crucial to the ability to do critically intentioned diversity work. But as I also noted in that chapter following Brown (1995), the recognition of pain and loss is not necessarily transformative. As well as potentially individualising and depoliticising the necessary repetition required for the translation of pain and suffering into the institutional space takes its toll on those doing the transformation work, it can be physically and mentally debilitating in ways which make it difficult to continue the struggle for social justice. The sorts of tiredness and exhaustion which pepper a range of accounts of activist politics (Gould, 2009; Newman, 2012; Staiger, Cvetkovitch and Reynolds, 2010) have lots in common with those told about institutional diversity work. Keeping up the momentum of pain and anger can be debilitating as well as energising.

As I have made clear from the beginning of my empirical analysis which began in Chapter 3 with the account of Bill, a white male middle class chief executive officer, retroactive positioning is not a practice confined to those who most obviously appear to be positioned through the pain of inequality, nor to those like diversity workers who are engaged in governing for institutional cultural change specifically. Nevertheless, diversity work does tend to be gendered and racialised in specific ways with Black, minority ethnic and women staff tending to fill these positions. This means that the work of transforming institutional cultures tends to fall disproportionately to staff who are already institutionally marginalised because of their gendered and raced positioning. On top of the affective toll incurred through retroactioning, processes of institutional marginalisation work in part through normative ideas of affect and emotion where certain forms of angry and politically dissenting action are socially over-determined and depoliticised, for example through the discursive coupling of 'riotous young Asian men', 'aggressive Black men', 'irrational women protesters' or 'angry Black woman' (see Chapter 2). Compounding this issue is the fact that diversity work itself is over-determined as a site of emotionality, rather than bureaucratic rationality. Particular forms of emotion like anger are expected to be enacted through diversity work and this very expectation can produce an institutional ignoring of the messages diversity workers are trying to put across (see Ahmed, 2010, 2012; Ahmed et al., 2006). This emotional over-determination forms a core part of the broader 'contemptuous tolerance' of liberal institutional space explored by Shirley Tate (2010) also considered in Chapter 5. It operates as a means to listen to pain, according it superficial institutional space whilst infantilising and ignoring the subjects of this pain. Under such circumstances the resistance to positioning through expectation can be an important opposition to objectification as well as an important means to confound well established racialising and gendering discourses. The development of different sorts of more ambivalent, less obviously agitating feelings may be crucial to producing successful challenges to this racialising *status quo*, especially so where they are taken up by subjects usually defined as disruptive.

In this chapter I am interested in responding to this set of issues by exploring the ways affect, as it relates to positioning, is mobilised as a means of sustaining diversity work as a politically and socially resistant practice. I draw on interviews with the same 11 members of the national educational network for Black and minority ethnic (BME) professionals and learners in adult and continuing learning (BME education network) which I introduced in Chapter 5 (see also Chapter 1). These interviews suggest that feelings of patience and impatience sustain what is often, over time, debilitating diversity work. It could be argued that frustration better captures a more agentic and potentially productive response to these diversity workers' predicaments, rather than the 'smaller' and somehow less active response to being thwarted suggested by the idea of impatience.[1] In line with this critique my aim here is to represent these diversity workers' potential for more radical and politicised action, challenging the idea that they are necessarily passive and disempowered in the context of monolithic and immovable inequalities. But I prefer to use the idea of impatience over frustration for two reasons. First, it is the term more readily used by participants. Second, I am looking to push the boundaries of assumptions about the sorts of feelings which have the potential to be politically productive. Keeping 'lesser' affects like impatience in the mix is important here. Inspired by Sian Ngai's (2005) argument about the contemporary importance of 'ugly feelings' or 'sentiments of disenchantment' within the contemporary context of neoliberalism's increasingly monolithic disciplinary power, I argue that these more ambivalent and less heroic feelings of patience and impatience are important aspects of sustaining critical capacity for transformative change in contemporary governance.

From the perspective of concerns around the potential for the institutionalised co-option of diversity workers outlined in Chapter 5, it is understandable that the feelings of patience and impatience, with their connotations of holding out, hanging on, waiting for rather than promoting change, are viewed with suspicion, as limited, enfeebled and even acquiescing forms of response to the repetitive persistence of such trenchantly institutionalised inequalities. But my argument in this chapter begins from the recognition that the subtle intricacies of repressive and contemptuous institutional tolerance do not necessarily lend themselves to the same sorts of overt forms of resistance which may be suitable to producing radical change and transformation outside the institutional space. Indeed, the perspective I have been developing to this point in *Power, Politics and the Emotions* is suspicious of such claims to the possibility of political clarity, and particularly suspicious of the supposedly unambiguous insider/outsider positions upon which this perspective is based and to which it can give rise. Institutional transformation does not have such clear lines, nor such obvious enemies or proponents. This is precisely because positionings are multiple and institutional realities are always on the move within and through them.

Through this discussion of patience and impatience this chapter is dealing more explicitly with ideas of affect than those of emotion *per se*, and in particular with the idea that affect can work 'outside' power's normativities. Affect and emotion are not qualitatively different, but work along a continuum where affect refers to:

> the unbound: it has no fixed object, no prior aim: rather, it is unattached free floating mobile energy . . . affect is bursting with potential . . . it can stir an inchoate sense that we are experiencing something, a vague stirring that if forceful enough, can induce efforts – more or less conscious – to figure out what we are feeling and how to express it.
>
> (Gould, 2009, pp. 20–21)

What is interesting about 'ugly feelings' as Ngai conceptualises them through affect is that they capture more of the melancholic ambiguity which underpins the institutional everyday than ideas of more clearly articulated emotions like anger. Ugly feelings do not have an obvious release or target. They do not facilitate action (one way or another). Instead they highlight states of suspended agency. They point to a pause in action, taking time out, to speculative potential rather than an already decided actual. Their relative unremarkability, their ordinariness is important for rethinking everyday life as part of resistance as well as agency. This everyday becomes part of the 'imperceptible politics' (Papadopoulos, 2008) necessary for resistance within the sorts of biopolitically disciplining contexts of neoliberal institutions.

One of the common and, in my view, legitimate critiques of the 'turn to affect' is the way in which some analyses can tend to overstate the supposedly free float-ing nature of agency suggested by the idea of potentialities, as though this exists dehistoricised, untouched by power's normativities. In contrast to such free float-ing analysis and in keeping with my argument against linear universalising time, my claim is that patience and impatience are feelings which pause progression, rather than break with the past. The affective continuum of im/patience discern-ible in participants' accounts of diversity work is what makes such work possible and through which it is located within histories of social justice struggles. Thus, in what follows I am claiming that it is through these affective relations that this work is always constituted as potentially politically resisting because affect maintains situatedness within historical struggles over (but not necessarily clearly for or against) social justice. Thus, it is historical positioning which produces the ambiguity framing multiple future possibilities for action. By paying attention to this affective ambivalence I want to show how it is possible to move beyond vili-fying or romanticising diversity work to more realistically represent the murkier political ambiguities and tensions which often lie at the heart of this. On the basis of the empirical data, this chapter argues that these 'ugly feelings' are not neces-sarily evidence of disconnection to ideals of equality. Patience and impatience are forms of relational connection which are potentially politically productive depending on the relational politics through which they are enacted. Taken together they are constitutive of the states of readiness which sustain critically oriented activist sensibilities within formalised professional contexts.

Following on from this, this chapter also explores the possibilities for the distribution of patience and impatience between those differentially positioned within the social relations of gender, ethnicity, class, generation or other forms of difference. Such distributions may constitute a means of relationally distributing resistance in order to enact durable shared equalities networks. Thus, rather than considering a decline in traditional forms of equalities activism as evidence of political inertia, Chapter 6 argues that ideas of political agency must be expanded to what Ngai thinks of as 'suspended agency', as forms of active inaction upon which more strategically driven, interdependently enacted collective action depends. Following this line of argument I suggest that this vacillation between feelings of patience and impatience keeps in play the possibility of more explicitly political action because they keep open an affective space from which more explicit resistance to inequality can be developed and shared between differently positioned staff.

Ugly diversity work

The personal fulfilment that diversity workers derive from positioning themselves socially and culturally, within history through their participation in diversity work which I discussed in Chapter 5, is paradoxically also diversity's downside. In part this is because the work of cognitively positioning the self within the relations of power, inequality and oppression is painful in terms of what it exposes about the self as 'victim'/'perpetrator'. We saw some of this in Bill's narrative in Chapter 3. However, this pain is experienced differently and often disproportionately depending on positioning. This is because some diversity workers are taken to embody the object of their work more than others. Diversity workers often do identify themselves in this way, as women, as Black or as disabled, for example. But, even if they do not position themselves in this way, they are often positioned like this by others as part of everyday gendering and racialising processes. Whether chosen or imposed, or both, such embodiments produce additional pressures for these workers because this exposes diversity work itself as a site of personal pain, loss and oppression as well as a means to personal empowerment. The work of positioning itself surfaces pain and surfaces the worker through pain. For example, as Gulshan, a Pakistani British woman in her early forties, teaching for 20 years in local authority adult education basic skills English for Speakers of Other Languages (ESOL) provision, says:

Extract 6.1
Although I'd experienced racism in its most overt form, the more subtle intricacies of race in a workplace setting, I hadn't really come across. And

when I was faced with it, it was a real shock to my system and it takes time for you to engage again, understand where people are coming from, to figure out ways that you can challenge it, to even be bold enough to question other people.

For diversity workers like Gulshan, where the 'subtle intricacies' of workplace racialising are experienced so forcefully and personally through her own body as a 'shock to my system', this produces a form of temporary recoil, a hiatus from which 'it takes time for you to engage again'. The paradox here is that for diversity workers positioned through their bodies in this way it is impossible to get away from the assumption that a collapse of the categorical (collective identity) and the ontological (self identity) (see Chapter 3) is inevitable. The freedom to situate the self historically within the social relations of inequality which can be so engaging and rewarding, as Anne described it in Chapter 5, 'a personal awakening', is forcefully curtailed when the self is reduced to the category of race through workplace racialising; when these diversity workers become (again) the object rather than the subject of diversity.

This contradiction between subtleties and physical visceral shock is important because it highlights the forcefulness of the reminder that the self has already been subject to and continues to be positioned through racialising dynamics, the strength of which are bolstered precisely by their subtlety, such that even those subjects most wise to the exigencies of the most overt violating forms of racism remain bewildered and disoriented by its reductive force within the institutional space. Shirley Tate writes incisively about the malevolent annihilating nature of these forcible reductions within the academic context, bringing home the contemptuous tolerance constitutive of organisational 'spaces of estrangement' (2011, p. 219). Under such circumstances the hiatus often brought on through the shock realisation as to the extent of racist objectification can serve as a form of protection maintaining the affective space for the sort of reorienting (see also Ahmed, 2006; Puwar, 2004), the re-stabilising, necessary to figuring 'out ways that you can challenge it [discrimination]' (Tate, 2011, p. 219). In such personally and professionally annihilating contexts this hiatus provides the space to literally reanimate, rejuvenate and gather the self together (again). But whilst this hiatus can be enabling, as I go on to consider below, this gathering and reorienting move is a particular sort of additional affective labour for these already unequally positioned workers to have 'to figure out ways that you can challenge [discrimination]'. For these workers this is not a question of how discrimination can be challenged in the general abstract, but how 'you', in this case Gulshan, are positioned forcefully within it and how 'you', Gulshan, might challenge it. It is a call with a different sort of immediacy and urgency for those diversity workers already positioned unequally through the social relations of gendered and racialised power in their everyday working contexts.

Conserving marginalised energy

The disproportionate affective labour produced through unequally positioned diversity workers' everyday feelings of shock, anxiety and fear creates fatigue, exhaustion and tiredness. Diversity work is surrounded, sometimes almost engulfed, by tiredness brought about by its repetitive, seemingly endless nature, where action for systemic change to challenge the unequal *status quo* is easily ignored or co-opted into the governmental frame identified by Anne and others in Chapter 5. Repetition gathers its own momentum. It necessitates repetition, but these repetitions reinforce the blockages they are intended to dislodge in the first place, in turn provoking further repeated challenge, creating more tiredness for the workers delivering the challenges and for those blocking them. Tiredness circulates, apparently concentrically, attaching itself to terms, actions and bodies. As Sara Ahmed notes, whole institutions as well as the people in them can be tired, experiencing 'equity fatigue', where, she claims:

> The circularity of this 'loop' is what produces the tiredness of the term [equality]: the term 'slows down', or gets weighed down, by acquiring too much baggage, which produces a kind of gut resistance ... Rather than terms acquiring currency through repetition, this implies that the more terms are repeated over time the more resistance there is to 'hearing them'. Indeed, such resistance also involves attributing the term to specific bodies: the practitioner who uses the term 'equity' is not heard precisely as the failure of the term is assigned to her.
>
> (Ahmed, 2007, p. 239)

Ahmed's use here of the idea of 'gut resistance' serves as a reminder that such tiredness is an integral part of the melancholic drama in which diversity work is bound up, where repeated attempts to deny unequal histories are forcefully viscerally resisted. Like indigestion, unequal histories repeat back on the institutional or individual self only creating the need for even more forceful resistance. To recapitulate Cheng's view described in Chapter 4 the melancholic is 'stuck – almost choking on [diversity] – the hateful and loving thing he or she just devoured' (Cheng, 2001, p. 9). Such tiredness reduces diversity workers' capacities for resistance, effectively operating as its own blockage. Resistance begins to appear futile, or at least as disabling as it is enabling.

Aadil, a Pakistani British FE lecturer and his college's race equality officer, talks a lot about being tired, and about being anxious and sometimes even scared over the time he has been doing diversity work. At the time of interview Aadil was in his late fifties and he took the opportunity of our conversation to reflect on nearly 30 years in equalities work which began on his immigration to the UK in the early 1960s when 'people expected some kind of leadership on these issues from someone like me' in terms of his skills as a youth worker and his qualifications as a Chemistry PhD. He says:

Extract 6.2

My introduction to [diversity work through my experience in] multicultural education, race relations, was a very tiring, and yet intellectually stimulating experience, it was a very very tiring and painful experience at a linguistic level and an academic level as well as a kind of cultural level. Having studied the sciences, and having some interest in the social world, they do not amount to knowing where people are coming from and what actually people mean, and not having the [understanding of the] historical baggage linked with the different mirrors, prisms, lenses that different people bring. [But over the years] it is nice to have learned how to problematise and then to learn through that by disentangling the factors which then contribute to making it [diversity work] look complex and difficult, because I think that's the result of all these processes which are operating on the situation at that time. So things may be complex and difficult but if you go through it and think through it then you can see the light at the end of the tunnel without having tunnel vision in the first place you are able to see from outside the box. I think it is a lot better that way, you find your own solutions, at least in the short term and the medium term if not for the long term, because for the long term strategic thinking is required, what kind of society do you want in the future? That is depending on your value system. If you don't believe in democracy then fine yeah, but to say either you are against us or with us is problematic because of the complexities.

The first half of this extract focuses on the challenges of diversity work framing them in terms of the tiring emotional and intellectual labour involved. Characterised by significant anxieties, diversity work is 'very very tiring and painful', as well as producing 'intellectually stimulating' highs. It is engaging with the complex contested and multiply sociohistorically enacted nature of diversity which makes it tiring. This complexity produces an ambiguity of meaning between what people who are multiply historically situated through 'the different mirrors, prisms, lenses that different people bring' convey and 'what people actually mean' which requires a particular form of 'deeper' form of learning which can only be achieved by 'going through', evocative of a more affective embodied reflexive experience, as well as 'thinking through' cognitively. There is no clear cut object for Aadil's struggles. This less clearly articulatable experience enables a morally agnostic stance. '[F]ind your own solutions . . . depending on your value system', he says. Thus, whilst it is the sociohistorically situated, experiential aspect to diversity work that is challenging and personally painful to navigate, this is necessary in order to see 'the light at the end of the tunnel' and escape the blockages encountered in diversity work. '[L]earning through' or 'going through' holds the possibility of something new, 'outside of the box' and 'better' in the future.

Overall, from this extract Aadil's approach appears calm, measured, even emotionally contained, more diagnostic than action oriented, but it does not feel completely blocked or thwarted. It conveys a sense of long durée which is pleasurable as well as confounding. His use of the term 'historical baggage' evokes the sort of melancholically framed ideas of history as a weight to understanding, slowing progress down, which gets attributed to diversity workers through diversity fatigue. However, the second half of the extract is more hopeful in tone, continuing with Aadil claiming a niceness to problematising, 'disentangling' and 'learning through' and unpicking such complexity. This slowing down could therefore also, as I pick up in more detail below, be considered an advantage, rather than a disadvantage. It potentially holds open ambivalence, enables inclusivity and refuses to reduce complexity; it seeks to 'problematise' and to 'learn through' it and 'disentangle' it. It opens up, rather than answers, the question of 'what kind of society do you want'?

There are different ways of interpreting Aadil's restrained even-handedness in Extract 6.2. Through an active/passive binary it could be read as the latter: unhurried, classically patient in the sentimental ethical tradition, representing 'tolerant and even tempered perseverance; the capacity for calmly enduring pain, trying situations' (Collins Dictionary, 7th edn). However, links between self sacrifice, tolerance and the calm endurance of pain and hurt are problematic in their associations with liberal moral pedagogies which see the endurance of pain as the means of conversion to the good and just life. For feminists and other critical cultural theorists scepticism is required here (Ahmed, 2004b; Berlant, 2008a, 2008b; Brown, 1995; Cvetkovich, 2007) (see also Chapter 5). This is because such sentimental logics neatly support conservative arguments justifying the exclusion and suffering of a range of marginalised subjects as a matter of endurance to be 'got over' by the individual, with no need for systemic adjustments. Aadil's comments might suggest such scepticism is justified in other ways. They feed into a sense of rational objective ('without having tunnel vision') level headed progression towards something 'better'; into ideas of individualistic personal struggle: 'you find your own solutions, at least in the short term' and pragmatic non-confrontational intervention; they also code issues of inequality and power through the ideas of 'culture' and 'history'. Whilst it potentially provides important historicisation and contextualisation, when viewed from within a binary, the sort of patient approach displayed by Aadil could easily be seen as politically conservative and reformist in ambition rather than desirous of more dramatic and clearly systemically transformative action for equality. From this perspective his approach would be considered 'failed' resistance, stuck in a never ending cycle of challenge and resistant response in the end leaving the basic parameters of the unequal *status quo* untouched.

Another way of interpreting Aadil's patience is from outside this sort of binary thinking as a form of suspended rather than spent or failed agency. From this point of view patience like Ngai's 'ugly feelings' (Ngai, 2005) and Tomkin's basic affects such as interest (Ngai, 2012; Tomkins, 1995) constitute a form of active inaction, neither fully active, nor entirely passive. Patience is diagnostic and sustaining and thus has value in at least three ways. First, having patience highlights the fact that there is something to be done, though it is not clear what that something might be. It is this indistinctness of purpose which 'enables the individual to sustain attention to complex objects' (Tomkins, 1995, p. 75) within a context where there is not necessarily any sense of a clear resolution, like the problem of equality with its multiple 'mirrors, prisms, lenses' (Extract 6.2). So, patience sustains a potential for action where it might otherwise stop. Finally, patience provides an important means to resist the universalising collapse of time in neoliberal institutional life characterised by the constant push to ever faster and more urgent forms of institutional activity in the service of institutional progress and modernisation (see Chapter 7). As such patience can constitute an important form of 'waiting power' (Sloterdijk, 2005), biding time, taking time out, stopping to think (Berlant, 2010), in more or less strategic ways. '[C]hoosing your moments when you want to pick the fight, to challenge' as Anne (see also Chapter 5) suggests or even avoiding challenge altogether is crucial to effective resistance. Patience is important when engaging with the multiplicity of reality, necessary for the sort of relational democratic practice I envisage in Chapter 2 (see also Chapter 7). It speaks to a different understanding of social change and transformation:

> transformative time doesn't always stop the world, as if it's an absolute break between now and then, but is a daily part of it, a way of being in the ongoing work of emancipation, a work which inevitably must take place while you're still enslaved, imprisoned, indebted, occupied, walled in, commodified etc.
>
> (Gordon, 2011, p. 8)

Rather than wasting time due to a lack of clear activity, the ongoingness and continuity is important as a way of 'carrying on regardless', of keeping going, which suggests an important indifference to the supposed emergencies, crisis and diminishing hopes. It links the past and the future through a prolonging of the present.

Furthermore, for diversity workers already positioned unequally patience is a powerful protective strategy because reacting quickly, without thought presents particular problems. As Anne says:

Extract 6.3
. . . particularly when something is racist and you know that it is clear but you are not in a position of power . . . if you challenge them what sort of reprisals are going to come from that? And you've really, really got to be very, very careful when it comes to issues of race.

To interpret all forms of hesitation, waiting, pausing, non-active actions that could be read through the frame of patience, in the same way would fail to take account of the much higher stakes for some diversity workers in contexts where they embody the work. Patience for these workers provides a very necessary hiatus in confusing and insecure circumstances where care must be taken around race. But such pauses are not only about reorienting for strategic action, it is affectively crucial to the ability to continue to work and exist within systemically repressively tolerant contexts, like the institutionally racist ones considered in the interviews discussed in this chapter and in Chapter 5. As Ngai suggests, the pauses enacted through ugly feelings are a means for Black subjects situated in such contexts to resist 'the forced choice' continually demanded of them, to identify ethnically and organisationally (where it is assumed that whiteness and organisational identification meet seamlessly) as either one way or the other.

Extending this line of argument about forced choice, for an already racialised diversity worker like Aadil in Extract 6.2, positioned through difference, but institutionally included, the refusal to be pressured into being either for or against a particular point of view, course of action or set of ideas can be read as constituting an important form of resistance to the dichotomising premises of such a system of contemptuous inclusion where choice is only ever framed through systemically predetermined ordering. Under such circumstances patience as a means of stepping back, creating the space for problematising, can be a means of dealing with the organisation's concerns for Black staff to position themselves one way or another, and thus to sustain the sort of bewildering shocks described by Gulshan in Extract 6.1. This resembles the difference between being 'forced to think' through shock, crisis or trauma and 'stopping to think' as a response to such shock as appreciated by Berlant. The latter relates to the struggle to maintain 'continuous experience' as an excess which cannot be reached by institutionalised calls to subjectification. This refusal to position one way or another brings an additional prospect of finding 'your own solution'. This is not necessarily an individualised response because for Aadil it is framed in terms of the broader collectively driven question 'what kind of society do you want?' But the response is not pre-ordered through institutional framing and it does not necessarily have to be responded to through recognition. Patience is therefore a means of holding open this space for debate, sustaining the political potential of equity-fatigued diversity workers in situations where they do not appear to be actively resisting systemic inequality, and where their inaction or even certain actions may appear to support the unequal *status quo*. Patience can provide the space to generate a different set of commitments to those around the organisation's definition of inequality, equality or diversity, thus already closing down any debate as to the nature of inequalities in this context.

Privileged impatience

For workers who are not taken to embody diversity/work, the experience of organisational demands is very different. Tony is a white man in his mid-forties, who has been working in the broad field of equalities in the archives libraries and museums service for over 20 years. At the time of interview he was the diversity lead for the service's London-based coordinating body. He presents himself as strident unequivocal uncompromising – apparently quite the opposite to the sort of careful patient restrained approach advocated by Anne and Aadil and Gulshan above. In Extract 6.4 he reflects on his present position after recently completing the diversity strategy for his service. He explains that he had made it 'a bit more harder hitting because I think we were all losing a bit of patience with this coded way of saying things and in fact no; we needed to be a bit more in your face I think'. He goes on to say:

Extract 6.4

I've lost patience. I've always been an impatient individual anyway, but I've always associated that with a lack of maturity. However, in this particular subject I think impatience shows extreme maturity rather than a lack of maturity. I think it shows the opposite because I think I've got to the stage now where the time we are in that we should express it in those terms. I think we all know what's right and wrong today, um, we've had a lot of examples of good and bad behaviour in the past so um, we can clearly make a very quick judgement I think. So instead of sort of sitting on the fence and saying that [those organisations that haven't done anything about diversity] are all kind of sweet really, well-meaning and 'oh they don't have much money do they'. Instead of sort of saying that and making excuses for the use of public money – they've been around for decades you know, they are educated, {raising voice} they should know bloody better! So all those sort of arguments that sort of come to the fore really and you think that group of arguments is a little strong about 'oh they are weak', but it's also because you know, they've been given enough chances as well and you don't see much evidence of change. That's when you begin to lose it, you still get people sort of making outrageous statements, it flips you really. You just lose it at that point. I was talking to someone at a well-established, centrally-funded organisation about diversifying their workforce, and this woman said to me, 'what's the point of doing that?' she said, because when people come in all they'll see is, 'they won't see these people because a lot of them work behind the scenes'. She said {raising voice} they won't see them so there's no point of doing it is there! ... I think people, are sort of tired of it all, well me anyway, and sort of therefore not prepared to sort of make excuses for people anymore, or organisations.

From the beginning of Extract 6.4, Tony's comments appear to set up a binary between being 'patient' and 'impatient'. His distinction recapitulates an active/passive binary where the former is valued over the latter. You are patient: indecisive, 'sitting on the fence' and 'making excuses' for inaction. Alternatively you are impatient: characterised by a strong 'in your face' and 'harder hitting' sense of moral judgement as to 'what's right and wrong today', what is 'good and bad' and the ability to come to judgement quickly one way or another on this basis, rather than by engaging with a more contextualised sort of debate around personal or organisational circumstances. This patience/impatience binary is formulated through the familiar liberal emotional maturity/immaturity binary. As such it works to counterpose an association between contextually driven indecisiveness ('sitting on the fence') and emotional immaturity, with an association between political maturity and clear cut decisiveness rooted in supposedly straightforward normative principles of right and wrong. Tony's claim that impatience is necessary 'in this particular subject' of equality appears to fit into traditional liberal ideas of the public/private divide between normative collective political judgement and more contextually dependent individual/personal issues. For him, impatience is justified normatively in terms of appeals to a unified collective understanding 'what we all know' therefore 'they should know bloody better!' because 'they've been around for decades', 'they are educated'. For Tony then, whether organisations are 'weak', or advantaged, equality should be obvious. Impatience has the moral high ground in this extract. On the other hand patience, in the subject of diversity in particular, is at the least ineffective in its slowness to reduce inequality, if not morally dubious in terms of its tendency to support excuses for inaction on inequality through its passivity. Thus, overall for Tony in this extract there is a strong sense of urgency for change informed by moral imperative juxtaposed with (and maybe even amplified by) a failure to effect change. Contrasting this extract with Aadil's carefully presented patient ambivalence in Extract 6.2, it is hard to ignore the ways in which Tony so easily adopts the position of universal knower and judger so representative of white masculinist liberal institutional epistemologies and from which he positions some issues as public and others as private, defining the parameters of relevance in the organisational sphere. This positioning even allows him to feel able to rework traditionally accepted infantilisations, shifting impatience from a sign of immaturity to maturity.

Whilst Tony's concern in Extract 6.4 appears to be to present himself as an active decisive agitator for equality, this presentation is underpinned by a strong sense of loss and potential defeat: 'people, are sort of tired of it all, well me anyway I am tired of it all'. Patience is not something Tony has actively rejected. It is something he has lost, which has been broken down. Taken in the context of the interview, his phrase 'the time we are in' is a reference to the ostensible strength of political support and high public profile of diversity at the time the interview was being conducted which, as Tony comments elsewhere in that broader discussion, has 'fundamentally changed [for the better] under the Blair Government, like it or not'. His loss of patience is all the more poignant within this ostensibly more diversity-friendly context – by implication it should have provided positive material change. His sense of exasperation is heightened at the ongoing resistance to the most superficial forms of diverse representation where people like the woman in Extract 6.4 still don't see the point. In contrast to anger which 'threatens violence for you, your family, your friends, and above all for society' (Tomkins, 1995, p. 198), Tony's impatience is ambiguously targeted, shifting between a range of objects – well-established organisations, under-resourced weak organisations, educated people. Nor does it immediately suggest clearly identifiable strategies for change. It contrasts the tone of his self-presentation, suggesting his very limited agency. Rather than positioning Tony as a straightforwardly radical resister, the patience/impatience binary he sets up in Extract 6.4 could also be read as depoliticising. Depoliticising in the sense that it serves to obscure the systemic aspects to ongoing inequality that Tony is so keen to address by locating the inability to effect change in the assumed passivity of more patient diversity workers. His insistence that 'education' should trump organisational context means that he appears to ignore the fact that the contexts he works within are already racialised and gendered with relatively large numbers of Black and women workers in relation to the rest of the learning and skills sector (Hunter, 2005c). Thus, his urge to forget organisational histories plays out as a failure to recognise the racialisation of that disadvantage. Resistance to patience reinforces ignorance of racialised disadvantage, enabled through positioning within power.

Extract 6.5 below comes towards the end of a long narrative in which Tony has been recounting an earlier professional experience than the ones he is discussing in Extract 6.4, working in an organisation that he accused of being racist, and where he 'felt really sick', 'that pit of your stomach feeling', 'seeing colleagues racially abused' and which he eventually left; 'got out because I had to get out', before getting 'done at some stage', like his other colleagues 'one by one'. It provides further important insight into the way in which his resistance to patience works as a function of privileged positioning.

Extract 6.5

[As a white man] the organisation had me marked down as one of them. So when [I started to challenge their blatant racism], I think they took some time to get to grips with that as an issue, which perhaps meant that they were slower to act than with [an Asian woman colleague of mine], in terms of taking action against me, so they made attempts to bring me back into the fold, as if I was Colonel Kurtz in *Apocalypse Now*.

Tony's recognition that the organisation 'took some time to get to grips with' his challenges to their blatant racism and that he thus had more time to think/act/ resist than his Asian woman colleague before it took 'action against me', because it 'had me marked down as one of them', is important because it is suggestive of the ways in which his impatience can be read as a sign of his empowerment as a white man. Because as a white man Tony's fitting into the organisational 'party line' is assumed, he escapes the constant pressure of being called on to position himself that Black and Asian workers experience so frequently. This insider positioning affords him orienting time not available to his racialised co-workers, whilst the organisation is busy reorienting its stance towards what it expects of him. His resistance to patience can, then, also be read from within the prior experience of being able to be patient, being afforded time as an organisational insider. In terms of what is expected of him as a white man worker who already has his organisational space, the expectation is of silent acquiescence to the party line because of his assumed agreement with it. Reluctance to be patient could be read as a form of resistance from within his particular positioning of power and privilege which as a white man is quite different from that of Gulshan, Anne and Aadil where challenges to racism within normatively white contexts are concerned.

Tony's self comparison to the image of Colonel Kurtz the main antagonist in the 1979 Francis Ford Coppola film *Apocalypse Now* is important because of the further light it sheds on how he experiences these tensions of racialised and gendered insiderness. It enables a comparison to Bill's narrative explored in Chapter 3 in terms of the ways in which his impatience could be read as a form of desperate reaction to being positioned as 'one of them'. Coppola's Colonel is based on the fictional character of Kurtz, the nineteenth century ivory trader from Joseph Conrad's 1902 novella *Heart of Darkness*. Set in Vietnam and the Congo Free State respectively, both Kurtzs are corrupted imperialists, beginning as multi-talented and exceptionally promising within their professional contexts as soldier and trader, before becoming degraded murderous psychopaths through the circumstances within which they find themselves. They both end up damaging the reputations of the institutions to which they belong by publicly flaunting their ability to take institutionalised atrocities to unacceptable extremes. In the 1979 film Colonel Kurtz is given an opportunity to return to the US Army's fold, before the Army authorities order his death, dispatching an assassin who eventually kills him. However, the assassin succeeds only because of Kurtz's fragile mental state and his own desire to be released from the savageries he has been involved in. The comparison Tony makes in Extract 6.5 invites association between Kurtz's rejection of the US Army's values and his own rejection of the racist values of his workplace, choosing instead to expose it. The comparison adds affective force to Tony's references in Extract 6.4 to 'when you begin to lose it' and 'it flips you'. It is evocative of the desperate, last resort nature of his struggle within the organisation and the inchoate ultimately failed emotional release that means the only option left open to him in the instance he is recalling was to accept defeat and leave.

It is important to take the force of Tony's anger at racist injustice at face value and to understand its power as part of relationally enacted resistance to institutional violence. I follow up on this point about relational enactment in the next section. Nevertheless, the discursive associations within his account are important. Both *Apocalypse Now* and *Heart of Darkness* have been criticised as forms of racially revisionist cultural products (Dyer, 1997). Both stories illuminate the unpleasant sickening realities of colonial degradation for the imperialists and from their perspectives, focusing on the lonely desperate downfall of a once promising white man, dragged down by systemic degradations of Imperialism.[2] Therefore, this comparison is not a straightforwardly heroic one. It serves to position Tony as a flawed man casting his impatience as born out of the desperate act of a lone male anti-hero, saving himself from the degradations of his racist organisation by leaving whilst he still can. Thus, this bears similarities to the sort of white masculine losses considered in Chapters 3 and 4. On the face of it Tony is, like Bill in Chapter 3, mourning the elusive prize of equality rather than loss of his power, like the GPs discussed in Chapter 4. However, the mourning relates more to the loss of control over achieving equality. In part then, Tony's disappointment and impatience here illuminate his frustration at not being able to direct the world as he might wish, the sense of entitlement to do which is in itself part of the power and privilege of white masculine positioning.

Connected resistance

Leaving, being forced out of one's professional context, could be interpreted as the successful curtailing and blocking of professional agency which maintains the unequal distribution of power and inequality within institutional cultures. But there are ways to understand leaving and its place within diversity work other than as a desperate individualistic nihilistic bid to save the self. Doreen is a West Indian head of service manager in one of England's largest inner-urban local education authority (LEA) adult learning services, with over 20 years' service, who was in the process of leaving the local authority setting to make the transition to private equalities consultancy. Over the course of our meetings she reflects on this:

Extract 6.6
. . . quite often for people like me it is a battle and we do leave and we do move on and we do move out and sometimes you don't get the benefits that you, it's a bit like Martin Luther King and people come behind and they get those benefits. And I think you have to recognise that otherwise you'll get burn-out, you know, you can fight this cause forever and you can try and get equalities embedded and things. But if you've got an organisation where the head isn't really interested in it, then you can fight until the cows come home and it wouldn't change it.

For Doreen the act of leaving was in some sense about self-preservation 'otherwise you'll burn-out', because diversity work 'is a battle'. But leaving is not viewed as an end point. It is part of a broader continuity in equalities work over time and in different contexts, and also relationally. This was the case for Iopia, another Black Caribbean woman whose perspective was considered in Chapter 5 (Extract 5.3) and who, after deciding to leave the prison education service for the FE community context, made her final and most effective (in term of organisational policy change) stand to support her new Asian colleague (see also Chapter 5 and Hunter and Swan, 2007). In relation to this particular issue within the broader context of our interviews outside the extracts presented in Chapter 5 she says, 'I had to support [my Asian colleague] openly *especially when I knew I was leaving* I couldn't leave her in an environment where she felt isolated or she felt um, at risk' (emphasis added). For Doreen also 'sometimes you don't get the benefits', 'people come behind and they get those benefits'.

From this point of view leaving can be seen as an enactment rather than an individual act, a relational enactment of care for self and other within the context of an overall network for equality. This is not necessarily a formal professional network like the one the practitioners in this chapter, and Chapter 5, belonged to, but an imagined symbolic affective network more like the one established through the dynamic collective unconscious considered in Chapter 4. But this time the network stretches further across time-space positioning participants collectively within a broader 'fight' or 'cause'. This broader cause is vividly symbolised for Doreen through an association with Martin Luther King, the Black Civil Rights leader spearheading non-violent politically and ethnically inclusive protest against segregation in 1950s and 1960s America rooted in his Christian practice as a pastor. Doreen's near self comparison with Martin Luther King could be read as self aggrandising. It is also potentially problematic in its association with the liberal mainstream methods of political resistance which so famously differentiated King from his peer Malcolm X, the more radically inclined Pan African Nationalist Muslim convert and minister. Nevertheless, Doreen's self positioning within a broader 'cause' means that the benefits, successes and failures of equalities work are not viewed as individualised but as more dispersed, longer range and generationally and spatially interdependent. This idea of leaving as an enactment across time and space is another example of the way in which relationality disrupts linear temporalities by bringing the past into the present through the enactment of intergenerational memory conceptualised through ideas of 'transgenerational haunting' where 'the generation finds itself performing the unspoken unconscious agendas of the one that went before', connecting across generations and families, rather than only down, 'creating a monstrous family of reluctant belonging' (Rose, 1996, p. 31; see also Cho, 2008; Gordon, 2008). This observation extends the arguments developed in Chapters 3, 4 and 5 around relationality's temporalities. In those chapters family, community and activist histories are brought into the institutional space as a means of bringing the outside sociohistorically enacted difference into the universal institutional space. But in each of those examples participants were symbolising from some form of face to face experience in order to enact a fantisised community. Doreen's example here suggests something slightly different and more expansive in terms of the potential created through the enactment of a dynamic collective unconscious through affective transfer working across continents and over time to create Doreen as 'one yet many' (Blackman, 2012).

Patience, 'not rushing things', 'seeing how things progress', waiting, is integral to this sort of longer range more dispersed relational enactment. It is what holds differentiated subjects together and keeps in play the future possibility of collective action. It is a means of expanding the present, and the space for thinking about what is to be done, rather than assuming an *a priori* solution. It does not solve inequality, but it means that its existence can be kept in mind, considered; 'diagnosed' in Ngai's terms. Within the context of a broader relational economy, patience is important because it prepares the way for more intentioned, more clearly object oriented and more obviously politically efficacious states like anger or love. As part of this economy im/patience is a continuum of emotionality which means that patience does not form part of a linear progression to unproblematic equal consensus driven collective action, but instead there is an oscillation between the struggle to maintain connection to others through differentiation and the inevitable periodic slide into categorical difference. Thus, patience comes from the desire to connect to others through an ideal like equality or diversity, but the struggle to maintain connection is continually punctuated by inevitable differences within those normative ideals; ideals which are related to, but not determined by, sociohistorical positioning. Thus, there are certain differences that cannot coexist effectively within the same space. Impatience indicates that the limits to difference are being reached. For example, for Tony in Extract 6.4, this happens when even the crudest issues of visible numeric representation and inclusion were not understood by the organisation. Therefore, whilst appearing unequivocal, even Tony's impatience has ambiguous potential because in the end it constitutes part of a continuum, as part of a broader system of affect. The possibility is always there to move from impatience back to patience, or maybe to more expressive anger, rather than his most frustrated recognition 'it flips you really' 'you just lose it at that point'; or even to somewhere else entirely, yet to be anticipated.

This recognition that diversity work is a relational enactment leads to the recognition that workers are differently empowered at different points (or at the same point, but within different relations); their positionings shift and oscillate (see Hunter and Swan, 2007). For Iopia things changed where another member of staff more vulnerable than her needed support; Iopia's leaving both prompted and enabled more radical challenges to her organisation. For Doreen her most 'inclusive' workplace experience was a 'responsive' one where, as she clarifies in another passage from our interview discussions, 'we agreed with other white research and development officers that I wouldn't always make the point about racism because then it made me look bad'. In this way, even Tony's apparently more problematic approach as relayed in Extract 6.4 can be viewed as helpfully resistant in its refusal of more genteel polite organisational norms. Relational enactments like this, where more enabled staff adopt more obviously resistant attitudes, can create space for those who are exhausted by constant organisational demands to position the self to conserve energy, take stock and engage in self care. Who takes up what issues and forwards which perspectives, at which points and in what ways, shapes shifting material enactments. It is the shape of these enactments which can challenge the uneven distribution of diversity work, and in particular the way in which it gets attached to certain bodies. But whilst the shifting of responsibility between differently positioned workers is important because of the ways in which it points to the potential for collective action enacted across difference, the potential for oppressions to be reproduced within this (most obvious within Tony's account in Extracts 6.4 and 6.5, but also in Aadil's account, Extract 6.2, and in Iopia's presented in Chapter 5, Extract 5.3) is always there to be recognised and negotiated through.

Conclusions

In this chapter I have looked at the ugly side of diversity work. I suggested it is ugly in the sense that it is hard, personally painful, anxiety-provoking and often thankless; a seemingly never ending struggle. But it is also ugly because those signed up to this work cannot lay claim to stories of straightforwardly heroic, noble acts of resistance. Everyday diversity work might not even always be couched within a broader systemic understanding of inequality, it might sometimes be individualistic, desperate or ineffective, or all three. The workers considered in this chapter are often enacting what appear to be tiringly familiar racialised formulations: white lone hero, Black workers confined to supportive or acquiescent background roles facilitating those more overtly agitating aspiring heroes. Diversity work itself can be as much about disempowerment, loss and historical repetition, as about challenge and change. There is the risk that these ugly affective formulations position Black and Asian workers as passive and accepting recipients, 'safely disattendable' (Tate, 2014; Ngai, 2005), reproducing their institutional marginalisation. Similarly, they risk reinforcing white male antagonists as central to diversity action. Whilst white women have not been present in this discussion, in Chapter 4 they played an active role in the reproduction of other problematically racialised formulations, avoiding their positioning within ugly affective formulations. All of these professionals doing diversity work are angry, tired and exhausted at different points. Some of their actions can appear self destructive, individualising and depoliticising. This is in stark contrast to the more active and energised tone of the discussions with the diversity workers presented in Chapter 5, though there too the issue of politicisation is more complex.

Despite the risks, exposing the debilitating paradoxical aspects of diversity work is important because it suggests that there is less difference than might be assumed between the welfare professionals in Chapters 3 and 4 and the workers discussed in this chapter, who are proactively positioning themselves as working for equality and diversity. They are all situated ambivalently, implicated in inequality's reproduction as well as its challenge. Whilst this poses difficult questions for those engaged in institutionally based diversity work around their role in reproducing the inequalities that they are seeking to challenge, it is an important aspect to understanding the puzzle of why inequality persists even in contexts where its reproduction is explicitly challenged. Rather than devaluing diversity work, this recognition of ambivalence could be taken as a positive sign for the broader potential to develop collective challenge to organisational inequality, as well as a warning as to the difficulties. Ambivalences provide opportunities for change. The question is how to hold onto them?

There is no doubt that feelings like patience and impatience can appear to support politically conservative agendas when their impact is considered alone. But this is not necessarily the case because it depends on how these feelings function within an overall system of affect, how they are enacted relationally, who takes them up, in what form and for what purpose. Thus, ugly feelings do not necessarily produce ugly enactments. Patience enacts a space of respite from where workers can refuse to be governed by familiar divisions sustained through the types of institutional blaming dynamics outlined in Chapter 4. Patience maintains an important ambivalence by resisting pressure to come to a decision to be one thing or another, being 'against us or with us' as Aadil puts this in Extract 6.2. Thus, as much as successful diversity work is about doing things, it is also about stopping things being done producing blockage and rupture to institutional 'business as usual' (see Ahmed, 2012). From the perspectives considered in this chapter an important form of 'inaction' is this refusal to come to a decision, to judge good/bad, this inaction maintains ambivalence and complexity.

An emotion like anger can be a politically productive force creating the momentum which invites an immediate action. For Black subjects whose agency is already negated through processes of exclusion anger can be a useful tool to puncture the sort of gentlemanly organisational practices which remain the somatic norm (Puwar, 2004) of many contemporary institutional settings. For Massumi it prompts reconfigurations, interruptions and eruptions because something does not fit. Thus, it creates a pause which 'forces an instantaneous calculation or judgement . . . But it's not a judgement in the sense that you've gone through all the possibilities and thought it through explicitly – you don't have time for that kind of thing' (Zournazi, 2002, p. 216). But, because anger seeks a clear target, it can enact unhelpful objectifications. Its intensity and demand for immediate action is difficult to sustain and can produce exhaustion, as well as release. For Black subjects it can also mean being 'put in the space of the "well-adjusted slave", a position from which [Black and Asian workers] can always already be understood, known, recognised and undermined with "see, what you can expect they are full of the same"' (Tate, 2012, p. 223). Expressions of anger very clearly single workers out with serious consequences, as Anne makes clear in Extract 6.3. My intention here is not to argue that anger is necessarily unhelpful, rather that it will not always be helpful. A focus on anger to the expense of other less obviously resistant emotions is problematic. In order to understand how it can work in politically efficacious ways it needs to be understood as part of an affective economy, produced through particular forms of relational politics. Thus, problematic as Tony's expressions of impatience in Extract 6.4 may appear in terms of the reinforcement of white masculine dominance over the field of resistance, as part of a broader relational network his impatience could play out helpfully. Whilst his irritation does not put him at the same sort of risks and as publicly out of place as his earlier experience, it provides a useful function. It keeps the idea of organisational failure in play, enabling Black subjects to take respite from personal attacks and the exhaustion of day to day struggle.

For Gordon the combination of 'acute timeliness and patience, of there being no time to waste at all and the necessity of taking your time' (Gordon, 2011, p. 8) is the mark of the abolitionist imaginary guiding a range of worldwide resistance movements. Following this line of argument, taken together expressions of patience and impatience enlarge the relational space for different potential to be enacted creating more not less radical forms of opportunity. It enlarges the space for remaining ambivalent, enabling different symbolic connections across context and over time, connecting past to present, rather than privileging action in the present. Patience sustains the pause crucial to renegotiating self and broader parameters of activity. Thus patience functions not to depoliticise, but to put the brakes on the too quick move to pit good against bad in racialised resistances. It operates at least as much as a means to prepare the way for anger as for acqui-escence. It potentially enriches anger's enactments in the sense that it provides room for preparation and respite. It sustains diversity workers' affective energies, keeping open a space for more explicitly politicised resisting hard hitting actions which can draw attention to the systemic reproduction of inequality. It is part of the ugly everyday work which sustains more obviously radical challenges to the *status quo*. It is necessary work if ideas of equality and diversity are to be kept in play at all in institutions which remain structured through inequality, but which envisage themselves through inclusion. As such it must be recognised as crucial to broader political projects for equality. In the next chapter I continue to explore this issue of holding ambivalence as central to the ability to do institutionalised forms of diversity work for critical social transformation which work through, but also against the normativities of institutional life. But I take this further to under-stand the process of policy development itself as a means of holding ambivalence, multiplicity and hope for something different.

Notes

1 This was suggested to me by Sara Ahmed and Elaine Swan in comments on a much earlier version of the working paper that became this chapter.
2 It is important not to underplay here that Kurtz is a grotesquely barbaric character. Representing the extreme violence of colonialism and the Vietnam War, it is his excessive revelling in and barbaric extension of the institutionalised violence of war which prompts the US Army's attempts to stop his activities. The critique within the film is ambivalent at best, as to whether the problem is of violent extreme, rather than the violent impulse in itself. Kurtz's turning away from the mainstream authorities is open to different readings, either as the result of his earlier ambitions to promotion being spurned by the military authorities, or as the result of the strug-gle to survive within the savageries of the necessary evils of war and colonialism which create their own madnesses to which Kurtz succumbs. The story perpetrates considerable symbolic violence to those it casts as 'natives', according little or no agency to subjects essentially construed as the savage 'victims' of colonial oppres-sion gone wrong. Indeed, the savageries of the 'natives' provide contextual justifi-cation for Kurtz's descent into violence.

Chapter 7

Equalities policy as relational hinterland

> Politics has many geometries, is never finally sure of its subjects and objects, and is premised on the virtues of difference and listening as well as on articulation – that is, boundary-making and domain connecting action in the world.
>
> (Haraway, 1997 p. 73)

Following Chapter 2's argument that politics is multiple, this chapter traces how policy decisions are neither located in one place, nor with one set of people. Instead, according to my analysis of its relational politics as outlined in Chapter 2, policy is enacted in the performative sense, through the ambiguous, often conflictual and always emotional interaction between various people, objects and ideas. Up to this point in the empirical chapters in *Power, Politics and the Emotions* my attention has been focused on the everyday institutional enactments which make up this relational politics, what more mainstream accounts might think of in terms of street level bureaucracy, or implementation. In this final empirically based chapter I explore more directly the process of policy making *per se*. Through this discussion I re-imagine this process as a *relational hinterland*. Rather than a means of problem resolution, policy constitutes a meeting point for different but interdependent and overlapping perceptions of 'reality out there' (Law, 2004), such as those constituted through ideas of equality and diversity respectively. Policy is a means of *cooperation*, not consensus. Thus, it does not direct behaviours within a given field, but constitutes the contested field itself.

In order for us to recognise these multiple people, objects and ideas working together as (if) a policy, they *appear* as collected in the same place, held together, singular. This chapter proposes that this is the important role of policy documents; they constitute a means of holding together disparately positioned people, objects and ideas across time and space. Thus, documentation practices (including but not confined to writing practices) form an important part of relational politics, with important symbolic, material and psychosocial functions. By this I mean that documents are constituted collectively through the emotions and they also constitute a means by which affect and the emotions move. Policy documents move us, we move them, they constitute points for collective investment and they connect us to others. They come to constitute part of the hinterland through which they are enacted. Once we understand them in this way we can begin to understand their important role in both sustaining and disrupting social relations through their very production.

Psychosocially, following my argument around melancholia, policy documents can be understood as melancholic objects (Navaro-Yashin, 2009) because of their mediating role. They are melancholic in the sense that they join together multiple differentiated subjects, providing a means to contain the losses produced through encounters with difference at the same time as they are constituted through multiple investments in some sort of future. They are constituted through the interdependence of absence and presence, bringing together past and present, insiders and outsiders. Due to this melancholic nature documents' meanings and uses are ambivalent and shifting, rather than fixed. As such, policy documents *may* constitute a means to work through loss, difference and division rather than to get over it, leave it behind and repress it.

Substantively, the chapter brings a number of themes considered in other parts of the book together. It returns to the relationship between equalities work, public sector modernisation and 'good' (neoliberal) governance as manifested in the conflation of quality and equality in the new equality regimes. This chapter comes up again against the claim considered in Chapter 5 that these regimes have produced a damaging shift away from principles of collective equality to those of individualising diversity (Squires, 2006) and that they promote an obsession with superficial process over action. It uses a case study of diversity policy documentation from the English learning and skills sector to challenge again notions of a straightforward shift. It considers one document in particular, *Leading Change in Diversity and Equality* (Centre for Excellence in Leadership, 2005), that I was involved in drafting as part of my work on the Integrating Diversity research project the findings of which inform Chapters 4 and 5. This document was published by the national leadership college for the learning and skills sector,[1] the Centre for Excellence in Leadership (CEL).[2] By situating this document within its conflicted context for production this chapter shows how equalities policy, far from being imposed 'top down', is constituted through a range of arm's length organisations, activists, colleges, chief executive officers, teaching professionals, diversity managers, diversity trainers, academic researchers and documents, all gathering to enact a particular, more specific and locally relevant 'matter of concern' (Latour, 2005a) – race equality/institutional racism. In this way, the chapter returns again to think specifically about the ascendency of neoliberal whiteness and its relationship to emotion and, in particular, 'bad' feeling.

From this, and in line with the melancholic point of view, this chapter argues that conflict can be rethought as a form of emotional connection, as a relation forming activity, conflict over the form of the new equality regimes is no different. Such an analysis broadens our understanding of what and who constitutes policy and in particular how policy objects, in this case policy documents developed as part of the new equality regimes, are productive, enabling, living; constituting components of the lived relations of governance. They can be important containers for the emotions, whether fear, despair or happiness, and can sustain as well as disrupt work for equalities. This brings into question assumptions as to the socially reductionist nature of the performance evaluation nexus. Following this, the case deepens the challenge I have been making to an assumed institutional insider/community outsider dichotomy upheld within the (neo)liberal state's personalities, and gestures again to a consideration of the place of hope (from outside of institutional spaces) inside institutional spaces which I draw together in the book's concluding chapter.

This chapter begins by situating the Leadership College as emblematic of the way in which New Labour positioned e/quality – the joining of quality and equality discourses – as central to 'good [educational] governance'. It moves on to consider how Macpherson's pronouncement of institutional racism and the subsequent Amendment to the 1976 Race Relations Act disrupted the smooth connections between e/quality discourses in the learning and skills context. The case study explores the way in which the relational politics of policy documentation practices worked with this disruptive grain, keeping ideas of institutional racism in play as a means to hold open a space for the acknowledgement of histories of difference, struggle, antagonism and power which resist any straightforward conflation of e/quality.

E/quality and diversity in the learning and skills sector

The Leadership College was established as part of what David Blunkett, the then Secretary of State for Education and Employment (1997–2001), described at the time of the College's proposal as 'the most significant and far reaching reform ever enacted to post-16 learning in the country' (Blunkett, 2000): the New Labour Government's effort to bring into one sector – the learning and skills sector – the wide range of learning opportunities existing in further education (FE), adult and community learning (ACL), work based training and learning (WBL), all under the remit of the Learning and Skills Council (LSC). Under the auspices of Third Way educational discourse around 'excellence for all', and in tune with broader modernisation impulses like those in the health services described in Chapter 3, the stated aims of this overhaul were organisational streamlining, bureaucratic reduction coupled with enhanced quality and standards and inclusion (see Coffield et al., 2005). Debates around these reforms, such as those over the modernisation of compulsory education (Ball, 1998; Gewirtz, 2002a, 2002b; Gunter, 2001), focus on the dangers of losing education's democratic and social mission in new versions of managerially performing educational institutions (Hunter, 2005a; Kerr, 2005). Third Way discourses around educational excellence for all have been analysed as particularly insidious in this regard because of their explicit reliance on the conflation of quality coming from the managerially inspired Total Quality Movement (Temple, 2005) and the politically inspired notion of equality. The former is operational, about standards and consistency of service provision with its roots in human resource management. Whereas the latter is ideological, in the English context it tends to be linked to social democratic ideals around equality of outcome. Within this English education context there have also at different times been strong pushes towards radicalism via the Workers' Education Movement and a strong socialist influence in inner urban LEAs (Bonnett, 1993, 2010). Overall, this excellence for all discourse operated in a similar way to that within the health services discussed in Chapters 3 and 4, to bring together equality and diversity within a mainstream educational governance agenda. But, in the case of education this is from within a stronger liberally inclined social justice agenda (Gillies, 2008).

The College's name, the Centre for Excellence in Leadership, positioned it quite clearly as an example of this managerial excellence and quality discourse. In practice too, the College followed a modernised partnership inspired organisational form, it was established as a consortium of three organisations: Lancaster University Management School, the Learning and Skills Development Agency (LSDA, the key advocacy agency for further education at that time) and Ashridge Business School, with a small central team of employees, chief executive, financial director, communications officer, etc., based at a central office in London. It was to be funded for three years by the Department for Education and Skills (DfES) (as was then, now Department for Community and Family Services (DCFS)) and to be self funding by its third birthday in October 2006. The central London team and the College's governing board included several civil service secondments from within the DfES. So from the start the College and its activities were constituted through various different organisational histories, cultures and principles. The LSDA, created in 2000 as a national strategic resource for the development of policy and practice for staff and government, had evolved out of the Further Education Development Agency (FEDA), known for its left liberal and sometimes more left radically informed ethos of learning and education as a social good. Whilst led by a team located in its Management School, Lancaster's research arm was proud of its critical and multidisciplinary ethos, including staff from Computer Sciences, Education, Sociology and Women's Studies. Nevertheless, the fact that the majority of the partnership was housed within business and management schools, rather than contexts more explicitly allied to education's social mission, suggested alignment with the business rhetoric of quality and standards and closer relations between business and management practices and educational mission (Ainley, 2005; Ball, 2007; Mccafferty, 2010).

Race equality as a particular matter of concern

As I also considered in Chapter 5 this potentially depoliticising managerialising moment was developing at the same time as a very different and potentially more radical shift towards the statutory recognition of institutional racism in the 2000 Amendment (RRAA 2000) to the Race Relations Act 1976, on the back of the publication of the Macpherson Report into the police investigation of the racist murder of the London teenager Stephen Lawrence. The Macpherson Report and its ongoing aftermath are significant for a number of reasons which are important for my analysis of the development of policy in the Leadership College so it is worth outlining in some detail.

Macpherson's institutional analysis was important because it 'brought home *to those who had not known it before* the extent of racist violence in Britain, the way miscarriages of justice could take place and the incompetence and racism of the police force' (Bourne, 2001, p. 13). For example, the mass circulation politically conservative press such as the *Daily Mail*, ordinarily hostile to Black and anti-racist concerns, took up the cause of the Lawrence family as a moral affront to 'middle England', 'shaming every law abiding Briton irrespective of race' (McLaughlin, 2005, p. 169; Gillborn, 2008). Some have gone as far as to trumpet the Macpherson Report as a triumph of the liberal elite to 'look institutional racism in the eye', 'level the charge' and 'create a sea-change in public attitudes to racial injustice' (Phillips, 2009, p.13).

This official recognition of institutional racism can be seen in one sense as fulfilling the longstanding anti-racist concern to reallocate responsibility for racialised inequality to white institutions and away from Black communities. At least as significant as this conceptual reversal was what this recognition suggested about the significance of Black and Asian struggles against state racism. 'For one miraculous moment it looked as though the black voice had been heard in the land' (Bourne, 2001, p. 9). In so far as I am claiming that voice, experience and feeling are related, this hearing meant the recognition of feeling, and in particular *bad feeling* in the public sphere. Prior to Macpherson the term 'institutional racism' was most closely associated with a growing Black self consciousness expressed in anti-racist and anti-colonial movements (Biko, 2004; Carmichael and Hamilton, 1976). In the UK this 'British Black Power activism' (Alleyne, 2002) is most closely associated with London (and other inner urban) focused activities in multicultural education and various grass roots projects to monitor racist incidents, support victims of racist violence and protect them against immigration and deportation. (For an overview, see Anthias and Yuval-Davis, 1993; Gilroy, 1989; Mirza, 1997; Sudbury, 1998.) Throughout the 1960s and 1970s this growing Black and Asian self consciousness around racial oppression ruptured political activity across Britain (Shukra, 1998). Anger was channelled into campaigning activity but erupted periodically in various protests and civil disobedience. It was in the state's official response to the most notorious of these protests in the South London borough of Brixton that the charge of institutional racism was denied by Lord Scarman's 1981 inquiry with his claim that: '"institutional racism" does not exist in Britain: but racial disadvantage and its nasty associate racial discrimination are yet to be eliminated' (Scarman, cited in Bourne, 2001, p. 11). In contrast Macpherson's acceptance of the term signalled a shift towards the recognition of Black agency, subjectivity and feeling which necessitated some level of acknowledgement of the collective systemic nature of racist oppression.

This is not to suggest that Macpherson's inquiry findings were an uncontroversial success for anti-racist campaigning. Getting the inquiry onto the government agenda in the first place was the result of a four year long campaign by the Lawrence family which hooked into other much longer standing local and anti-racist campaigning around racist policing, and which was marred in 1996 by a failed private prosecution against Lawrence's alleged killers (Bhavani, 2001; Hamaz, 2008; Shukra, 1998).[3] Throughout the life of the actual inquiry, there were tensions. Some of the harder hitting analysis of British race relations' relationship to slavery and imperialism made by the Lawrence family, and Lawrence's mother, Doreen, in particular, early on in the inquiry were glossed over (McLaughlin, 2005). Nevertheless, I am suggesting that part of the significance of the inquiry and the RRAA 2000 is in terms of their official recognition of feeling, and in particular the validity of bad feeling, struggle and anger on the part of minority ethnic people living in Britain. An important aspect of this was the maintenance of a relationship between these struggles for social justice to the dynamics of institutional life.

Out of this very particular moment heralded by Macpherson came space for a range of organisations to openly recognise the need to address deep seated racialised inequalities. This opportunity was greeted with particular gusto within the learning and skills sector context, where, following the publication of the Inquiry Report in 1999, '[k]ey organisations in Further Education recognised the pressing need to tackle institutional racism and set up the Commission [for Black Staff in Further Education (CBSFE)] as an independent body' (Commission for Black Staff, 2002, p. 2).

The Commission was a collaborative effort between a consortium of anti-racist educators, activist groups and Black professionals. They included the Network for Black Managers together with trades unions, such as the GMB and UNISON, and further education principals' associations, such as the LSC and the Association of College Management (AoC). The Commission's findings detailed the ways in which institutional racism was manifest in FE in terms of the gross underrepresentation of Black and Asian staff in senior management and leadership positions and the differential achievement and uneven distribution of minority ethnic students.

As well as drawing on extensive quantitative evidence the CBSFE also drew on qualitative evidence from ten witness day events held throughout the country over 2000–2001 and involving more than 200 Black staff. The foreword to the Commission's report began with reference to Martin Luther King on the importance of education for equality and freedom. The witness day accounts of individual experiences were highlighted 'as deeply moving and often painful' and the report is dedicated to:

> those who have helped to take forward the struggle for social justice and for the dignity of Black staff, especially those people who trusted us enough to come and give their accounts during the Commission's witness

days, in the hope and expectation that their evidence would help to make a difference.

(Commission for Black Staff, 2002, p. 9)

Thus, similar to Macpherson, the CBSFE presented itself as allied with, listening to and in many senses coming from the experiences and struggles of Black staff, whose feelings of pain, loss and anger were apparently to be given high priority in the policy process moving forward.

From its investigations, the Commission produced a number of wide ranging recommendations for FE colleges, principals, managers, teaching staff, the LSC, inspectorates, trade unions, the Commission for Racial Equality (CRE), and for the DfES who should, amongst other things:

[r]equire the future director of the proposed Leadership College [CEL] to embed best Race Equality practice in all its activities and ensure that its programmes equip participants to manage diversity in the learning and skills sector.

(Commission for Black Staff, 2002, p. 82)

Accordingly in its 2002 strategy document *Success for All* (*SFA*), the DfES laid out its commitment to take advice from the Commission's findings as to how best to increase the diversity of leaders and managers, address equal opportunities and reduce racial discrimination across the learning and skills sector (Department for Education and Skills, 2002). Thus, the CBSFE, positioned in alliance with some quite radically anti-racist perspectives, can be seen as an important influence on the mainstreaming of equality and of *race equality specifically* into the core 'business' of the learning and skills sector. With this, it could be argued, came a space for the expression of bad feeling about the harm and violent losses suffered through state racism.

Documenting against the grain of diversity

In what follows I show how the space held open by Macpherson's pronouncement of institutional racism is a space for *the chance* to change practices and enact new presents which are rooted in the idea of equality *as a transformative social ideal*. This is the sort of space that I claim is enacted through the production of the Leadership College's diversity strategy *Leading Change*. This space is relational because the recognition of racism demands an acknowledgement of the histories of pain, anger and conflict that have been so necessary to achieving the struggle to meaningfully configure equality in terms of social transformation. Such relational enactments resist the exclusion of feeling; more than this though, as I have been arguing throughout *Power, Politics and the Emotions*, they bring new feelings and struggles to the fore.

The learning and skills sector and its constituent parts, ACL, HE and WBL, as well as FE, are configured through particular histories of power and disadvantage with specific impacts for the differential distribution of inequality across the sector. For example, ACL has a relatively high proportion of Black and minority ethnic staff in contrast to other parts of the sector. This is at least in part related to ACL's marginalised position within the learning and skills sector as provider of basic skills, English as a Second Language and informal community-led provision for disadvantaged students often returning to learn (see Hunter, 2005c, 2005d). Thus, it occupies a similar position to general practice and certain Cinderella specialisms within medicine. In line with the aims outlined for the Leadership College in *SFA*, the College's strategy document describes its remit to:

> promote and support leadership improvement, transformation and capacity building across the sector, to provide leadership for learners and employees. A key aim is to *improve the diversity profile and talent pool* of leaders in the sector.
>
> (Centre for Excellence in Leadership, 2004, p. 3; emphasis added)

In this strategy document, the Integrating Diversity Project (the project which I was part of and the largest of the College's Lancaster based 'flagship' academic research projects) was positioned as one of the key mechanisms for delivering these organisational aims both within the College and sector wide. From the beginning the provision of research informed knowledge, diversity (and in particular race equality as framed through Macpherson and then CBSFE) as an organisational ideal were high up the College's remit. Our project was commissioned to conduct qualitative research into how the term 'diversity' and its associated practices were being taken up within the sector and the effects on staff across the learning and skills sector, with a particular focus on women and Black staff. From very early on in the research the Diversity Project team were in the unenviable position of being called on to input into diversity policy on the basis of our research findings. Through these experiences the difficulties of maintaining equality as a transformational ideal while negotiating an organisational discourse of diversity became apparent. I say unenviable here, not because I am against increasing endogenous reflexivity (see May, 1998) in research practice: this would be strange given the feminist voice centred relational approach I adopt to academic research and writing which calls for the recognition of multiple positioning (see Chapter 1 and the preamble to Part II). I say this on the contrary because I am aware of the considerable complexities.

Unsurprisingly our research team's positioning of ourselves as explicitly feminist and critical race diversity researchers/workers/users further only compounded the sorts of pressures often experienced by researchers engaged in conducting critically informed applied research (Bannister, Hill and Scott, 2007; Burawoy, 2005; Burnett and Duncan, 2008; Keith, 2008; Nixon, 2007; Wetherell, 2008). During our research we used a private electronic discussion space as a supplement to face to face meetings to discuss the research and other related issues. The following analysis draws on posts from this discussion space, email records and, less directly, from other forms of informal research team briefings, research notes. Rooted in this type of data this chapter presents the most obvious example of 'anecdotal theorising' (Gallop, 2002) in *Power, Politics and the Emotions*. That is theorising subject to incident, out of life experience which 'teaches us to think in precisely those situations which tend to disable thought, forces us to keep thinking even when the dominance of our thought is far from assured' (Gallop, 2002, p. 15). This writing is only possible after having had some distance and time to reflect on the challenges and difficulties of our experiences. Writing about such experience is certainly born out of the desire to recoup something from what was a very difficult and debilitating situation for all those involved (see also Neal and McLaughlin, 2009) for an interesting view from the perspective of policy makers themselves). Any such reflexive analysis needs to be undertaken with care, disclosure of secrets is never straightforward because of power's multiplicities (see Ryan-Flood and Gill, 2010). But given that a feminist psychosocial analysis challenges the view of research and researcher experience as somehow outside of the policy process it is important to begin to subject my own voice to the same sort of more sustained analysis as the one I have undertaken with participants (see also Hunter, 2005b).

Despite some positive starting points for the development of diversity policy in the learning and skills sector in terms of institutional racism and the positive duty to promote equality, from early on the Diversity team identified the dominant unspoken narrative (Fotaki, 2006) within the College beginning to articulate much more clearly with the notion of 'management' and the control of minoritised subjects (see also Lewis, 2000; Puwar, 2004) more common in the HRM inspired enactments of diversity management. The replacement of the College's Equal Opportunities Officer was an early sign of this sort of more managerialist consolidation. This person was an LSDA secondment who had been very active and well respected in 'grass roots' terms for their earlier work in Inner London Education Authority and anti-racist community initiatives throughout the 1980s and 1990s. The replacement of this worker within CEL's first six months of operation with a civil service secondee coming from the Home Office with no previous experience in the areas of education or equality presented an early indication of the nature of the shift underway. This articulation with managerial control continued to manifest in the familiar paradoxical tendency for diversity to be, on the one hand, about everyone and thus no-one in particular therefore avoiding association with systemically unequal groups such as women or Black and minority ethnic staff, which would risk attesting to histories of structural inequalities. Or, on the other, for the idea of diversity to be hyper visibilising and objectifying of systemic difference and inequality, rooting it in a deficit model of disadvantaged staff (and in particular of Black and minority ethnic staff) constructing these staff as lacking capacity which it is assumed can be 'released' through confidence and aspiration raising. From this early point in the College's existence there was a push towards 'practical' positive action provision responding to this supposed deficit including a range of special professional development initiatives such as mentoring, coaching and subsidised places on the College's certificate in leadership course.

On the basis of our theoretical perspectives, our political commitments and our developing research findings, the Diversity team's basic position was one of resistance to this dominant managerialist narrative of diversity. A core part of our concern over the insidious shift towards diversity as depoliticised 'inclusivity' was the erasure of Black and Asian subjectivities, experiences and struggles which had been so evident in the CBSFE's findings, propelling the case for working towards equality. Within this there were problems with the promotion of certain forms of initiative and certain people as the 'acceptable faces of diversity' and others as not. For example, through the commissioning of Black led organisations and staff to deliver the diversity agenda, but from within a limited positive action perspective, the tendency was to reinforce a managerially driven approach. This sort of promotion of acceptability was an issue that was *widely though informally* recognised as having reared its head in the final stages of the completion of the CBSFE report. These were especially difficult areas of concern for us to navigate as a team of researchers multiply positioned through relations of racialised power and inequality (three of us identifying outside of whiteness as British Asian, Turkish and Caribbean heritage, and three within) and from within the relatively privileged professional context of a university setting (I say relatively here as four of the team were in short term contract research posts, and one project director in a teaching only post), given that it meant engaging directly with a variety of different, some more and others less, politicised Black led organisations. From a feminist psychosocial perspective critiques of tokenism or co-optation have limited utility, they also damage research relations and the fragile gains made by Black staff working in the sector. As a team we were careful not to become caught up in such critiques. Nevertheless, our response to our concerns over the managerial creep was to attempt to re-attach diversity to particular meanings, identities and interests and in particular recent histories of Black activism in FE, lost in the rush to proclaim the College's success at diversity. Our aim was to connect this idea of diversity to broader claims for equality rather than confining them to the limits of managerial professional development processes. I consider the racialised specificity of these complexities in more detail later, but first I turn to explore how these struggles over meaning came to be funnelled through *Leading Change*, and the effects.

How documents matter

Ongoing and increasingly acrimonious struggles between the Diversity team and other parts of the College took an increasing toll. Resisting dominant diversity narratives was a frustrating, relentless and emotionally fraught task. In this sense it resembles the work of diversity practitioners in our research whose experiences I discussed in Chapters 5 and 6. Relations between the team and other College partners, and especially the central London team, became increasingly strained, much of this related to the involvement of the research team in organisational and policy development in the area of equality and diversity. One of the many points at which these struggles came to a head was over the development of the College's diversity strategy *Leading Change in Diversity and Equality* (Centre for Excellence in Leadership, 2005).

The following extract (Post 7.1 below) is an electronic posting from one of the research team members about nine months into our research. It concerns a meeting held at Lancaster in September 2004, between our research team, the College's new Diversity Officer and a consultant for Ashridge Business School who ran Diversity Master Classes for the College. Not able to be present, but involved in subsequent discussion around *Leading Change* was the College's Communications Manager, a secondment from the LSDA. The meeting had been called by the Diversity Officer, the aim being to consider her first draft of the document *Improving Diversity and Extending Opportunity: A CEL Strategy for Leadership in the Learning and Skills Sector* which in successive drafts became *Leading Change*.

In the meeting members of our research team were highly critical of the approach to diversity adopted in the draft document. It reflected the clear shift towards managerial definitions of diversity around which we were already expressing concern. Our criticisms in the meeting focused on three core related areas: the negligible references to notions of equality and structural disadvantage; the failure to refer to the CBSFE and their findings on institutional racism, despite being peppered with references to Black and minority ethnic (BME) staff to the exclusion of other categories of staff who may experience discrimination; the failure to consider the specific character of the learning and skills sector and its constituent parts, ACL, HE and WBL, as well as FE, and how power and disadvantage are configured through particular histories with specific impacts for the differential distribution of inequality across the sector. By the end of the three hour meeting, it felt to us as though little headway had been made in relation to our concerns. The following post was written by one of the team members reflecting on this experience.

Post 7.1 19/09/04

I have been thinking a lot about that meeting and how it left us all with a generalised sense of anxiety and depression in the face of it. I have been thinking that the best way to convert this experience of negation (of not being listened to, of institutional and personal violence that enables that non-listening, of the constant presumption that we can facilitate the branding of [the College] as good/diverse, of the appropriation involved in all that etc.) is to research the process itself as part of what happens when diversity 'gets taken up'. I was thinking of the whole question of documents for instance, and what they do. We could think more on 'diversity documents', which take the place of action, rather than being forms of action . . . As [one of us] pointed out, in the meeting there was a constant 'return' to the document [the draft diversity strategy], as a way of blocking conversation about 'diversity'. There is a difference then between documenting diversity and the transformation of diversity into a document. What does it mean that good citizenship for researchers in [the College] is about being readers of such documents, in which the reading is 'already' read as a form of legitimation (if they have seen it, it must be ok, we want them to read it, so it can be 'seen' as ok). Maybe if we could write about how [the College] is using diversity (in a separate set of publications!) then we can feel that even seemingly useless diminishing encounters can get us somewhere? Or is that simply being hopeful in the face of the lost object?

This post suggests the various ways in which documents mattered. Broader epistemological struggles over managerialist versus more egalitarian versions of diversity became funnelled through certain documents. It is clear from the post how our experiences of transforming diversity into *Leading Change* provided a focal point for our struggles. It suggests multiple ways in which documents reach out to create realities, configuring the relations of the research team, the Leadership College and 'the sector' hierarchically as author-writers, citizen-readers. The post attests to the way in which documents became very concrete and real blocking mechanisms for us, the way in which documents stood in for diversity. The organisational subtext being 'we don't want to talk about the meaning of diversity we want to do the writing of policy', 'you stop us getting our documents out and so stop us doing things for race equality'. Our demand for discussion around diversity and its meanings is constructed as the barrier to organisational progress.

What is also clear from this post is the ways in which emotions are funnelled through documents, the way they figure in the configuration of documents and are configured through them. We can see our investments in this document: 'the lost object' and the real sense of grief, failure and anxiety in 'useless diminishing encounters'. But the failure of course is not in the document in and of itself, rather it is *in our perceived failure* to grab the chance to reconfigure unequal social relations; the chance that we imagine lies with the document and our interaction with it. However, the post also suggests the ways in which documents and documenting, in the form of publications, might also be enabling, a means to sustain emotional attachment to equalities work, in order to keep working at social transformation.

After this initial meeting our struggles over the document rumbled on. A key part of our concern after the meeting was that in revision there still appeared to be no clear basis for how the organisation understood the relations between equality and diversity. Of particular concern to us was the way in which the lack of ethnic minority staff occupying leadership positions was still being conceptualised in terms of a deficit, a problem of individual (and collective) aspiration and capacity releasing on the part of Black staff, rather than as structural issues produced through organisational blockages. In email correspondence feeding back further comment on the post meeting redraft of the Strategy I wrote:

Email 7.1 08/10/04

Whilst I was not holding out for a document which was effectively externally grounded [in current equalities policies and sector context], I am also dismayed by the lack of internal consistency within the document as a whole. For instance even on the first page 1.2. 'the current landscape' the second sentence implies the rejection of a deficit model of minority ethnic staff. The third sentence in this same paragraph then goes on to use a deficit model as its starting point, continued in the fourth sentence and then contradicted again in the 5th! Just for example. I want to be clear that this is not a quibble over semantics, these are not issues that 'only' a researcher would recognise.

After much more machination between our team and the College Diversity Officer and CEO, two subsequent redrafts and a cancelled launch event, *Leading Change* was eventually published quietly by the College in March 2005. It still contained many of the managerialist individualising neutralising flaws that we had identified in 'consultation'. As Post 7.1 above suggests 'equality' as a transformative ideal at this point seemed in many ways to be an object completely lost to us. The cancellation of the planned launch event was at least in part because of our team's eventual refusal to publicly endorse the final version of *Leading Change*. Indeed, conflict over our more systemically informed understanding of diversity and the College's more managerially inclined take only increased in frequency and intensity as time went on. As a later post from another team member suggests:

Post 7.2 24/11/05

The very brief evaluation [we] did of [the College's positive action programme for Black and minority ethnic staff] . . . I could critique this to death because of the way it infantilizes ethnic minorities and tells them that they have a self esteem problem. This is just utter rubbish! And once again this policy and the program that it is tied to are deeply rooted in whiteness which has a particular perception of people from minority ethnic backgrounds – Can I say this at the [cross sector dissemination] workshop? Obviously not.

There are two points of additional interest in Post 7.2. It shows how our growing frustration (at times it is not too strong to say an indignant rage, at least for my own part) was related in large part to what we felt that we *could not say* about the reproduction of racialising practices internally within the College and to some extent (at least in so far as we were seen *by the College* to speak for the College) across the wider learning and skills sector, even where we felt that our research findings called for a harder hitting response. The use of 'obviously' is telling here, as it compounds the sense of futility to our efforts. But it is also important because it shifts the debate in a slightly different direction away from race and towards an acknowledgement of whiteness rather than Blackness and, therefore, away from the experience of disadvantage and marginality to a critique of an investment in power and domination. This shift is important because it points to the limits to resistance within that context. I return to this issue of whiteness and the limits of critique below. But for now I want to continue to consider the emotional function of the document within this unhappy context.

Despite our almost overwhelming sense of 'failure' at the time, looking in retrospect at what we managed to *write* rather than what we managed to say, we did make significant gains. For all its managerialist conceptualisations of diversity the final published version of *Leading Change* contained multiple traces of the different voices contributing to its production, including that of the College's Communications Manager and the Management Consultant from Ashridge, but also from the organisations we had informally invited to comment on the draft document after our initial meeting with the College's Diversity Officer. These included the network of Black Practitioners and Learners participating in the ACL research. This therefore opened out the previously limited consultation to learners as well as a broader Black staff base than up to that point. On page 3 of that final document it stated that:

> We acknowledge that there are challenges in interpreting the evolving termi-
> nology of 'diversity' and 'equality', their application, and in understanding
> the case for positive action. We look to legislation, government commissions
> and representative groups for advice and guidance on defining diversity and
> equality across all areas of under-representation including gender, disability,
> race, sexual orientation, religion, age, working patterns, socio-economic
> background and human rights.
>
> (Centre for Excellence in Leadership, 2005, p. 3)

There is an explicit recognition of complexity, change and shift in diversity's meanings. However, in some senses *Leading Change* actually strengthened dis-tinctions in more managerialist and egalitarian perspectives, in its final incarna-tion outlining *four different* cases for the strategy: social, legal, business and educational (2005, p. 4). At different points it referred to 'structural inequality', 'denial of access' as related to 'power' and 'institutional discrimination' (2005, p. 5). It also highlighted the work of the CBSFE as the 'definitive guide and the driver for change with regards to Black and minority ethnic staff in the sector' (2005, p. 3). Small as the significance of some of these phrases may seem, their inclusion in the document was hard won, and their presence attests to the exist-ence of multiple and contested perspectives on diversity circulating within the College and across the learning and skills sector more broadly.

Rethinking policy documents as transitional phenomena

In this story of how *Leading Change* came to be, diversity documents, far from being static objects, form part of a complex relational web around diversity and equality. Rather than forging a single perspective on diversity, *Leading Change* constitutes a meeting point for the multiple perspectives on diversity *and* equality constituted through that web. In this sense it could be viewed as a more inclusive mode of ordering, a 'boundary object', which:

> . . . inhabit[s] several intersecting social worlds . . . and satisf[ies] the informational requirements of each of them. [Boundary objects] are both plastic enough to adapt to local needs and the constraints of the several parties employing them, yet robust enough to maintain a common identity across sites. They are weakly structured in common use, and become strongly structured in individual site use.
>
> (Star and Greisemer, 1989, p. 393)

As boundary objects then, policy documents constitute both means and ends (Riles, 2006a). *Leading Change* is the product of collaborative work on diversity and the means by which collaboration on diversity is to be achieved in future. So documents like this one are the heart of the organisation *in action* (Callon, 2002). Their power is not in an ability to communicate a definitive normative truth about the world, but as fictions between what 'is' and what 'might be'; temporary definitions of purpose which serve to bind the organisation for a while. There is a contested but interdependent relationship between documentary processes, their substance and action. The substance is enacted relationally through the material, symbolic and affective process of documenting. Its shape both attests to and redistributes the ordering of power and vulnerability.

Focusing on these interdependencies in the way that I am suggesting raises a number of uncomfortable issues for our positioning as diversity researchers as well as for the organisation we were working for. Boundary objects keep matters open in as much as they constitute points of connection. From this perspective it is crucial that *Leading Change* was not *tied up* according to *ours* or *any one particular constituency's* view on diversity. It highlights the validity of multiple truths on diversity *and* equality. Because the very techniques and practices of diversity documentation are what constitutes doing diversity in action, this story blurs the boundaries between doing diversity work, diversity research and diversity policy. In blurring those boundaries this sort of perspective further blurs the boundaries for expertise and authority in diversity work. Such documents, then, can make for uncertain, shifting and ambiguous ground on which to do diversity work/policy. This lack of certainty in itself produces its own anxieties. This uncertainty is part of what we can read from my anxious self positioning as '"only" a researcher' in Email 7.1 above.[4]

Paradoxically the very *coexistence* of this *multiplicity* of different views can also be seen as crucial to our team's continued ability to do equalities work in conditions of profound uncertainty and conflict. Here, I am moving to develop the point I made in Chapter 2 on the unconscious as a transitional space through which subjects and worlds come to be through the simplification of complex multiple experiences which enables the integration of good and bad objects. For Winnicott (2000, 2005 [1971]), whose work informed this observation, material objects had a crucial role in achieving this transition. Such 'transitional objects', as he called them, enable the move from absolute to relative dependence, from fusion to separation. They sit between objects as neither inside nor outside constituting an in between space where objects can be one, but also many (see Blackman, 2012). As such transitional objects are a means by which the paradox of difference and sameness, the way subject-objects are interdependent (multiple) but also individuated (singular); and the related uncertainty and anxiety produced can be withstood and the associated limits to individual omnipotence can be acknowledged. I am suggesting here that *Leading Change* fulfilled this important role. Rather than seeing an object-subject such as a document as a pause point, finished, to be changed in the future, such objects are a space for activity, an agentic space where things go on, just outside the realms of clear conceptualisation. As a space for activity documents are therefore a place of creating new configurations of the equalities landscape, materially as well as epistemically. They are therefore places of potential, opportunity and thus for hope in the vein of my argument in Chapter 6 about suspended agency.

Leading Change became so important to us as a research team precisely because it constituted a space to conceive together the multiple sites, subjects and objects through which equality and diversity were being formed; sites often too complex and contradictory to consider at once. As with other transitional objects over the course of the Diversity Project our relationship with this document ranged from identification to love and hate. But it was not so malleable that we felt magically in control of it, it survived the rough treatment of our split relating to it; idealisation, denial, refusal, rage. The document was able to withstand and contain multiple apparently paradoxical perspectives on diversity *and* equality and the related uncertainty and anxiety that disagreements over these perpetuate. Thus, through *Leading Change* we were able to realise the limits to our own powers in relation to equalities work. So, like other transitional phenomena *Leading Change* eventually enabled the psychic move from absolute to relative dependence, from fusion with the document to separation. In Freudian melancholic terms this shift represents the move from violent unprocessed melancholia towards the internal object, to the mourning and reprocessing of grief over what is lost. As another member of our team writes elsewhere of other diversity documents 'writing documents means giving them up, or giving them over to the very organisations we wish to change' (Ahmed, 2007, p. 236). In a similar way we had to give up *Leading Change* recognising that it had a substance and *life of its own*.

This shift begs the question of what we were giving up and why this was so difficult to relinquish. As my analysis above begins to suggest this reluctance was at least in part reticence to give up the Diversity team's claims to expertise. This is because these claims to expertise are not neutral matters of the rightness or wrongness of evidence, of fact over fiction; they are rooted in issues of social power and positioning. The giving up of expertise, therefore, potentially blurs a positioning on the side of the 'right', 'outside' the College's mainstream, more managerialist view. Such a giving over of the document risks challenging the straightforward idea of the heroic benevolent diversity researchers battling on behalf of the sector, and Black staff within it. Our difficulties attest to the difficulties of letting go of such a vision of ourselves and our role in diversity work within the College, as much as they attest to our role in challenging the reproduction of racialising practices within the document.

Hinterland

The issue I am pressing home in this discussion relates to one I raised at the end of Chapter 2 about the significance of the incoherent partial nature of power and invulnerability and what this means for resistance and change and the role of policy in this. Within *Leading Change* equality and diversity were not two great 'ontic-epistemic' systems counterposed in any clear way which could be challenged, bad diversity, good equality or vice versa. Rather they were patchworked together through the coexistence of overlapping and often contradictory educational, business, moral and legal ideas; different group claims for equality on the grounds of social identity, different sectoral claims such as from ACL, ideas of individual capacities and ideas of positive action programmes. It is this patchworking which makes them durable but also challengeable.

John Law uses the notion of hinterland as a 'concrete metaphor' for the paradoxical coexistence of absence and presence, the way in which everything can never be known all at once, reality always depends on what is not there. A hinterland is 'a bundle of indefinitely extending and more or less routinised and costly' symbolic and material relations that *include statements about reality* (such as those contained in *Leading Change*) and the *realities themselves* (Law, 2004, p. 160). In my terms it is a way of considering the conscious and unconscious together. Objects do not exist in and of themselves, but are being crafted *as part of a hinterland*, and, once produced, constitute part of the hinterland enacting other new objects. The objects in this sense *are the hinterland*. In this way hinterland operates as a relatively stable 'topography of reality-possibilities', whereby 'some classes of possibilities are made thinkable and real. Some are made less thinkable and less real. And yet others are rendered completely unthinkable and completely unreal' (Law, 2004, p. 34). The limits to hinterland are defined through historical repetition and relate to power.

In the Diversity team's example this leads me to two important observations. First, the struggle for the meaning of equality and diversity is not a struggle in the abstract. It occurs within and against a discursive context as this is lived out through the document's enactment. Second, in this particular case the ways in which racialised histories constitute the limits to the diversity and equality hinterland can be traced through what is communicable within *Leading Change* and what in the end is not. Matters of ethnic underrepresentation, institutional discrimination and even some ideas around systemic power are communicable, through *Leading Change*. However, what 'lies behind' these realities, the referents and relations such as whiteness, are not so. As Post 7.2 makes clear the Diversity team's frustration relates to this unsayability of whiteness, which attests to our failure to radically reorganise the equality and diversity hinterland by naming whiteness as a socially constructed relation of power and a broader institutional ideal within the College and broader learning and skills sector. But what precisely is the problem with whiteness here?

Sara Ahmed in her book *On Being Included* captures some of the troubles we had as a team around naming racism as a specific relation of inequality:

> The word 'racism' is very sticky. Just saying it does things. Constantly I am witnessing what the word 'racism' does. We speak of racism in our papers, which we give at research meetings to an audience made up of other project teams. I can feel the discomfort. . . . We stop, and someone asks a question about class. It happens over and over again. We speak about racism, and they ask questions back to us about class. Not just class but something more specific: they ask the same question about the complicity of middle-class Black professionals almost as if they have to re-imagine Black subjects as the ones with relative privilege. They displace the attention.
>
> (Ahmed, 2012, pp. 154–155)

This recollection serves as a reminder that talk of racism has very specific effects: it 'does things' in a way that talk about other social relations does not appear to have the power to. In this example class is legitimately sayable whereas other ideas like race or racism are not. Elsewhere, Elaine Swan (2010a) recalls how the Diversity team's findings on experiences of racism are met with questions about the absence of an analysis of disability. These examples point to the ways in which calls to shift attention between apparently different relations of inequality can become a means of displacement shifting attention away from race and racisms. However, here I am interested in unpicking what such displacements tell us about the interconnections between social relations as they work to produce racism as the constitutive limit to the equalities and diversity hinterland.

From my point of view Ahmed's reflection tells us something important about the terms of neoliberal institutional power's displacement which I drew attention to in Chapter 1 via the idea of the ascendency of whiteness. This displacement works to *redefine* the parameters of governmental privilege, power and inequality through the careful management of difference, by bringing it into sameness, thus hiding the complicated intersections, bargains and alliances which are crucial to comprehending its durability and which position race as a fundamental fault line for inclusion/exclusion; the fundamental difference, the principle social division. Thus, race is never general, it is only ever particular. We can see this general particular tension at work in this example from Ahmed's reflection on this experience of presenting our work, where class is read through race as a means to redefine institutional inequality as institutional privilege. Class is prioritised as the defining inequality which means that *Black* subjects who (supposedly) don't understand their experience in terms of generalised material class disadvantage are automatically considered to be powerfully complicit in the reproduction of inequality *in general*. This (supposed) complicity in general inequality is understood to cancel out their unequal positioning as raced. There is no concern as to the role of white middle classed professionals. The implication of this omission is multiple. It reinforces the view that race (only ever viewed through Blackness) is viewed as a divisive force and class as a generalising one; a means to bring people together, a bringing together which racism prises apart. Difference is only Black, never white, and it is always problematic. This means that some subjects are raced as Black and powerful others, but powerful white others, because they are not defined through raced difference, *can become powerless* in the vein of 'me too' I suffer discrimination. This is similar to the way in which Bill's claims to classed disadvantage work in Chapter 3. But racialised others, because of their relation to particularity, *must always be raced problematically* and associated with the reproduction of dominance. Whiteness, the general remains outside.

The point I am making here is not that expressions of classed inequalities are not legitimate, nor even that critiques of the development of a Black middle class are not legitimate, both are important to anti-racist goals as part of an intersectional analysis of power and inequality. Nor am I suggesting that there are no differentiations within these positions. Instead I am arguing that under circumstances where racism is publicly recognised it tends to be delegitimised through an emphasis on classed inequality as about everyone and that this delegitimisation relies on a silence about whiteness as a form of power which functions to ensure that *racism* is only ever conceptualised through the minority position. Holding onto racism therefore becomes positioned as the cause for difference and division, for bad feeling. Back to the zero sum where power can only ever be understood negatively, through reference to inequality, pain and loss and never through advantage or investment. Thus, as Goldberg claims, it is through this conceptual removal of race that the stigmatisation of racism as something only racists are concerned with occurs; a stigmatisation which means that it is racism which is unspeakable and that racisms operate *without racism*. By pointing out the contradiction that racisms operate without racism Goldberg means that 'racisms [are] cut off from their historical fertiliser. Racisms born again, renewed. But shorn of the referential language' of race, and without racists (Goldberg, 2009, p. 362). This brings an analysis back to how the prioritisation of positivity and good feeling work to reproduce power through the promotion of sameness. This is because bad feeling is linked to difference, and good feeling, by implication, to sameness. If the mention of racism brings with it bad feeling as I am suggesting it does in this example, then not wanting to raise the bad feeling implied through racism means not talking about race (as a relation of difference). Resistance to voicing bad feeling becomes crucial to sustaining the invisibility of the *whiteness* of the general liberal governmental ideal. Outrage levied at the speaking of whiteness is not because it serves as a disruption to the particular, but because it disrupts the general tenets of the governing order. The implications of voicing bad feeling are wider than drawing attention to one form of inequality, but have the potential to unravel the liberal governmental ideal itself.

As I mentioned earlier in this chapter, the take-up of the idea of institutional racism in public culture and in law was thought to be so important because it sought to work against this grain of erasure through its keeping bad feeling in play. As such it constituted the short lived 'radical hour' (Pilkington, 2008) for race equality. As I argued above this radicalism was related to its relationship to a wide range of activist 'bottom-up' struggles associated with the anger, pain, shame, violence and discord constitutive of campaigns for social justice. Centralising Black subjectivities shifts meanings and definitions through a focus on pain. It links pre and post-Macpherson struggles, violences, pain and antagonisms.

This connection between race discrimination and violence is a far cry from the development of other equalities issues under the new equalities regimes, presented in the more positive terms of 'work life balance', 'pay equality', 'gender diversity'. This is something recognised by the Advisory Conciliation and Arbitration Service (ACAS) who say:

> Unlike the subject of pregnancy discrimination that employers are quite happy to talk about, race is a topic that employers would rather avoid. One of the main reasons for this appears to be their fear of the stigma of being labelled *racist*, above all other accusations of prejudice. The approach of ACAS advisers is to cloak advice on race discrimination within more general advice on equality and diversity. This, they say, helps to put employers at their ease when discussing their concerns.

Here it is not a shift from equality to diversity which makes social inequality more or less achievable, but the resistance to connect it to a particular referent, race, because of its association with racism.[5]

The notion of institutional racism is powerful precisely because it constitutes a reminder of this history and brings emotions, violence and struggles into the public sphere, it constitutes this (neo)liberal public sphere as an *uncomfortable* place. So the discomfort felt when institutional racism is raised is not about the naming of difference or racialised difference *per se*, but about the recognition of *feeling* and responsibility which comes with the acknowledgement of historical relations constitutive of raced social division. What is difficult to take on board is its associations with public pain, voice, feeling and the possibility of *bad feeling*. Thus, it serves as a reminder that social transformation cannot be achieved without antagonism, or governance outside of this necessarily antagonistic social context.

This puts a slightly different complexion on the animosity and difficulties we experienced in the Diversity team as in fact about our attempts to reattach diversity to recent histories of struggle around *racism*. Highlighting racism in particular serves as an especially stark reminder that equality *as a transformative ideal* could not be achieved without facing up to antagonisms, struggles which produced those relations. The idea of institutional racism enables precisely such a keeping open of subjectivities, emotions and a potentially reconstituted hinterland for equality and diversity work because of the way systems, power and feeling are related. This meant that as a team we were able to name racism as more than individual ethnic and cultural differences, able to generate arguments in support of subsidised positive action programmes for Black staff, including mentoring and coaching schemes. However, in keeping institutional racism in play we failed when it came to going against the grain of established hinterland by bringing individuals and the institution into relationship with these broader issues of inequality. We were neither able to name whiteness *as the institutional ideal*, nor in the end even to go so far as naming racism as the relation producing inequalities.

Conclusions

My point in telling this story is not to suggest that the document *Leading Change* is in itself pivotal to equalities policy across the learning and skills sector. The DfES, LSC, College for School Leadership and a range of other bodies were all busy creating their own documents and statements of good diversity governance, all with their own partialities, bearing the traces of special interests and concerns. But these documents and their writers are all interconnected, speaking to, around and over each other in a broader equality and diversity policy network, which is rarely exposed or commented on in traditional stories around policy development. The writing and connections, whilst they may from a distance seem to be relatively orderly, or well ordered, are in practice chaotic, structured through personal and professional positioning as much as strategic intent.

Similarly, my intention is not to claim that this document, the Diversity Project or indeed CEL as such, made any significant material differences in the experiences or employment prospects of Black and minoritised staff across the learning and skills sector. This sort of argument, as well as being self important and overblown on our part, would be to miss the point that I am making about politics and governance as relational, the effects of which occur through the multiple shifting connections, interrelations and interdependencies. This is precisely the point that was missed by CEL in its pronouncements as to its *own* capacities to 'improve the diversity profile' of staff and which is misunderstood in the current 'calls to documentation' (Riles, 2006b) so prevalent in recent equalities work.

The power of documents lies in the ways in which they enable forms of resistance. They are the tangible 'real' aspects of policy, but not in the sense that they communicate decisions made and fought over. They constitute one part of a broader hinterland, enacting change relationally through the creation of a common ground in the present through writing. They constitute collective forms of witnessing (Verran, 2002) through which communities come to life 'through the collective act of remembering in the *absence of a common terrain*' (Ahmed, 1999, p. 345). This collective witnessing is another way of thinking about writing as an ethical practice, a 'third area', a *relational space* between the individual and the collective where emotions, practices and subjectivities come into play. This is in their ability to enact a reality which keeps open a space for different action in the future. The document serves as a promise of something different to come in the future, around which multiple parties can become invested.

What I am suggesting is that our involvement in writing *Leading Change* constituted such a relational space for equalities work. Not only did it give our research team the opportunity to challenge the College's construction of its diverse self, but it also gave the team the opportunity to challenge our varied experiences of *negation* as minoritised, queered and/or feminised subjects, but also as researchers aligned with feminist and critical race perspectives. It was because struggles for equality were bound up in our own struggles for recognition, of course, that the negation, or deletion, of 'our' perspectives was felt to be so frustrating and violent as it reproduced the very hierarchical organisational relations that we sought to challenge. Writing provided a space from which we could recuperate emotionally and intellectually from the challenges of the paradoxical personal erasures and hypervisibilities involved in doing equalities work which I discussed in Chapter 6. It also worked to contain our anxieties and enabled us to imagine change even when it seemed least likely to materialise, to go on doing this work and writing other documents.

Writing also gave us space in which to hold the ambivalence and uncertainty produced by inequalities within our research team. This is not to deny the complexities and difficulties of the various ways in which we as a team reinforced and resisted 'fantasy's of understanding between us' (Treacher, 2006, p. 32). Positioned as we were differently and *unequally* in relation to the social and institutional practices which objectified all of us differently by turns, but some of us less than others in relation to the specific politics of racism in the College, we have to ask why should there have been ethical understanding between us? (Puwar, 2003). Perhaps this is why feminist writing is less straightforward than other writing, because it persists in complex expositions of positionality where the question is always '*how* can we write [as] a collective given the absence of a common terrain?' (Ahmed, 1999, p. 345; see also Ali, 2007). Lack of common starting points always creates uncertainty as to inclusion in the community of writers, or in our case as researchers, but this lack of clarity about who writes also 'makes a definition and redefinition of the community possible'. It allows the group to emerge through a constant need to redefine group identification (Ahmed, 1999, p. 345). In this way writing and the *focus* for our writing constitute an important means of working through some of these fantasies some of the time, and the process of writing *Leading Change* was no different in this.

Exploring writing and documentation practices in this way prevents us from idealising equalities policy. Instead we can view policy as the relational hinterland, the space for *temporary* connections made in practice between those differentiated through power relations and profound inequalities. Policy is not about solving inequalities, but about creating space to better deal with their effects. Refusing such certainties might enable a more realistic view of what it is possible to achieve through policy, enabling us to create more constructive alliances between practitioners, researchers and policy makers around theory and practice connections. It helps us to understand why in our case a focus on institutional racism was both necessary and futile in terms of our attempts to address social inequalities in the learning and skills context. It was necessary in terms of fulfilling our commitments to maintaining a political resistance to socially conservative appeals to diversity, bringing emotion, bad feeling and conflict into the policy arena. It was futile in that the institutional power and idealisation of whiteness would always have remained unsayable and in that this was at least in part because of our own ambivalences as a team to the need for multiplicity. This is because a commitment to multiplicity makes it impossible to make general claims for the good. In a context where fighting for change, in the sense of a clear set of goals as to what it is that needs to change, produces a generalising pressure around the goal itself. This generalising impulse works the other way to produce a clear sense of what one is against. This generalising impulse was underpinning our own resistances to diversity as much as it was our own commitment to a systematised understanding of inequality. In this sense what it does is prevent the sort of reinterpretations of diversity through practice that were so important to the governing subjects speaking in Chapters 5 and 6. Thus, this generalising impulse on our part potentially constitutes an important part of the (neo)liberal will to govern that we are engaged in challenging.

Notes

1 The notion of the learning and skills sector in England shifts depending on the political priorities of the day, but it generally refers to all forms of post-16 education and training, apart from universities. Over the period 2003–2006 covered in this chapter, universities were initially included, but excluded by the end of the project.
2 For ease of reference, where appropriate I also refer to CEL as the Leadership College, the College as well as CEL. The College merged with the Quality Improvement Agency in 2007, reorganising again in 2008 to become the Learning and Skills Improvement Service, finally closing its virtual doors in 2013 (Learning and Skills Improvement Service, 2013).
3 Whilst two of the perpetrators were finally convicted and sentenced to life imprisonment in 2012, other evidence has since come to light that the Lawrence family themselves were the victims of illegal police wire tapping, and that some of this was probably known though not disclosed in the Macpherson inquiry itself.
4 The generally hostile attitude towards academic research and the more general questioning of the utility of academic research and academic researchers' ability to know 'what it's like on the ground' was rife across the College. This overlaid and bolstered the critical narrative arising around the Diversity team and our research as misunderstanding and detracting from the 'real' business of doing diversity.
5 It is important to be clear that I am not suggesting that this elision of bad feeling is

representative of less antagonistic histories and experiences as constitutive of other social divisions such as gender, disability and sexuality. Each is constituted through serious antagonisms, premature and violent death and protest included. But these are at least within the present UK context more muted within the public imagination, perhaps as Angela McRobbie (2009) suggests of feminist struggles for gender equality, they have been better 'made over' than racialised antagonisms.

Chapter 8

Conclusions: mobilising hopeful fictions through differentiated uncertainties

The worst is always what the hopeful are prepared for.

(Lasch, 1991, p. 81)

[W]e like to have hopes, they are amongst the things that keep us going . . . . There might be periods in our lives, after the disappointment of hope, when we try to give up all future hopes, not being able to face again even the possibility of the pain of disappointment. Some people despair and do not return to hope; but many will despair in the hope that hope will return. . . . [T]here are processes which encourage us to hope for too much, not to surrender our hopes when they prove unrealistic or to surrender them, as far as possible, without experiencing the pain and despair that follow. The search for somebody or something to blame when hopes are frustrated can help to avoid the pain and has become intimately bound up with modern politics.

(Craib, 1994, pp. 4–5)

There is no need for the excessive optimism that will inevitably end in disappointment, but neither is there an excuse for fatalism. Give up dreams of perfection or control, but keep on trying. But who is addressed; who should keep on trying; who should act? The answer is: everyone and everything . . . The 'we' who does the doing may shift.

(Mol, 2008, p. 107)

Much of what has been at stake for me in writing *Power, Politics and the Emotions* has been the desire to offer a potentially reconstructive approach to a critique of the state. A reconstructive approach that responds to the complex and often confounding experience of institutional life as this has been communicated to me by research participants across a range of welfare contexts; but also as I experience this myself. My aim has been to provide a realistically reconstructive critique of the state that provides hope for change in the face of loss. There is a growing body of work which has started to capture aspects of the loss, anxiety and fear present in the everyday struggles involved in striving to survive, as well as to do a good job in complicated and contradictory neoliberal institutional spaces where ideas of economy and efficiency jostle with others like diversity and equality, social justice and care. Janet Newman's recent analysis of feminist women's 'border work' (Newman, 2012, 2013a, 2013b), undertaken through their straddling of positionings across formal 'insider' and less formal activist 'outsider' politics, is an important contribution to this body of work in its emphasis of these women's neither one nor the other both/and ambivalent resistance to neoliberalised institutions. Yet, there is very little work which gets to grips with the way fear and anxiety reproduce themselves through those sorts of ambivalent resistances to the creation of normative insider institutional cultures. The issue is to recognise practices of ambivalence as part of a powerful blame culture which blocks and disadvantages *governing subjects themselves* as well as the range of others they are looking to help, fixing them into good/bad silos, user/professional policy maker/activist. Ambivalent shifting practices do not in themselves remove governing subjects from institutional blame cultures.

In *Power, Politics and the Emotions* I see the negotiation of fear and anxiety not as a matter of managing and negotiating the contours of *already existing institutional space* between 'inside' and 'outside' which enables governing subjects to somehow stand outside of power and responsibility for the reproduction of unequal institutional orderings. Instead this negotiation of fear and anxiety is a matter of *making the institutional space itself* as an entity which exists between 'outside' and 'inside'; the negotiation of fear and anxiety is thus, *productive* of 'inside' and 'outside'. This is a subtle, but important distinction which points to the ways in which personal power and agency must be understood as *constitutive of* the institutional world without individualising or romanticising this power. As I outlined in Chapter 2 this distinction between negotiating already existing entities and the negotiations themselves as bringing the entities into being is a distinction that begins from the Foucauldian idea of the *relation* (between subject and object or individual and group) as the unit of social science analysis. Prioritising the relation means that the person as much as the group is the product of relations. Groups *and people* are multiple, they are entities which appear singular from the outside, but are made up of difference from the inside which is already understood through a *taken for granted* outside.

This starting point is crucial for the ability to disrupt institutional blame cultures because it insists on the multiple enactment of responsibility and innocence as located *between* individuals. Meanings are always contestable which in turn means that judgement of responsibility for 'right' and 'wrong'/'good' and 'bad' is not straightforward. This is because a practice, like governance, can never be 'owned', actioned or located in a singular and therefore objective sense (whether this singular is thought of in terms of the individual or the collective object, or as the micro or the macro). It also means that governance can never be one thing, for example, *either* neoliberal *or not*; it is always produced through its many relations. As well as producing possibilities for change, this multiple in betweeness produces a range of fears and anxieties which are constitutive of institutional life where the nature of 'the good', who is 'on its side' and who is not, is uncertain and whereby it is therefore possible, even inevitable and maybe perhaps desirable, to be wrong *and* right at the same time. It is the inevitability of oscillations of 'wrong' and 'right' together which produces change. This approach to relational multiplicity is not reconstructive in the sense of seeking to satisfy the desire to develop a new idea of a better way of ordering the state. Its reconstructive potential lies in its ability to understand the way the state becomes fixed as a thing in itself as a function of this desire to do better and the role of uncertainty within this desire.

The struggle over the attachment of the emotions of fear or anxiety, or others like love and care, to ideas of good and bad is the means of producing the institution practically, as a material entity, by bringing people (and other entities) together, but this struggle is also the means of producing the institution *morally* through positioning these people (and other entities) as 'good' and 'bad' insiders and outsiders. It is a paradoxical struggle around the creation of normative ideals of good and bad which order the institutional space in multiple ways at the same time, and which bring outsiders inside and shift insiders out. *The interdependence between* the maintenance of ambivalence *and* the desire for closure around meaning are core to understanding resistance and reproduction *as part of this same process* of creating the good and bad, institutional inclusions and exclusions. As such cultures of resistance can form part of the cultures of blame sustaining neoliberal governing projects.

My desire to understand this paradoxical *inevitability* of doing 'bad' as you are seeking to do 'good' is what first brought me to consider psychosocial approaches (Cooper and Lousada, 2005; Froggett, 2002; Hoggett, 2000a, 2009, 2010) and then to my analysis of the liberal state's potential neoliberal suicide. As part of this analysis the power of the concept of melancholia lies in its potential for understanding the moral distinctions between 'good' and 'bad' as a way to attempt to manage the practical impossibility of group relations without some form of exclusion which, because of the interdependence of good and bad within the same subject, will always fail because of the way in which exclusions of the Other must always constitute a form of self exclusion. The problem from a melancholic point of view is that the self is always on the side of good, and the Other is always positioned as a potential threat to the self, therefore with the bad. Following this sort of dynamic responsibility for the reproduction of exclusion is always mislocated as *exclusively* elsewhere, rather than as a product of the relation of interdependence between inside and outside, self and other. From a specifically feminist and postcolonial perspective my aim has been to contribute an analysis of the ways that this good/bad paradox is enacted through a range of dichotomies (insider/outsider, sameness/difference) which work to distribute multiple intersecting social relations (of race, gender and class, as well as generation and sexuality) unequally within governance. From the point of view of bringing these feminist and psychosocial approaches together it is this struggle with the paradoxical interdependence of ideas of good and bad which creates toxic debilitating institutional contexts characterised by anxiety and fear of social difference, rather than any *sui generis* external threat. If there is no way out of this good/bad paradox, as I am suggesting in *Power, Politics and the Emotions*, there are important questions to be answered around what this paradox means for the possibility of institutional change and transformation and the roles and responsibilities for any such change. It is to answering these questions that I turn in this final concluding chapter. My main aim is to draw out the implications of the arguments I have been developing in the previous chapters for conceptualising relational politics as a reconstructive politics of hope which, because of the way it sits between the ideal and the real in institutional life, holds open closure on the good and the bad, without rejecting the possibility of ordering. But before I do this, I make one more detour to recap a couple of related points about the state as an everyday enactment that I am making in *Power, Politics and the Emotions*.

The relational everyday

The picture I painted of (neo)liberal governance at the beginning of *Power, Politics and the Emotions* was fairly bleak. This was a picture of a conflicted institutional space characterised by internal crisis, where the human agency generated through the experience of social difference that is essential to the state's enactment was perceived as a threat to institutional stability. As such, difference is systematically repressed, constrained or split off as external and Other to the state, to the extent that the state itself is in danger of being snuffed out. I conceptualised this internal crisis as a form of potential suicide of the liberal state achieved via *neo*liberal managerial methodologies which defended against the expression of difference. Paul Hoggett develops a complementary line of argument, claiming that welfare governance increasingly takes on the form of perverse 'virtual reality' whereby there is an organised denial of the emotional experience central to the effective working of the state, and the relationship between cognition and feeling is split. The new managerial performance evaluation nexus mediates between 'the state, its managers and policy makers on the one hand, and the many seas of social suffering characteristic of increasingly socially polarised democracies, on the other' (Hoggett, 2010, p. 62). This mediation operates like a 'thick skin' to create an 'as if' relation between the state and its citizens where auditable performance stands in for an often less palatable reality of social suffering and inequality. For Hoggett this development 'was not primarily cynical, government and the political elites, which circulated through it, believed in the illusion that they had created' (Hoggett, 2010, p. 62) . But it contributes nevertheless to the splits between rationality/feeling, inside/outside, good/bad, reality/illusion which work to support blame, rather than to promote understanding between differently positioned (governing and governed) subjects. In *Power, Politics and the Emotions* my concern has been to understand the ways in which the association between particular forms of social difference and bad feelings works to position such differences as normatively external to the state. From this point of view, the management of social difference becomes fundamental to the creation of a thick skin of governance by sustaining *the idea* that the state is one sort of technical bureaucratic reality, distinct from a messier lived social and cultural reality outside of the state. The resolution of the bad feeling on the lived sociocultural outside is dependent on the ability to keep it out of the state's rational technical inside.

From my point of view this issue of a thick skin is complicated and interesting to explore because it is not only a space of separation and denial but one of potential understanding, connection and creativity. I like the idea of the state's skin because it is suggestive of my focus on lived enactments, the state's personality and its feelings, it draws our attention to the 'livedness' of the technical bureaucratic in a way I find helpful. Conceived of relationally (rather than anthropomorphically) skin is a form of paradoxically enacted border space like the hinterland discussed in Chapter 7. It is living, active, it grows and changes. It is 'a border that feels' (Ahmed, 2000, p. 45). Its form is a living history of its encounters with others *and their others* (Ahmed, 2002). It contains the subject and holds them together to create an inside, whilst simultaneously opening out to the world of the Other. Skin therefore exposes the inside to the outside as much as it provides protection from it. It materialises the body through the enactment of porous borders. In terms of the state's enactment as a body politic then, this 'thick skin' of governing is the border space that I have been thinking about in terms of relational politics, the place where the *everyday* state is enacted through practice, where practice is conceived of as a sort of border, a relational crossing point or meeting place for differentiated subjects. This is an everyday state different to the 'real', where the real is something internally experienced as cognitively meaningfully understood as present in the here and now. But this everyday state is also different to the ideal as an external projection yearned for imaginatively as a possibly present in the future. Instead, this everyday state is *practised*, materially, symbolically and affectively *between* insider reality in the sense of a taken for granted shared understanding and the external world of difference. Thinking of the relational skin of governance as the location for governing practices means that thickness may be an advantage, rather than a disadvantage. This is because the thickening of relational skin extends the border space where inside and outside become blurred rather than fixed, it extends the space of relational interdependence (of inside/outside, similarity/differentiation, included/excluded) through which creativity and change are enacted through everyday practice.

This notion of everyday livedness that I have been trying to capture through the idea of relationality in relational politics is recognisable in Claire Colebrook's idea of the 'radical everyday'. According to Colebrook, this is an everydayness that can be conceived of as a 'disruptive force', rather than a conservative one. This everydayness is a 'way of thinking beyond the closure of constituted powers' (2002, p. 699) which is *already evidenced* in lived practice as a positive, or in my terms performative, ethics, it is a way of perceiving and engaging in the world which does not necessarily stem from the expression of an underlying continuous or coherent logic. It works through bodily powers like affect. This everyday is a space of productivity, a space of utopian potential and promise which escapes (*a priori*) definition (Cooper, 2014). Its meaning is only interpretable through enactment, through relational practice. As such, the everyday may be thought of as a space of 'unintention' (see Garforth, 2009); neither properly conscious, nor unconscious, but in between, a space of *relationally practised activity*. It is this unintentioned character which makes the everyday a space of hope. It is hopeful precisely because its ends are not established *a priori*; its pathway is not set with clear intention framed through taken for granted normativities.

Hope in the institutional present

Understood through this idea of the everyday, hope is an 'event' enacted relationally through commonplace encounters between subjects (where, as I outlined in Chapter 2 and pursued more fully via empirical discussion in Chapter 7, these subjects can be material objects, people and ideas). Hope is not located in a thing, but occurs in the practice of encountering others. '[T]he very fact that we can be transformed by what we encounter, or what we participate in is a matter of hope' (Stengers, 2002, p. 247). Hope is not a matter of optimism as such, but a matter of more agonistic relational practice which is only achievable within the context of difference, disagreement and uncertainty over the nature of reality. This is the distinction between hope as blind faith in a knowable goal or form of resolution, or hope as an openness to the risk of relationships, to the risk of being changed and therefore to the *certainty* of loss and fear and to the illusory nature of omnipotence; to the certainty of uncertainty. In the latter case hope sits in the contested space between a knowable and achievable *shared* reality and a projection of something else that might *be*, where that something else cannot be known either in advance or retrospectively, it can only be playfully fantasised about and tested out through practice in the present.

Donald Winnicott (2005 [1971]; see also Chapters 2 and 7) understood children's play in precisely this way, as a hopeful space for shared reality making. Hope enacts a space of play for working through the contested illusory nature of reality, reality's unreality. By reality's unreality I mean the fact that a shared reality exists *only* in so far as it is signed up to and invested in by differentiated subjects. Therefore, it only exists in so far as the desire for contact and understanding between subjects is hoped for. Reality is only created in the act of hopefulness, brought about in the act of hoping, an act which assumes, but cannot know another's reality. This is the paradoxical nature of reality where in Winnicott's observations 'the baby creates the object, but the object was there waiting to be created and to become a cathected [emotionally imbued] object' (2005 [1971]), p. 119). This unreality of reality means that hope is about being able to withstand the ongoing experience of failure to fully grasp the nature of the external world and others in it, and to invest in the possibilities for joint action in spite of this failure. It is this sort of hope as the process of encountering the failure to fully understand other subjects which lies at the heart of what I have been analysing in terms of relational politics. This recognition of the necessity of failure as lying at the heart of relationally practised activity is a way of thinking about collective action occurring through the everyday lived relations of difference. It contrasts with a view of collective action occurring on the basis of abstracted ideals of categorical similarity. Relationally enacted collective practice relies on hope because there is not an assumption of shared knowledge of the other in order to act in concert, action proceeds *as if* there is shared knowledge. The taken for granted nature of the rules of the game which constitute the illusory nature of reality for Winnicott are important under these circumstances because 'we know that we will never challenge the baby to elicit an answer to the question: did you create that or did you find it?' (see Chapter 2). How the rules of the game came to be *in the first place* is not at issue. Therefore, from within this sort of hopeful engagement there is no need to find out, to paraphrase Winnicott, did you create that problem or did you find it? Are you or your behaviours the cause of racism, or was it already there? The impossibility of drilling down to a singular location for agency means that there is no *automatic* drift to the pinpointing of responsibility and blame.

In Chapter 7 I looked at how policy documents can constitute the sort of relationally realistic hopeful encounter as part of an uncertain policy hinterland where various differently positioned actors meet, a sort of relational borderland space of collectively enacted unreality between state institutional inside and outside. The document, like other objects in the policy hinterland, was a space of unreality in the sense that whilst the material document existed in the present in an apparently singular form, as a statement of a diversity policy ideal to be worked on, redrafted and continually re-enacted, its meanings (diversity as structural inequality, as ethnicity, as institutional racism) and uses (as a means to hold individuals or groups to account, to engage staff or for institutional promotion or survival) were differentiated and distributed intersubjectively throughout the relationships, ideas and other objects (professionals, users, Black staff groups) which made it up. As such, the document brings multiple past and future absences (in the sense of ideas about what might be) into that present enactment of diversity. It is simultaneously fixed and changeable; one document containing multiple changeable ideas and investments in how the world could be. Hope is invested *in the present encounter*, enacted through the document (its making and its distribution), rather than via any fixed idea of outcome in the future. From this point of view *the encounter itself* can be thought of as a form of hopeful 'mobilising fiction' (Hoggett, 2000); an image or an ideal which can be collectively held as a means to *enabling a transition* from the fear of difference to the ability to withstand differentiation within the same space. The document enacts cooperation through difference. As such, it is a way of transitioning from individual to collective via the experience of different attachments to the same taken for granted thing. In that example of the document, this transition came about through the shift away from a single continually frustrated idea of a certain sort of categorically equal institutional order towards a coexistence of multiple ideas about diversity and equality which kept the question of equality itself open. The hopeful encounter enacted through the document offers the potential for a change, the enactment of new possibilities where existing ones appear to have been exhausted. It protects from the uncertain certainty of no hope where there is no investment in the possibility of connection via the collective practising of taken for granted reality. From this point of view the opposite of hope is not despair, but *complacency* and inaction (Duggan and Muñoz, 2009). Hope is *not waiting inactive* for something fully imagined, but yet to come. It is a way of *actively suspending closure* on the present through everyday encounters with difference.

The melancholic promise of illusion

This transition from individual to collective (singular to multiple) via hope is the promise of identification as it is understood relationally through the idea of melancholia. Identification itself is a form of hopeful encounter where individual difference is phantasmicly crossed in order to get to be closer to the other, to become part of a collective through communion with another subject who is already communing with its own other subjects enacted through gendered, raced or other forms of social difference. Relational identifications conceived of as the sorts of continually staged enactments between multiply enacted subject contain the *promise* of creating a self; one that can be lived through everyday experience as a singular self, an apparently ontologically unique 'I', but which is enacted in relational practice through its multiple external others, as a sister, brother, mother, friend, for example. There is an external collective otherness within internal subjective reality. This otherness of subjective internal reality is the relational 'back' story of differential positioning through history and power/vulnerability. This is a back story in the absent presence sense in that it is temporally 'behind' the self as it is experienced, but also in the sense that it provides a taken for granted 'explanation' for the self's positioning within power and vulnerability, for *how* it fits within various social orders.

The promise of liberal modernist politics is the *resolution* of this individual collective divide through the promise of traversing difference; the promise that in the end we can become the others external to us and thus understand and know them. This is the liberal modernist promise to bring the outsider inside, taking them out of difference, bringing them into sameness in the sense of taking them in or replicating the other object *within* the subject. This promise of bringing difference into sameness is the promise of belonging to a group, a profession or an organisation, or more broadly a state or nation, through the practice of subjective recognition. But this is a promise that can never be fulfilled because of the conceptual closure achieved through recognition. Part of you gets to come inside, may even be invited into the collective space, like the institution (Tate, 2013) but other aspects of yourself need to be smuggled in via the back door, hidden, not faced and encountered; which identifications you bring in, which you leave behind, how they intersect and configure are matters of power and choice.

There will always be some form of loss to encounter. However, the idea that the loss brought about through the closures of recognition *can be avoided* either by maintaining multiple aspects of the self in ambivalent play, or by developing new forms of *common* identification is a form of delusion which differs in two key ways from the helpful idea of illusion that I considered above. Both differences are related to the anticipatory logic of delusion.

As we saw in Chapter 4, delusion involves the tight coupling of individual subject and collective object which creates a confirmatory rather than inquisitive approach to the external world, where the nature of this external world is always already anticipated in advance. The processes of assimilation or cloning, like those considered in Chapter 3, operate in this way through replication, the collapsing of subject and object which happens through bringing difference into sameness. The dynamic contestations over positioning within the organisational space of the primary care trust in Chapter 4 elaborate the collective dynamics supporting assimilation. These dynamic contestations suggested that threats to institutional harmony which were produced through the reproduction of inequality were located within continued investments in a (white) heterosexual masculine institutional ideal of power and omnipotence, yet this threat of the reproduction of white heteronormative masculinity came to be understood through the presence of older Asian man GPs. This latter subject position is always read as grouped; tightly coupled in the sense that there are no subjects positioned within the group allowed to be defined outside of that position, as exceptions, as different. The group and the subjects within it are understood through the group's (absent/present) back story of colonial racialised-gendered difference. This is a back story perceived to be replicated in group members' unequal institutional behaviours which are then taken to explain the members' *own* exclusions from the new managerial institutional space. It is through this tight coupling of subject and object that cause and effect are linked so the dynamic becomes circular.

This circular anticipatory logic of the colonial back story of racialised-gendered difference replicates a broader cultural fetishisation of the normative splits between Black and white. This split turns race (rather than ethnicity) into a sort of overarching undifferentiated 'meta'-threat which becomes *the ultimate* taken for granted (unconscious/absent) explanatory device for outside of the norm, supposedly disruptive difference. It is important to emphasise that I am not using the notion of an ultimate explanatory device to suggest that race is more important than other forms of social difference. Rather, race becomes the idea of difference *that brings other differences into the modernist myth of the group*. It constitutes an 'ideological stress point' (Cheng, 2000; Silverman, 1992) which works through an alliance of repressions, like masculinity and age in Chapter 4, and through the more explicit additional intersections with heterosexuality in Chapter 3. As such race constitutes a fantasy structure which frames the terms on which life is worth living. But as a fantasy *structure* race has none of the looseness of everyday illusion that I considered above, it maps the ordering of dominance and vulnerability tightly through *governmental* power in the sense I am using this notion in *Power, Politics and the Emotions*. That is to refer to the enactment of the formal state and its policy processes, but also in the more general sense following Foucault where the point under emphasis in this idea of governmental power is one of *omnipotence* where governmental power works *biopolitically* to define the field of life *performatively* through conceptual accumulation. Within the context of the Western European tradition of colonial modernity out of which I am currently writing and through which, as I argued in Chapter 1, liberal institutions like the state came to be, this omnipotent power is white, where the idea of whiteness stands in for a particular Judaeo-Christian masculine ideal.

Going back to where I began in Chapter 1 then, whiteness ascends as *the* cultural manifestation of governmental power through a delusional fantasy structure enacted through paranoid forms of belonging via feelings of persecution, jealousy and exaggerated self importance which relate to the illusory nature of governing omnipotence. Ghassan Hage argues that national identifications work in this sort of paranoid threatened way where in the case of Australia, for example, 'Whiteness operates as a symbolic field of accumulation where many attributes such as looks, accent, "cosmopolitanism", or "Christianity" can be accumulated and converted into Whiteness' (Hage, 1998, p. 232). In *Power, Politics and the Emotions* the tight coupling of subject and object in Chapter 4 exemplifies the way in which paranoid belongings enact the institutional space as white. Such forms of paranoid belonging are cumulative where fantasies of *control over the other* lead to the fear of *being controlled by the other* as a form of retaliation which in turn begets more aggressive attempts to control the other. It is through this paranoid structure that good and bad become progressively more split, projected into good subjects, bad objects, until the ability to collectively symbolise (in the sense of recognising the space *between* the subject and object) is lost altogether. What is interesting here is the way that belonging to a governing ideal, as a certain sort of governing subject, as a professional, general practitioner or nurse, for example, is differentiated as good and bad through a *cultural common sense* that ensures threats to the governing order are managed through cultural means. This shows very powerfully the paranoid fantasy structure of whiteness in its *institutional* operation.

This understanding of the paranoid enactment of institutional space demonstrates the important difference between melancholy and melancholia which has underpinned the approach developed in *Power, Politics and the Emotions*. As Derek Hook notes:

> Freudian melancholia necessarily involves hostility towards a lost object that has been withdrawn into the ego. It entails the sufferer's assault upon this lost object which, via the means of narcissistic regression, has been incorporated into the ego. These then are the conditions under which a relation to the lost object may be maintained, conditions which amount to a crippling state of internalized aggression. A constituent component of melancholia – far more difficult to romanticize than states of ungrieved loss – is the fact of a loathing, self-*abjecting* relation to one's own ego that has been deemed

worthless and opened up to the punitive fury of the super-ego. . . . A form of suffering tantamount to being buried with the dead, melancholia cannot be summarily equated merely with blockages of identification, with states of unending remembrance.

(Hook, 2012, p. 7)

Whilst I am not claiming that *all* institutional spaces are literally deathly, I am interested in the ways that they can become toxic, materially, as well as symbolically and psychically. The enactment of institutions can debilitate governing subjects, making them generally fearful and self as well as other abjecting. It is this point about the violent enactment of loathing and self abjection in institutional space which I have been aiming to highlight in *Power, Politics and the Emotions* via the idea of a potential neoliberal suicide. I have been seeking to do this precisely because the sorts of traumatic toxic violences understood through melancholia, rather than melancholy, are generally viewed as *separate from*, rather than *integral to*, institutional life. Institutional spaces, as they are defined in modernist rationalist terms via a public/private split, are imagined through their ability to control inappropriate, privately, supposedly individually generated emotionalities, like hate, fear, loathing. This control is dependent on the externalising of violence which, from a melancholic point of view, is already always there; constitutive of institutional space. My analysis of relational politics is an attempt to represent governing subjects' struggles with this absent sociocultural past in the institutional present as a form of struggle which makes visible this absent presence of violence that relationally enacts, but is symbolically written out of (neo)liberal institutional spaces through the practices of cultural forgetting. The more this presence is materially and symbolically repressed within the institutional space the more violently it constitutes it. The racist murder of South London teenager Stephen Lawrence continues to remain emblematic of the struggles to make this link between supposedly externalised trauma and the inside of the institutional space. It looms very obviously in Chapters 5 and 7, but this is only one of a number of back stories through which governing subjects in *Power, Politics and the Emotions* disrupt linear institutional time which presents the past as over in order to suppress difference in the institutional present.

This brings me to the second related problem with this circular anticipatory logic whereby the world's topography is already anticipated, assumed to be known, ready to be confirmed *in practice*, rather than *changed through it*. This problem is the tendency within this logic towards intensification, amassing taken for granted assumptions and *solidifying them* into an object through the practices of forward momentum, progression and speed. Speed promotes routinisation, quick, quick, hurry; more repetition, forward momentum and therefore paradoxically institutional replication and stasis, rather than change through the promotion of an engagement with difference. This is because it compresses the opportunity for stopping to think differently through encounters with others (Stengers, 2002). Speed is what holds what are relationally uncertain entities together in a form already assumed to be known. It is therefore easy to imagine that we already know what the institutional problems to be faced are. As Tony says in Chapter 6 'we all know what's right and wrong today', the solutions themselves are understood to be self evident; they don't require thought, but quick and decisive action for resolution. There is an assumption here that the potential consequences of action are already known. This takes me back, yet again, to the linearity of cause and effect logics which assume a rationalist pre-emptive power rooted in the potential for governing omnipotence; the potential to know the world and the others in it. The problem of paranoid delusion from this point of view is a hyperreflexivity which knows all, but which is coupled with an ever increasing sense of demoralisation because, in spite of an overall intensification of problem solving activity, nothing changes. It is this mix of hopelessness for the possibility of something different *and* growing sense of helplessness to change which produces the conditions for suicide.

Feeling disappointed

Other aspects of relational politics that I have explored in *Power, Politics and the Emotions* challenge this sort of cumulative circular paranoid intensification, suggesting the capacity for much more hopeful encounters between governing subjects. My argument in Chapter 6 focused on the ways in which relational politics is about slowing down *through the practice* of patience, as a challenge to romanticised notions of radical ruptural social transformation supposedly achieved through quick, decisive and coherent forms of categorically ordered political action. Patience puts the brakes on the push to decide and to act one way or another. It sits between activity and complacency, keeping open the question about what sort of action works, under which circumstances and for whom. This slowing down is a sort of inactive action which holds off the tight coupling produced through paranoid ways of knowing. It produces a looser set of more ambivalent relations between subjects. This sort of practice produces a *space* that, following Winnicott again, 'link[s] the past, the present and the future; . . . take[s] up time and space. . . . demand[s] and get[s] our concentrated deliberate attention, deliberate but without too much of the deliberateness of trying' (2005 [1971], p. 147). It is a space which encourages resting with the difference of the other, attempting to inhabit it for a while, rather than crossing over into the other. Melanie Klein's ideas about the 'depressive position' rely on this sort of ability to rest with difference. This position is achieved for the self through the ability to perceive the other's existence as a whole object within a relational field, through the recognition of the other's connection to others, rather than only to the self. It is the means by which objects are seen to become subjects in their own right. The growth of the subject only occurs as part of the multiple extended relational field to which the self also belongs, but not in the same way, or even through the same configuration of connections. It is only through the 'painstaking labour' of resting as a form of 'getting closer, of speaking to each other, and of working for each other, that we get closer to "other others"', therefore to their pasts and potential futures and not only the person that we take for granted in front of us (Ahmed, 2002, p. 570). This resting involves an extension to the community of the institutional space via bringing more relations of difference inside, via families, friendships, communities. Whilst this labour is painstaking in terms of its understanding of pain and loss, it is dependent on the capacity for love, in the sense of the ability to love the other as a whole object, as someone who suffers loss in their own right. The patient subject is not a 'well adjusted' subject (Munoz, 2006, p. 680), but one that is often disappointed, sometimes sad, and maybe even depressed 'feeling down' about the inescapable difficulties of difference and our inability to get over them and to feel coherently securely bonded to others. The risk of fracture is always present.

The ambivalence of patience is not a means of resisting responsibility, but taking it more seriously by taking time to understand its multiple lines and configurations. This is what is implied by Donna Haraway's metaphor of the cat's cradle game that I called up at the end of Chapter 2 which involves the creation of figures and patterns through the collective work of multiple players. It is a game for 'nominalists like me who cannot *not* desire what we cannot possibly have' (Haraway, 1997, p. 268). For as soon as 'possession enters the game' the strings tying the figures together freeze into a flat lying, one dimensional pattern. From my point of view ambivalence points precisely to a collective form of responsibility in the sense that it is incumbent on all the players within the game to cooperate despite difference, to work through and maintain connections which enable a shifting dynamic entity to be enacted. This ability to shift relies on the willingness to rest with difference, to engage with it, rather than to imbibe it or to allow oneself to be collapsed into it.

Playing with institutional reality

Where does all of this leave me on the state and its formal institutions? If I were asked outright whether I believe in the state as a positive form of illusion, a mobilising fiction, rather than a form of paranoid delusion, I would have to say that I do believe in something like it, in some place where I could invest my energies and cares, confront my fears and anxieties with others who, whilst positioned differently, and maybe even oppositionally, wanted to do the same for our common benefit (though of course in the acknowledgement that these ideas of benefit surely wouldn't be the same). But this state would be very different from the (neo)liberal *ideal* I currently find myself wrangling through. In my playful imaginings it would be more like the state envisaged by Jacqueline Stevens in her 'thought experiments' in her book *States without Nations* (Stevens, 2011). For Stevens that state is one which understands that fantasies of life and death are what drive the sorts of divided (neo)liberal (and also those currently positioned by the West as 'illiberal' or 'failed') states which incite war violence and premature death, including their own. The creation of communities of practice, rather than ones reliant on forms of 'accidental' belonging like lineage or nationality, lies at the heart of this sort of state. Whilst thought experiments like Stevens' rooted in abolitionist philosophies may appear to be very far away from the possible, they are a crucial form of hopeful playing with our current reality as we face it; they are an important form of mobilising fiction. Such thought experiments might also seem far off my focus on the mainstream of governing practices. But my aim has been similar to Stevens' in the sense that I am identifying the everyday relational politics which enacts contemporary institutional life as an important location for such hopeful play and reality testing which extends the imaginary of what could constitute the institutional present. William Connolly (2013) advocates role experiments undertaken in institutions within the 'slack' between how a role is to be performed and its performer. The accumulation of difference within this slack, across several interconnected spaces, can make a difference. Formal institutions have a thirst for life as well as a fear of death which drives them, and it is this thirst for life enacted through such experimentation around the fear of death which is a crucial place to start when thinking of revisioning these spaces less unequally.

References

Ahmed, S. (1999). Home and away: narratives of migration and estrangement. *International Journal of Cultural Studies, 2*(3), 329–347.

Ahmed, S. (2000). *Strange Encounters: Embodied Others in Post-coloniality*. London: Routledge.

Ahmed, S. (2002). This other and other others. *Economy and Society, 31*(4), 558–572.

Ahmed, S. (2004a). Declarations of whiteness: the non-performativity of anti-racism. *Borderlands, 3*(2), 1–54.

Ahmed, S. (2004b). *The Cultural Politics of Emotion*. Edinburgh: Edinburgh University Press.

Ahmed, S. (2006). The non-performativity of anti-racism. *Merideans: Journal of Women, Race and Culture, 7*(1), 104–126.

Ahmed, S. (2007). The language of diversity. *Ethnic and Racial Studies, 30*(2), 235–256.

Ahmed, S. (2010). Killing joy: feminism and the history of happiness. *Signs: Journal of Women in Culture and Society, 35*(3), 571–594.

Ahmed, S. (2012). *On Being Included: Racism and Diversity in Institutional Life*. Durham, NC: Duke University Press.

Ahmed, S., and Swan, E. (2006). Introduction: doing diversity. *Policy Futures in Education, 4*(2), 96–100.

Ahmed, S., Hunter, S., Kilic, S., Swan, E., and Turner, L. (2006). *Final Report on the Centre for Excellence in Leadership Research Project: Integrating Diversity: 'Race' and Leadership in the Learning and Skills Sector*, Lancaster: Lancaster University Management School.

Ainley, P. (2005). The new 'market-state' and education. *Journal of Education Policy, 19*(4), 497–514.

Akhtar, S. (2009). *Comprehensive Dictionary of Psychoanalysis*. London: Karnac Books.

Alexander, C. (2004). Imagining the Asian gang: ethnicity, masculinity and youth after 'the riots'. *Critical Social Policy, 24*(4), 526–549.

Alexander-Floyd, N. (2012). Disappearing acts: reclaiming intersectionality in the social sciences in a post-Black feminist era. *Feminist Formations, 24*(1), 1–25.

Ali, S. (2007). Feminism and postcolonial: knowledge/politics. *Ethnic and Racial Studies, 30*(2), 191–212.

Allen, T. W. (1975). *Class Struggle and the Origin of Racial Slavery: The Invention of the White Race*. New York: Hoboken.

Allen, T. W. (1994). *The Invention of the White Race, vol.1: Racial Oppression and Social Control*. London: Verso.

Alleyne, B. W. (2002). *Radicals Against Race: Black Activism and Cultural Politics*. Oxford: Berg.

Anthias, F. (1999). Institutional racism, power and accountability. *Sociological Research Online* (Vol. 12): Sociology online http://ideas.repec.org/a/sro/srosro/1999-21-1.html.

Anthias, F. (2013). Moving beyond the Janus face of integration and diversity discourses: towards an intersectional framing. *The Sociological Review, 61(2)*, 232–343.

Anthias, F., and Yuval-Davis, N. (1993). *Racialised Boundaries: Race, Nation, Gender, Colour and Class and the Anti-racist Struggle*. London: Routledge.

Bacchi, C., and Eveline, J. (2009). Gender mainstreaming or diversity mainstreaming? The politics of 'doing'. *NORA – Nordic Journal of Feminist and Gender Research, 17(1)*, 2–17.

Bagilhole, B. (2009). *Understanding Equal Opportunities and Diversity: The Social Differentiations and Intersections of Inequality*. Bristol: Policy Press.

Ball, S. J. (1998). Performativity and fragmentation in 'Postmodern Schooling'. In J. Carter (Ed.), *Postmodernity and the Fragmentation of Welfare*. London: Routledge.

Ball, S. J. (2007). *Education Plc: Understanding Private Sector Participation in Public Sector Education*. London: Routledge.

Bannister, J., Hill, M., and Scott, S. (2007). More sinned against than sinbin? The forgetfulness of critical social policy? *Critical Social Policy, 27(4)*, 557–560.

Barnes, M., and Prior, D. (Eds.). (2009). *Subversive Citizens: Power, Agency and Resistance in Public Services*. Bristol: Policy Press.

Barnes, M., Bauld, L., Benzeval, M., Judge, K., Mackenzie, M., and Sullivan, H. (2005). *Health Action Zones: Partnerships for Health Equality*. London: Routledge.

Barnes, M., Newman, J., and Sullivan, H. (Eds.). (2007). *Power, Participation and Political Renewal: Case studies in Public Participation*. Bristol: Policy Press.

Benschop, Y. (2001). Pride, prejudice and performance. *International Journal of Human Resources Management, 12(7)*, 1166–1181.

Berlant, L. (2008a). Cruel optimism: on Marx, loss and the senses. *New Formations, 63*(Winter), 33–51.

Berlant, L. (2008b). *The Female Compaint: The Unfinished Business of Sentimentality in American Culture*. Durham, NC: Duke University Press.

Berlant, L. (2010). Thinking about feeling historical. In J. Staiger, A. Cvetovich and A. Reynolds (Eds.), *Political Emotions: New Agendas in Communication* (pp. 229–245). London: Routledge.

Berman-Brown, R., and McCartney, S. (2000). Professionalism definitions in 'managing' health services: perspectives on the differing views of clinicians and general managers in an NHS Trust. In N. Malin (Ed.), *Professionalism, Boundaries and the Workplace* (pp. 178–194). London: Routledge.

Bhabha, H. (2004 [1994]). *The Location of Culture*. London: Routledge.

Bhavani, K.-K. (2001). *Rethinking Interventions in Racism*. Stoke on Trent: Trentham Books.

Bhavnani, R., Mirza, H. S., and Meetoo, V. (2005). *Tackling the Roots of Racism: Lessons for Success*. Bristol: Polity Press.

Biko, S. (2004). *I Write What I Like*. Johannesburg: Picador Africa.

Blackman, L. (2012). *Immaterial Bodies: Affect, Embodiment, Mediation*. London: Sage.

Blakemore, K., and Drake, R. (1996). *Understanding Equal Opportunity Policies*. London: Prentice Hall/Harvester Wheatsheaf.

Blenkisnopp, A., and Bond, C. (2003). The future healthcare workforce in pharmacy. In C. Davies (Ed.), *The Future Health Workforce* (pp. 199–221). Basingstoke: Palgrave Macmillan.

Blunkett, D. (2000). *Remit Letter to Learning and Skills Council*. London: Department for Education and Skills.

Bondi, L. (2005). Making connections and thinking through emotions: between geography and psychotherapy. *Transactions of the Institute of British Geographers, 30*(4), 433–448.

Bonnett, A. (1993). *Radicalism, Anti-racism and Representation*. London: Routledge.

Bonnett, A. (2010). Radicalism, antiracism, and nostalgia: the burden of loss in the search for convivial culture. *Environment and Planning A, 42*(10), 2351–2369.

Bornat, J., Leroi, H., and Raghuram, P. (2009). 'Don't mix race with the specialty': interviewing South Asian overseas-trained geriatricians. *Oral History, 37*(1), 74–84.

Bourne, J. (2001). The life and times of institutional racism. *Race Class, 43*(2), 7–22. doi: 10.1177/0306396801432002

Bowling, B. (1998). *Violent Racism: Victimization, Policing and Social Context*. Oxford: Oxford University Press.

Brah, A., and Phoenix, A. (2004). Ain't I a woman? Revisiting intersectionality. *Journal of International Women's Studies, 5*(3), 75–86.

British Medical Association. (2010, 12 July). Press release: BMA response to the health White Paper.

Brown, L. M. (1998). Voice and ventriloquation in girls' development. In K. Henwood, C. Griffin and A. Phoenix (Eds.), *Standpoints and Differences: Essays in the Practice of Feminist Psychology*. London: Sage.

Brown, L. M., and Gilligan, C. (1992). *Meeting at the Crossroads: Women's Psychology and Girls' Development*. New York: Ballantine Books.

Brown, L. M., Debold, E., Tappan, M., and Gilligan, C. (1991). Reading narratives of conflict and choice for self and moral voices: a relational method. In W. Kurtines and J. Gewirtz (Eds.), *Handbook of Moral Behaviour and Development*. Hillsdale, NJ: Erlbaum.

Brown, W. (1995). *States of Injury*. Princeton, NJ: Princeton University Press.

Brown, W. (2003). Neo-liberalism and the end of liberal democracy. *Theory and Event, 7*(1), 1–508.

Brown, W. (2008). Regulating Aversion: Tolerance in the Age of Identity and Empire. Princeton, NJ: Princeton University Press.

Buckman, L. (2010, 18 July). Letter from the GPC chairman to all GPs in England regarding the NHS White Paper.

Burawoy, M. (2005). 2004 American Sociological Association Presidential Address: For Public Sociology. *British Journal of Sociology 56*(2), 259–294.

Burchell, G., Gordon, C., and Miller, P. (Eds.). (1991). *The Foucault Effect: Studies in Governmentality*. Chicago: University of Chicago Press.

Burnett, J. (2013). *Racial Violence: Facing Reality*. London: Institute of Race Relations.

Burnett, J., and Duncan, S. (2008). Reflections and observations: an interview with the UK's first Chief Government Social Researcher. *Critical Social Policy, 28*(3), 283–298.

Burton, J., Nandi, A., and Platt, L. (2008). *Who are the UK's Minority Ethnic Groups? Issues of Identification and Measurement in a Longitudinal Study.* Colchester: Institute for Social and Economic Research, University of Essex.

Butler, J. (1997). *The Psychic Life of Power: Theories in Subjection.* Stanford, CA: Stanford University Press.

Butler, J. (2004). *Precarious Life: The Powers of Mourning and Violence.* London: Verso.

Callon, M. (2002). Writing and (re)writing devices as tools for managing complexity. In J. Law and A. Mol (Eds.), *Complexities: Social Studies of Knowledge and Practices* (pp. 191–217). London: Duke University Press.

Cameron, A., and Masterson, A. (2003). Reconfiguring the clinical workforce. In C. Davies (Ed.), *The Future Health Workforce* (pp. 68–86). Basingstoke: Palgrave Macmillan.

Cameron, D. (2010, 11 May). Speech outside 10 Downing Street.

Carmichael, S., and Hamilton, C. (1976). *Black Power: The Politics of Liberation in America.* New York: Vintage Books.

Carver, T., Torfing, J., Mottier, V., and Hajer, M. A. (2002). Discourse analysis and political science. *European Political Science, 2*(1), 48–67.

Centre for Excellence in Leadership. (2005). *Leading Change in Diversity and Equality.* London: Centre for Excellence.

Cheng, A. A. (2000). *The Melancholy of Race: Psychoanalysis, Assimilation, and Hidden Grief.* Oxford: Oxford University Press.

Cho, G. M. (2008). *Haunting the Korean Diaspora: Shame, Secrecy, and the Forgotten War.* Minneapolis: University of Minnesota Press.

Cho, S., Crenshaw, K. W., and McCall, L. (2013). Toward a field of intersectionality studies: theory, applications, and praxis. *Signs, 38*(4), 785–810.

Choo, H. Y., and Marx Ferree, M. (2010). Practicing intersectionality in sociological research: a critical analysis of inclusions, interactions and institutions in the study of inequalities. *Sociological Theory, 28*(2), 129–149.

Chow, R. (2002). *The Protestant Ethnic & The Spirit of Capitalism.* New York: Columbia University Press.

Clarke, J. (2004). *Changing Welfare Changing States: New Directions In Social Policy.* London: Sage.

Clarke, J., and Newman, J. (2012). The alchemy of austerity. *Critical Social Policy, 32*(3), 299–319.

Clarke, M. (2012). Talkin' 'bout a revolution: the social, political and fantasmic logics of education policy. *Journal of Education Policy, 27*(2), 173–191.

Clarke, S. (2001). Projective identification: from attack to empathy? *Journal of Kleinian Studies.* http://www.human-nature.com/ksej/vol2.htm.

Clarke, S. (2003a). Psychoanalytic sociology and the interpretation of emotion. *Journal for the Theory of Social Behaviour, 33*(2), 145–163.

Clarke, S. (2003b). *Social Theory, Psychoanalysis and Racism.* London: Palgrave Macmillan.

Clarke, S., Hoggett, P., and Thompson, S. (2006). Moving forward in the study of emotions: some conclusions. In S. Clarke, P. Hoggett and S. Thompson (Eds.), *Emotion, Politics and Society* (pp. 162–175). Basingstoke: Palgrave Macmillan.

Clough, P. T. (2007). Introduction. In P. T. Clough and J. Halley (Eds.), *The Affective Turn: Theorising the Social* (pp. 1–33). Durham, NC: Duke University Press.

Clough, P. T. (2009). Reflections on sessions early in an analysis: trauma, affect and 'enactive witnessing'. *Women & Performance: A Journal Of Feminist Theory, 19*(2), 149–159.

Coffield, F., Steer, R., Hodgson, A., Spours, K., Edward, S., and Finlay, I. (2005). A new learning and skills landscape? The central role of the Learning and Skills Council. *Journal of Education Policy, 20*(5), 631–656.

Colebrook, C. (2002). The politics and potential of everyday life. *New Literary History, 33*(4), 687.

Commission for Black Staff. (2002). Challenging racism: further education leading the way. *The Full Report of the Commission for Black Staff in Further Education.* London: Association of Colleges.

Commission for Racial Equality. (1995). *Racial Equality Means Quality: A Standard for Racial Equality for Local Government in England and Wales.* London: Commission for Racial Equality.

Connolly, W. E. (2013). *The Fragility of Things: Self Organizing Processes, Neoliberal Fantasies, and Democratic Activism.* Durham, NC/London: Duke University Press.

Cooper, A., and Lousada, J. (2005). *Borderline Welfare: Feeling and Fear of Feeling in Modern Welfare.* London: Carnac.

Cooper, D. (1994). Productive, relational and everywhere? Conceptualising power and resistance within Foucauldian feminism. *Sociology, 28*(2), 435–454.

Cooper, D. (2009). Intersectional travel through everyday utopias: the difference sexual dynamics and economic dynamics make. In E. Grabham, D. Cooper, J. Krishnadas and D. Herman (Eds.), *Intersectionality and Beyond: Law, Power And The Politics Of Location* (pp. 299–325). London: Routledge.

Cooper, D. (2011). Reading the state as a multi-identity formation: the touch and feel of equality governance *Feminist Legal Studies, 19*(1), 3–25.

Cooper, D. (2012). Public bodies: conceptualising active citizenship and the embodied state. In S. Roseneil (Ed.), *Beyond Citizenship?: Feminism and the Transformation of Belonging.* Basingstoke: Palgrave Macmillan.

Cooper, D. (2014). *Everyday Utopias: The Conceptual Life of Promising Spaces.* Durham, NC/New York: Duke University Press.

Craib, I. (1994). *The Importance of Disappointment.* London: Routledge.

Craib, I. (1998). *Experiencing Identity.* London: Sage.

Crenshaw, K. (1989). Demarginalising the intersection of race and sex: a black feminist critique of antidiscrimination doctrine, feminist theory and antiracist politics. *The University of Chicago Legal Forum, 89,* 139–167.

Crociani-Windland, L., and Hoggett, P. (2012). Politics and affect. *Subjectivity, 5*(1), 161–179.

Cussins, C. (1996). Ontological choreography: agency through objectification in infertility clinics. *Social Studies of Science, 26*(3), 575–610.

Cvetkovich, A. (2007). Public feelings. *South Atlantic Quarterly, 106*(3), 459–468.

Cvetkovich, A. (2012). Depression is ordinary: public feelings and Saidiya Hartman's *Lose Your Mother*. *Feminist Theory, 13*(2), 131–146.

Dadzie, S. (1997). *Adult Education in a Multi-ethnic Europe: A Handbook for Organisational Change*. Leicester: NIACE.

Davies, B., and Bansel, P. (2010). Governmentality and academic work: shaping the hearts and minds of academic workers. *Journal of Curriculum Theorizing, 26*(3), 5–20.

Davies, C. (1995). *Gender and the Professional Predicament in Nursing*. Buckingham: Open University Press.

Davies, C. (Ed.). (2003). *The Future Health Workforce*. London: Palgrave Macmillan.

Davies, K. (2003). The body and doing gender: the relations between doctors and nurses in hospital work. *Sociology of Health & Illness, 25*(7), 720–742.

Davis, K. (2008). Intersectionality as buzzword: a sociology of science perspective on what makes a feminist theory successful. *Feminist Theory, 9*(1), 67–85.

Dean, J. (2009). *Democracy and Other Neoliberal Fantasies: Communicative Capitalism and Left Politics*. London: Duke University Press.

Dean, M. (1999). *Governmentality: Power and Rule in Modern Society*. London: Sage.

Dean, M. (2010). *Governmentality: Power and Rule in Modern Society* (Second ed.). London: Sage.

Degnen, C. (2013). 'Knowing', absence, and presence: the spatial and temporal depth of relations. *Environment and Planning D: Society and Space, 31*(3), 554–570.

Deleuze, G., and Guattari, F. (2004). *Anti-Oedipus: Capitalism and Scizophrenia* (R. Hurley, M. Seem and H. Lane, Trans.). London: Continuum.

Department for Education and Skills. (2002). *Success for All: Reforming Further Education and Training*. London: DfES.

Department for Trade and Industry. (2002). *Equality and Diversity: Making it Happen*. London: HMSO.

Department for Trade and Industry. (2003). *Fairness for All*. London: HMSO.

Department of Health. (1997). *The New NHS: Modern, Dependable*. London: The Stationery Office.

Doyal, L., and Pennell, I. (1994). *The Political Economy of Health*. London: Pluto Press.

Du Bois, W. E. B. (1935). *Black Reconstruction in America, 1860–1880*. New York: Harcourt Brace.

Du Gay, P. (Ed.). (2005). *The Values of Bureaucracy*. Oxford: Oxford University Press.

Dugdale, A. (1999). Materiality: juggling sameness and difference. In J. Law and J. Hassard (Eds.), *Actor Network Theory and After* (pp. 113–135). Oxford: Blackwell.

Duggan, L. (2003). *The Twilight of Equality? Neoliberalism, Cultural Politics and the Attack on Democracy*. Boston: Beacon Press.

Duggan, L., and Muñoz, J. E. (2009). Hope and hopelessness: a dialogue. *Women & Performance: A Journal of Feminist Theory, 19*(2), 275–283. doi: 10.1080/07407700903064946.

Dyer, R. (1997). *White*. London: Routledge.

Edkins, J. (2003). *Trauma and the Memory of Politics*. Cambridge: Cambridge University Press.

Eng, D. L., and Han, S. (2003). A dialogue on racial melancholia. In D. L. Eng and D. Kazanjian (Eds.), *Loss: The Politics of Mourning* (pp. 343–371). Berkeley: University of California Press.

Eng, D. L., and Kazanjian, D. (2003). Introduction: mourning remains. In D. L. Eng and D. Kazanjian (Eds.), *Loss: The Politics of Mourning* (pp. 1–25). Los Angeles: University of California Press.

Essed, P. (2002). Cloning cultural homogeneity while talking diversity: old wine in new bottles in Dutch work organizations? *Transforming Anthropology, 11,* 2–12.

Essed, P. (2004). Cloning amongst professors: normativities and imagined homogeneities. *Nordic Journal of Women's Studies, 12,* 113–122.

Essed, P. (2005). Gendered preferences in racialized spaces: cloning the physician. In K. Murji and J. Solomos (Eds.), *Racialization: Studies in Theory and Practice* (pp. 227–247). Oxford: Oxford University Press.

Evetts, J. (2009). New professionalism and new public management: changes, continuities and consequences. *Comparative Sociology, 8*(2), 247–266.

Evetts, J. (2011). A new professionalism? Challenges and opportunities. *Current Sociology, 59*(4), 406–422.

Fanon, F. (1986). *Black Skin, White Masks.* London: Pluto Press.

Ferguson, J., and Gupta, A. (2005). Spatializing states: toward an ethnography of neoliberal governmentality. In J. X. Inda (Ed.), *Anthropologies of Modernity: Foucault, Governmentality, and Life Politics* (pp. 105–131). Oxford: Blackwell.

Fitzpatrick, M. (2001). *The Tyranny of Health: Doctors and the Regulation of Lifestyle.* London: Routledge.

Flax, J. (1990). *Thinking Fragments: Psychoanalysis, Feminism, and Postmodernism in the Contemporary West.* Berkeley: University of California Press.

Flax, J. (2004). What is the Subject? Review essay on psychoanalysis and feminism in postcolonial time. *Signs: Journal of Women in Culture and Society, 29*(3), 905–923.

Fortier, A.-M. (2008). *Multicultural Horizons: Diversity and the Limits of the Civil Nation.* London: Routledge.

Fortier, A.-M., Ferreday, D., and Kuntsman, A. (2011). Interview: Anne-Marie Fortier in conversation with Debra Ferreday and Adi Kuntsman. *Boarderlands e-journal, 10*(2), 1–17.

Fotaki, M. (2006) Choice is yours: a psychodynamic exploration of health policy-making and its consequences for the English National Health Service. Human Relations, 59(12), 1711–1744.

Foucault, M. (1991). Politics and the study of discourse. In G. Burchell, C. Gordon and P. Miller (Eds.), *The Foucault Effect: Studies in Governmentality.* Chicago: University of Chicago Press.

Foucault, M. (1994). *The Order of Things: An Archaeology of Human Sciences.* New York: Vintage Books.

Fraser, M., Kember, S., and Lury, C. (2005). Inventive life: approaches to the new vitalism. *Theory, Culture Society, 22*(1), 1–14.

Fredman, S. (2011). The public sector equality duty. *Industrial Law Journal, 40*(4), 405–427.

Freud, S. (2006 [1917/1915]). Mourning and melancholia. In A. Phillips (Ed.), *The Penguin Freud Reader.* London: Penguin.

Freud, S. (1959 [1912]). The dynamics of the transference. In R. Joan (Ed.), *Collected Papers, Vol 2*. New York: Basic Books.

Friedson, E. (1970). *Profession of Medicine: A Study of the Sociology of Applied Knowledge*. New York: Dodd and Mead.

Froggett, L. (2002). *Love, Hate and Welfare: Psychosocial Approaches to Policy and Practice*. Bristol: Policy Press.

Frosh, S. (1987). *The Politics of Psychoanalysis*. London: Macmillan.

Gallop, J. (2002). *Anecdotal Theory*. Durham, NC: Duke University Press.

Garforth, L. (2009). No intentions? Utopian theory after the future. *Journal of Cultural Research 31*(1), 5–27.

Garner, S. (2012). A moral economy of whiteness: behaviours, belonging and Britishness. *Ethnicities, 12*(4), 445–464.

Garner, S., Clarke, S., and Gilmour, R. (2009). Imagining the 'Other'/figuring encounter: white English middle-class and working-class identifications. In M. Wetherell (Ed.), *Identity in the 21st Century* (pp. 139–156). London: Palgrave Macmillan.

Gewirtz, S. (2002a). Can managerialism be harnessed to social democratic ends? Critical reflections on New Labour's 'Third Way' policies for schooling in England. *Prospero: A Journal for New Thinking in Philosophy for Education 8*(3), 36–47.

Gewirtz, S. (2002b). *The Managerial School: Post-welfarism and Social Justice*. London: Routledge.

Gill, R. (2008). Culture and subjectivity in neoliberal and postfeminist times. *Subjectivity, 25*, 432–445.

Gillborn, D. (2008). *Racism and Education: Coincidence or Conspiracy?* London: Routledge.

Gillies, D. (2008). Quality and equality: the mask of discursive conflation in education policy texts. *Journal of Education Policy, 23*(6), 685–699.

Gilligan, C. (1993). *In a Different Voice: Psychological Theory and Women's Development* (Second ed.). Cambridge, MA: Harvard University Press.

Gilligan, C. (1994). After word: the power to name. *Feminism & Psychology, 4*(3), 420–424.

Gilligan, C., Brown, L. M., and Rogers, A. G. (1990). Psyche embedded: a place for the body, relationships, and culture in personality theory. In A. I. Rabin, R. Zucker, R. Emmons and S. Frank (Eds.), *Studying Persons and Lives*. New York: Springer.

Gilroy, P. (1989). *There Ain't No Black in the Union Jack*. London: Routledge.

Gilroy, P. (2004). *After Empire: Melancholia or Convivial Culture?* London: Routledge.

Goldberg, D. (1993). *Racist Culture: Philosophy and the Politics of Meaning*. Oxford: Blackwell.

Goldberg, D. T. (2002). *The Racial State*. Oxford: Blackwell.

Goldberg, D. T. (2009). *The Threat of Race: Reflections on Racial Neoliberalism*. Oxford: Wiley – Blackwell.

Gomez, L. (1996). *An Introduction to Object Relations*. London: Free Association Books.

Gordon, A. F. (2008). *Ghostly Matters: Haunting and the Sociological Imagination* (2nd ed.). Minneapolis: University of Minnesota Press.

Gordon, A. F. (2011). Some thoughts on haunting and futurity. *Borderlands e-journal*, *10*(2), 1–21.

Gould, D. (2009). *Moving Politics: Emotion and ACT Ups Fight Against AIDS.* Chicago: University of Chicago Press.

Gould, D. (2012). Political despair. In S. Thompson and P. Hoggett (Eds.), *Politics and the Emotions: The Affective Turn in Contemporary Political Studies* (pp. 95–114). New York/London: Continuum.

Grabham, E., Herman, D., Cooper, D., and Krishnadas, J. (2009). Introduction. In E. Grabham, D. Herman, D. Cooper and J. Krishnadas (Eds.), *Intersectionality and Beyond: Law, Power and the Politics of Location* (pp. 1–17). London: Routledge.

Greco, M., and Stenner, P. (2008). Introduction: emotion and social science. In M. Greco and P. Stenner (Eds.), *Emotions: A Social Science Reader* (pp. 1–21). London: Routledge.

Gunaratnam, Y. (2001). Eating into multiculturalism: hospice staff and service users talk food, 'race', ethnicity, culture and identity. *Critical Social Policy, 21*(3), 287–310.

Gunaratnam, Y. (2003). *Researching 'Race' and Ethnicity: Methods, Knowledge and Power.* London: Sage.

Gunaratnam, Y. (2004). 'Bucking and kicking': 'race', gender and embodied resistance in healthcare. In U. Apitzch, J. Bornat and P. Chamberlayne (Eds.), *Biographical Methods and Professional Practice: An International Perspective* (pp. 205–219). Bristol: Policy Press.

Gunaratnam, Y. (2012). Learning to be affected: social suffering and total pain at life's borders. *The Sociological Review, 60,* 108–123.

Gunaratnam, Y., and Lewis, G. (2001). Racialising emotional labour and emotionalising racialised labour: anger, fear and shame in social welfare. *Journal of Social Work Practice, 15*(2), 131–148.

Gunter, H. M. (2001). *Leaders and Leadership in Education.* London: Paul Chapman Publishing.

Hage, G. (1998). *White Nation: Fantasies of White Supremacy in a Multicultural Society.* Annandale, VI: Pluto Press.

Hall, S. (1996). The meaning of New Times. In D. Morley and K.-H. Chen (Eds.), *Stuart Hall: Critical Dialogues in Cultural Studies* (pp. 223–237). London: Routledge.

Hamaz, S. (2008). How do diversity trainers and consultants embody antiracism? Constructions of antiracism in the United Kingdom. *International Journal of Sociology, 38*(2), 30–42.

Haraway, D. (1991). *Simians, Cyborgs and Women.* New York: Routledge.

Haraway, D. J. (1997). *Modest_Witness@Second_Millennium.FemaleMan©_Meets_OncoMouse™: Feminism and Technoscience.* London: Routledge.

Harding, J., and Pribram, D. E. (2002). The power of feeling: locating emotions in culture. *European Journal of Cultural Studies, 5*(4), 407–426.

Harris, A. (2013). The house of difference, or white silence. *Studies in Gender and Sexuality, 13*(3), 197–216.

Haylett, C. (2001). Illegitimate subjects?: abject whites, neoliberal modernisation, and middle-class multiculturalism. *Environment and Planning D: Society and Space, 19*(3), 351–370.

Henriques, J., Hollway, W., Urwin, C., Venn, C., and Walkerdine, V. (1998). *Changing the Subject: Psychology, Social Regulation and Subjectivity* (Second ed.). London: Routledge.

Henry, L. (2007). Institutionalized disadvantage: older Ghanaian nurses' and midwives' reflections on career progression and stagnation in the NHS. *Journal of Clinical Nursing, 16*(4), 2196–2203.

Hesse, B. (2000). *Un/settled Multiculturalisms: Diasporas, Entanglements, Transruptions*. London: Zed Books.

Higginbotham, E. B. (1992). African-American women's history and the metalanguage of race. *Signs, Winter*, 251–274.

Hill Collins, P. (2000). *Black Feminist Thought: Knowledge, Consciousness, and the Politics of Empowerment* (Second ed.). London: Routledge.

Hinshelwood, R. D. (1989). Social possession of identity. In R. Barry (Ed.), *Crisis of the Self: Further Essays on Psychoanalysis and Politics* (pp. 75–83). London: Free Association Books.

Hoggett, P. (1989). The culture of uncertainty. In B. Richards (Ed.), *Crises of the Self: Further Essays on Psychoanalysis and Politics* (pp. 27–39). London: Free Association Books.

Hoggett, P. (2000a). *Emotional Life and the Politics of Welfare*. London: Palgrave Macmillan.

Hoggett, P. (2000b). Social policy and the emotions. In G. Lewis, S. Gewirtz and J. Clarke (Eds.), *Rethinking Social Policy* (pp. 141–155). London: Sage in association with Open University Press.

Hoggett, P. (2009). *Politics, Identity and Emotion*. New York: Paradigm Publishers.

Hoggett, P. (2010). Perverse social structures. *Journal of Psycho-Social Studies, 4*(1), 57–64.

Hoggett, P., Beedell, P., Jimenez, L., Mayo, M., and Miller, C. (2006a). Identity, life history and commitment to welfare. *Journal of Social Policy, 35*(4), 689–704.

Hoggett, P., Mayo, M., and Miller, C. (2006b). Private passions, the public good and public service reform. *Social Policy & Administration, 40*(7), 758–773.

Hoggett, P., and Miller, C. (2000). Working with emotions in community organizations. *Community Development Journal, 35*(4), 352–364.

Hollway, W., and Jefferson, T. (1996). PC or not pc: sexual harassment and the question of ambivalence. *Human Relations, 49*(3), 373–393.

Hollway, W., and Jefferson, T. (2000). *Doing Qualitative Research Differently: Free Association, Narrative and the Interview Method*. London: Sage.

Holmes, M. (2004a). Feeling beyond rules: politicizing the sociology of emotion and anger in feminist politics. *European Journal of Social Theory, 7*(2), 209–227.

Holmes, M. (2004b). The importance of being angry: anger in political life. *European Journal of Social Theory, 7*(2), 123–132.

Holmes, M. (2012). 'Building on a firm foundation of tolerance and love?' Emotional reflexivity in feminist political process. In S. Thompson and P. Hoggett (Eds.), *Politics and the Emotions: The Affective Turn in Contemporary Political Studies* (pp. 115–136). London/New York: Continuum.

Hood, C. (1991). A public management for all seasons? *Public Administration, 69*(1), 3–19.

Hook, D. (2012). Apartheid's lost attachments (2): Melancholic loss and symbolic identification. *Psychology in Society, 43*, 54–71.

Hughes, C. (2004) Class and other identifications in managerial careers: the case of the lemon dress, *Gender, Work and Organisation, 11*(5), 526–543.

Hunter, S. (2003). A critical analysis of approaches to the concept of social identity in social policy. Critical Social Policy, 23(3), 322–344.

Hunter, S. (2005a). *Negotiating Professional and Social Identities: 'Race', Gender and Profession in Two Primary Care Organisations.* Birmingham: University of Birmingham.

Hunter, S. (2005b). Negotiating professional and social voices in research principles and practice. *Journal of Social Work Practice, 19*(2), 145–158.

Hunter, S. (2005c). Adult and community learning: subjugated knowledges and the possibilities for diversity, *Centre for Excellence in Leadership.* Lancaster: Lancaster University Management School.

Hunter, S. (2005d). *An Introduction to the Field of Adult and Community Learning.* Paper presented at the Centre for Excellence in Leadership, Lancaster University Management School.

Hunter, S. (2006). Working for equality and diversity and adult and community learning: leadership, representation and racialised 'outsiders' 'within'. *Policy Futures in Education, Special Issue on 'Doing Diversity Work', 4*(1), 114–127.

Hunter, S. (2008). Living documents: a feminist psychosocial approach to the relational politics of policy documentation. *Critical Social Policy, 28*(4), 506–528.

Hunter, S. (2009a). Feminist psychosocial approaches to relationality, recognition and denial. In M. F. Ozbilgin (Ed.), *Theory and Scholarship in Equality and Diversity, Inclusion and Work: A Research Companion* (pp. 179–192). London: Edward Elgar.

Hunter, S. (2009b). Subversive attachments: gendered, raced and professional realignments in the 'new' NHS. In M. Barnes, and D. Prior (Eds.), *Subversive Citizens: Power, Agency And Resistance Among Public Service Users and Workers* (pp. 137–153). Bristol: Policy Press.

Hunter, S. (2010). What a white shame: race, gender, and white shame in the relational economy of primary health care organizations in England. *Social Politics: International Studies in Gender, State & Society, 17*(4), 450–476.

Hunter, S., and Swan, E. (2007). Oscillating politics and shifting agencies: equalities and diversity work and actor network theory. *Equal Opportunities International, 26*(5), 402–419.

Husband, C. (1996). Defining and containing diversity: community, ethnicity and citizenship. In W. I. U. Ahmad and K. Atkin (Eds.), *'Race' and Community Care.* Milton Keynes: Open University Press.

Husso, M., and Hirvonen, H. (2009). Feminism, embodied experience and recognition: an interview with Lois McNay. *NORA – Nordic Journal of Feminist and Gender Research, 17*(1), 48–55.

Illouz, E. (2007). *Cold Intimacies: The Making of Emotional Capitalism.* Cambridge: Polity Press.

Inter Ministerial Group on Equalities. (2010). *The Equality Strategy – Building a Fairer Britain.* London: HMSO.

Jaworski, K. (2010). 'Elegantly wasted': the celebrity deaths of Michael Hutchence and Paula Yates. *Continuum: Journal of Media and Cultural Studies, 22*(6), 777–791.

Jaworski, K. (2012). The 'mad' intentions of those who suicide. In F. Alves, K. Jaworski and S. Butler (Eds.), *Madness in Plural Contexts: Crossing Borders, Linking Knowledge*. Oxford: Inter-Disciplinary Press.

Jones, E., and Snow, S. (2009). *Against the Odds: Black and Minority Ethnic Clinicians and Manchester, 1948–2009.* Manchester: Manchester NHS Primary Care Trust.

Jones, R., Pykett, J., and Whitehead, M. (2011). Governing temptation: changing behaviour in an age of libertarian paternalism. *Progress in Human Geography, 35*(4), 483–501.

Jones, R., Pykett, J., and Whitehead, M. (2013). Psychological governance and behaviour change. *Policy & Politics, 41*(2), 159–182.

Kandola, R., Fullerton, J., and Ahmed, Y. (1995). Managing diversity: succeeding where equal opportunities has failed. *Equal Opportunities Review, 59*(January/February), 31–36.

Keith, M. (2008). Public sociology? Between heroic immersion and critical distance: personal reflections on academic engagement with political life. *Critical Social Policy, 28*(3), 320–334.

Kerr, R. (2005). *Education and Social Justice: CEL Policy Briefing Paper.* Lancaster: CEL.

Khanna, R. (2012). Touching, unbelonging, and the absence of affect. *Feminist Theory, 13*(2), 213–232.

Kimura, M. (2013). Non-performativity of university and subjectification of students: the question of equality and diversity in UK universities. *British Journal of Sociology of Education, 35*(4), 1–18.

Kirkpatrick, I., Dent, M., and Jespersen, P. K. (2011). The contested terrain of hospital management: professional projects and healthcare reforms in Denmark. *Current Sociology, 59*(4), 489–506.

Klein, M. (1986 [1935]). A contribution to the psychogenesis of manic-depressive states. In J. Mitchell (Ed.), *The Selected Melanie Klein.* London: Penguin.

Klein, M. (1986 [1952]). The origins of transference. In J. Mitchell (Ed.), *The Selected Melanie Klein.* London: Penguin.

Knowles, C. (2003). *Race and Social Analysis.* London: Sage.

Konrad, A. M., Prasad, P., and Pringle, J. K. (Eds.). (2006). *Handbook of Workplace Diversity.* London: Sage.

Koshy, S. (2001). Morphing race into ethnicity: Asian Americans and critical transformations of whiteness. *Boundary 2, 28*(1), 153–194.

Kyriakides, C. (2008). Third Way anti-racism: a contextual constructionist approach. *Ethnic and Racial Studies, 31*(3), 592–610.

Kyriakides, C., and Virdee, S. (2010). Migrant labour, racism and the British National Health Service. *Ethnicity and Health, 8*(4), 283–305.

Larner, W. (2006). Global governance and local policy partnerships. In G. Marston and C. McDonald (Eds.), *Analysing Social Policy: A Governmental Approach* (pp. 49–65). Cheltenham: Edward Elgar.

Lasch, C. (1991). *The True and Only Heaven: Progress and Its Critics.* New York: Norton.

Latour, B. (2005a). From Realpolitik to Dingpolitik or how to make things public. In

B. Latour and P. Weibel (Eds.), *Making Things Public: Atmospheres of Democracy* (pp. 14–41). Cambridge, MA: The MIT Press.

Latour, B. (2005b). *Reassembling the Social: An Introduction to Actor-Network-Theory*. Oxford: Oxford University Press.

Law, J. (2004). *After Method: Mess in Social Science Research*. London: Routledge.

Law, J. (2008). On sociology and STS. *The Sociological Review, 56*(4), 624–649.

Lawler, S. (2012). White like them: whiteness and anachronistic space in representations of the English white working class. *Ethnicities, 12*(4), 409–426.

Layton, L. (2008). What divides the subject? Psychoanalytic reflections on subjectivity, subjection and resistance. *Subjectivity, 22*, 60–72.

Le Feuvre, L. (2010). Introduction: strive to fail. In L. Le Feuvre (Ed.), *Failure: Documents of Contemporary Art* (pp. 12–21). London: Whitechapel Gallery/The MIT Press.

Lea, T. (2008a). *Bureaucrats and Bleeding Hearts: Indigenous Health in Northern Australia*. Sydney: University of New South Wales Press.

Lea, T. (2008b). Housing for health in indigenous Australia: driving change when research and policy are part of the problem. *Human Organization, 76*(1), 77–85.

Lea, T. (2012). When looking for anarchy, look to the state: fantasies of regulation in forcing disorder within the Australian indigenous estate. *Critique of Anthropology, 32*(2), 109–124.

Learning and Skills Improvement Service. (2013). *A Legacy of Learning*. Coventry: Learning and Skills Improvement Service.

Lees, J., and Stimpson, Q. (2010). A psychodynamic approach to suicide: a critical and selective review. *British Journal of Guidance & Counselling, 30*(4), 373–382.

Leonard, P. (1997). *Postmodern Welfare Restructuring: an Emancipatory Project*. London: Sage.

Leonard, P. (2003). Playing doctors and nurses? Competing discourses of gender, power and identity in the British National Health Service. *Sociological Review, 51*(2), 218–237.

Lewis, G. (2000). *Race, Gender, Social Welfare Encounters in a Postcolonial Society*. Cambridge: Policy Press.

Lewis, G. (2005). Welcome to the margins: diversity, tolerance, and policies of exclusion. *Ethnic and Racial Studies, 28*(3), 536–558.

Lewis, G. (2007). Racializing culture is ordinary. *Cultural Studies, 21*(6), 866–886.

Lewis, G. (2013). Unsafe travel: experiencing intersectionality and feminist displacements. *Signs, 38*(4), 869–892.

Lewis, H. B. (1990). Shame, repression, field dependence and psychopathology. In J. L. Singer (Ed.), *Repression and Dissociation: Implications for Personality Theory, Psychopathology, and Health* (pp. 233–257). Chicago: The University of Chicago Press.

Leys, C., and Players, S. (2011). *The Plot Against the NHS*. Pontypool, Wales: Merlin Press.

Liff, S. (1997). Two routes to managing diversity: Individual differences or social group characteristics. *Employee Relations, 19*(1), 11–26.

Light, D. (2010). Health-care professions, markets, and countervailing powers. In C. Bird, P. Conrad, A. Fremont and S. Timmermans (Eds.), *Handbook of Medical Sociology*. Nashville, TN: Vanderbilt University Press.

Lipsitz, G. (1995). The possessive investment in whiteness: racialized social democracy and the 'white' problem in American studies. *American Quarterly, 47*(3), 369–387.

Lister, R. (2011). The age of responsibility: social policy and citizenship in the early 21st century. In C. Holden, M. Kilkey and G. Ramia (Eds.), *Social Policy Review 23: Analysis and Debate in Social Policy, 2011* (pp. 63–84). Bristol: Policy Press.

Lorde, A. (1984). *Sister Outsider: Essays and Speeches.* Trumansburg, NY: The Crossing Press.

Lury, C. (2012). Going live: towards an amphibious sociology. *The Sociological Review, 60*, 184–197.

Lutz, C. (2008). Engendered emotion: gender, power and the rhetoric of emotional control in American discourse. In M. Greco and P. Stenner (Eds.), *Emotions: A Social Science Reader* (pp. 63–71). London: Routledge.

Lutz, H., Herrera Vivar, M. T., and Supik, L. (Eds.). (2011). *Framing Intersectionality: Debates on a Multi-faceted Concept in Gender Studies.* Farnham: Ashgate.

Mabbett, D. (2008). Aspirational legalism and the role of the Equality and Human Rights Commission in equality policy. *The Political Quarterly, 79*(1), 45–52.

Macpherson, William. (1999). *The Stephen Lawrence Inquiry Report.* London: HMSO.

Malik, S. (2013). 'Creative Diversity': UK public service broadcasting after multiculturalism. *Popular Communication, 11*(3), 227–241.

Malin, N. (Ed.). (2000). *Professionalism, Boundaries and the Workplace.* London: Routledge.

Mama, A. (1995). *Beyond the Masks: Race, Gender and Subjectivity.* London: Routledge.

Mann, R. (2012). Uneasy being English: the significance of class for English national sentiments *Ethnicities, 12*(4), 484–499.

Marcuse, H. (1965). Repressive tolerance. In R. P. Wolff, B. J. Moore and H. Marcuse (Eds.), *A Critique of Pure Tolerance.* Boston: Beacon Press.

Massey, D. (2012). Ideology and economics in the present moment. In J. Rutherford and S. Davison (Eds.), *Soundings On: The Neoliberal Crisis* (pp. 97–107). London: Lawrence and Wishart.

Massumi, B. (2002). *Parables for the Virtual: Movement, Affect, Sensation.* Durham, NC: Duke University Press.

Mauthner, N. S and Doucet, A. (1988) Reflections on a voice-centred relational method analysing maternal and domestic voices. In J. Ribbens and R. Edwards (Eds.) *Feminist Dilemmas in Qualitative Research Private Lives and Public Texts* (pp. 119–144), London: Sage.

May, T. (1998). Reflexivity in the age of reconstructive social science. *International Journal of Methodology: Theory and Practice 1*(1), 7–24.

Mbembe, A. (2001). *On the Postcolony.* Berkeley: University of California Press.

Mccafferty, P. (2010). Forging a 'neoliberal pedagogy': the enterprising education agenda in schools *Critical Social Policy, 30*(4), 541–563.

McLaughlin, E. (2005). Recovering blackness/repudiating whiteness: the *Daily Mail*'s construction of the five white suspects accused of the racist murder of Stephen Lawrence. In K. Murji and J. Solomos (Eds.), *Racialization: Studies in Theory and Practice.* Oxford: Oxford University Press.

Mclean Taylor, J., Gilligan, C., and Sullivan, A. M. (1996). *Between Voice and Silence: Women and Girls, Race and Relationship*. Cambridge, MA: Harvard University Press.

McRobbie, A. (2009). *The Aftermath of Feminism: Gender, Culture and Social Change*. London: Sage.

Mello, R. A. (2002). Collocation analysis: a method for conceptualising and understanding narrative data, Qualitative Research, 2(2), 231–243.

Menzies Lyth, I. (1960). A case study in the functioning of social systems as a defence against anxiety. *Human Relations, 13*, 95–121.

Mikhailova, O. (2006). Suicide in psychoanalysis. *Psychoanalytic Social Work, 12*(2), 19–45.

Miller, P., and Rose, N. (2008). *Governing the Present: Administering Economic, Social and Personal Life*. Cambridge: Polity Press.

Mirza, H. S. (1997). Black women in education: a collective movement for social change. In H. S. Mirza (Ed.), *Black British Feminism: A Reader*. London: Routledge.

Mohanty, C. T. (2013). Transnational feminist crossings: on neoliberalism and radical critique. *Signs, 38*(4), 967–991.

Mol, A. (1999). Ontological politics: a word and some questions. In J. Law and J. Hassard (Eds.), *Actor Network Theory and After* (pp. 74–89). Oxford: Blackwell.

Mol, A. (2002). *The Body Multiple: Ontology in Medical Practice*. London: Duke University Press.

Mol, A. (2008). *The Logic of Care: Health and the Problem of Patient Choice*. London: Routledge.

Moon, D. (1999). White enculturation and bourgeois ideology: the discursive production of 'good' (white) girls. In T. K. Nakayama and J. N. Martin (Eds.), *Whiteness: The Communication of Social Identity*. London: Sage.

Mouffe, C. (2000). *The Democratic Paradox* (First ed.). London: Verso.

Mouffe, C. (2005). *On the Political*. London: Routledge.

Mouffe, C. (2013). *Agonistics: Thinking the World Politically*. London: Verso.

Munoz, J. E. (2006) Feeling brown, feeling down: Latina affect, the performativity of race and the depressive position. *Signs, 31*(3), 675–688.

Navaro-Yashin, Y. (2009). Affective spaces, melancholic objects: ruination and the production of anthropological knowledge. *Journal of the Royal Anthropological Institute, 15*(1), 1–18. doi: 10.1111/j.1467–9655.2008.01527.x

Nayak, A. (1999). 'Pale warriors': skinhead culture and the embodiment of white masculinities. In A. Brah, M. J. Hickman and M. Mac an Ghaill (Eds.), *Thinking Identities: Ethnicity, Racism and Culture*. London: Macmillan.

Nayak, A. (2003a). Last of the 'Real Geordies'? White masculinities and the subcultural response to deindustrialisation. *Environment and Planning D: Society and Space, 21*(1), 7–25.

Nayak, A. (2003b). *Race, Place and Globalization: Youth Cultures in a Changing World*. Oxford: Berg.

Neal, S., and McLaughlin, E. (2009). Researching up? Interviews, emotionality and policy-making elites. *Journal of Social Policy, 38*(4), 689–707.

Newman, J. (1995). Gender and cultural change. In C. Itzin and J. Newman (Eds.),

Gender, Culture and Organizational Change: Putting Theory into Practice (pp. 11–29). London: Routledge.

Newman, J. (2004). Constructing accountability: network governance and managerial agency. *Public Policy and Administration, 19*(4), 17–33.

Newman, J. (2005a). Enter the transformational leader: network governance and the micro-politics of modernization. *Sociology, 39*(4), 717–734.

Newman, J. (2005b). Regendering governance. In J. Newman (Ed.), *Remaking Governance: Peoples, Politics and the Public Sphere* (pp. 81–99). Bristol: Policy Press.

Newman, J. (2012). *Working the Spaces of Power: Activism, Neoliberalism and Gendered Labour* London: Bloomsbury Academic.

Newman, J. (2013a). Spaces of power: feminism, neoliberalism and gendered labor. *Social Politics: International Studies in Gender, State & Society, 20*(2), 200–221.

Newman, J. (2013b). Performing new worlds? Policy, politics and creative labour in hard times. *Policy & Politics, 41*(4), 515–532. doi: 10.1332/030557312x655693

Newman, J., and Clarke, J. (2009). *Publics, Politics and Power: Remaking the Public in Public Services.* London: Sage.

Ngai, S. (2005). *Ugly Feelings.* London: Harvard University Press.

Ngai, S. (2012). *Our Aesthetic Categories.* Cambridge, MA: Harvard University Press.

Niven, B. O. B. (2008). The EHRC: transformational, progressively incremental or a disappointment? *The Political Quarterly, 79*(1), 17–26.

Nixon, J. (2007). Deconstructing 'problem' researchers and 'problem' families: a rejoinder to Garrett. *Critical Social Policy 27*(4), 546–564.

Osborne, A., and Gaebler, T. (1992). *Reinventing Government: How the Entrepreneurial Spirit is Transforming the Public Sector.* Reading, MA: Addison Wesley.

Ost, D. (2004). Politics as the mobilization of anger: emotions in movements and in power. *European Journal of Social Theory, 7*(2), 229–244.

Papadopoulos, D. (2008). In the ruins of representation: identity, individuality, subjectification. *British Journal of Social Psychology, 47*(1), 139–165.

Parker, I. (1992). *Discourse Dynamics.* London: Routledge & Kegan Paul.

Pedwell, C. (2008). Weaving relational webs: theorizing cultural difference and embodied practice. *Feminist Theory, 9*(1), 87–107.

Pedwell, C., and Whitehead, A. (2012). Affecting feminism: questions of feeling in feminist theory. *Feminist Theory, 13*(2), 115–129.

Perfect, D. (2011). *Gender Pay Gaps.* Manchester: Equality and Human Rights Commission.

Phillips, T. (2009). *Stephen Lawrence Speech: Institutions Must Catch Up with Public on Race Issues* Paper presented at the Race in Britain: Ten years since the Stephen Lawrence Inquiry, London.

Pickard, S. (2009). The professionalization of general practitioners with a special interest: rationalization, restratification and governmentality. *Sociology, 43*(2), 250–267.

Pile, S. (2012). Distant feelings: telepathy and the problem of affect transfer over distance. *Transactions of the Institute of British Geographers, 37*(1), 44–59.

Pilgrim, D. (1992a). Psychotherapy and political evasions. In W. Dryden and C. Feltham (Eds.), *Psychotherapy and Its Discontents* (pp. 225–243). Buckingham: Open University Press.

Pilgrim, D. (1992b). Rebuttal. In W. Dryden and C. Feltham (Eds.), *Psychotherapy and Its Discontents* (pp. 249–252). Buckingham: Open University Press.

Pilkington, A. (2008). From institutional racism to community cohesion: the changing nature of racial discourse in Britain. *Sociological Research Online 13*(3), 1–12.

Pitcher, B. (2009). The problem with white trash. *Cultural Studies, 23*(3), 446–449.

Pollitt, C. (2013). 40 years of public management reform in UK central government; promises, promises. *Policy & Politics, 41*(4), 465–480.

Pollock, A., and Price, D. (2011). How the Secretary of State for Health proposes to abolish the NHS in England. *British Medical Journal,* (342), 800–803.

Power, M. (1994). *The Audit Explosion.* London: Demos.

Power, M. (1999). *The Audit Society: Rituals of Verification.* Oxford: Oxford University Press.

Prasad, P., and Mills, A. J. (1997). From showcase to shadow: understanding the dilemmas of managing workplace diversity. In P. Prasad, A. J. Mills, M. Elemes and A. Prasad (Eds.), *Managing the Organizational Melting Pot – Dilemmas of Workplace Diversity* (pp. 3–39). Thousand Oaks, CA: Sage.

Pringle, R. (1998). *Sex and Medicine: Gender, Power and Authority in the Medical Profession.* Cambridge: Cambridge University Press.

Probyn, E. (2005). *Blush: Faces of Shame.* Minneapolis/London: University of Minnesota Press.

Puar, J. K. (2007). *Terrorist Assemblages: Homonationalism in Queer Times.* London: Duke University Press.

Puar, J. K. (2011). 'I would rather be a cyborg than a goddess': intersectionality, assemblage, and affective politics. *Transversal, August,* http://eipcp.net/transversal/0811/puar/en.

Puwar, N. (2003) Melodramatic postures and constructions. In N. Puwar and P. Raghuram (Eds.), *South Asian Women in the Diaspora* (pp. 21–41), Oxford: Berg.

Puwar, N. (2004). *Space Invaders: Race, Gender and Bodies Out of Place.* Oxford: Berg.

Puwar, N., and Rhaghuram, P. (2003). (Dis)locating South Asian women in the Academy. In N. Puwar and P. Rhaghuram (Eds.), *South Asian Women in the Diaspora.* Oxford: Berg.

Pykett, J. (2012). The new maternal state: the gendered politics of governing through behaviour change. *Antipode, 44*(1), 217–238.

Pykett, J. (2013). Neurocapitalism and the new neuros: using neuroeconomics, behavioural economics and picoeconomics for public policy. *Journal of Economic Geography, 13*(5), 845–869.

Rabinow, P., and Foucault, M. (1984). Politics and ethics: an interview. In P. Rabinow (Ed.) *The Foucault Reader: An Introduction to Foucault's Thought* (pp. 373–380). London: Penguin.

Race Relations Amendment Act. (2000). London: HMSO.

Reay, D. (2008). Psychosocial Aspects of White Middle-Class Identities: Desiring and Defending against the Class and Ethnic 'Other' in Urban Multi-Ethnic schooling. *Sociology, 42*(6), 1072–1088.

Reay, D., Hollingworth, S., Williams, K., Crozier, G., Jamieson, F., James, D., et al. (2007). `A Darker Shade of Pale?' Whiteness, the middle classes and multi-ethnic inner city schooling. *Sociology, 41*(6), 1041–1060.

Redman, P. (2009). Affect revisited: transference-countertransference and the unconscious dimensions of affective, felt and emotional experience. *Subjectivity, 26*(1),
51–68.

Richardson, D. (2005) Desiring sameness? The rise of a neoliberal politics of normalisation, *Antipode, 37*(3), 515–535.

Richman, J. (2004). 'Modern language' or 'spin'? Nursing, 'newspeak' and organizational culture: new health scriptures. *Journal of Nursing Management, 12*(5),
290–298.

Ridell, S., and Watson, N. (2011). Introduction: equality and human rights in Britain.
Social Policy & Society, 1(2), 191–192.

Riles, A. (2006a). Introduction: in response. In A. Riles (Ed.) *Documents: Artifacts of
Modern Knowledge* (pp. 1–38). Ann Arbour: University of Michigan Press.

Riles, A. (2006b). [Deadlines]: removing the brackets on politics in bureaucratic
and anthropological analysis. In A. Riles (Ed.) *Documents: Artifacts of Modern
Knowledge* (pp. 71–92). Ann Arbour: University of Michigan Press.

Rizvi, F., and Lingard, B. (2010). *Globalizing Education Policy*. New York:
Routledge.

Roediger, D. (1991). *The Wages of Whiteness: Race and the Making of the American
Working Class*. London: Verso.

Rose, J. (1996). *States of Fantasy*. Oxford: Oxford University Press.

Rose, N. (1998). *Inventing Our Selves: Psychology, Power, and Personhood*. Cambridge:
Cambridge University Press.

Rose, N. (1999). *Powers of Freedom: Reframing Political Thought*. Cambridge:
Cambridge University Press.

Rosenberg, P. M. (1997). Underground discourses: exploring whiteness in teacher
education. In M. Fine, L. Weis, L. C. Powell and L. Wong, M (Eds.), *Off White:
Readings on Race, Power, and Society*. London: Routledge.

Roseneil, S. (2006). The ambivalence of Angel's 'arrangement': a psychosocial lens
on the contemporary condition of personal life. *The Sociological Review, 54*(4),
847–869.

Ruane, S. (2012). Division and opposition: the Health and Social Care Bill 2011. In
M. Kilkey, G. Ramia and K. Farnsworth (Eds.), *Social Policy Review 24: Analysis
and Debate in Social Policy 2012* (pp. 97–114). Bristol: Policy Press.

Rustin, M. (1991). *The Good Society and the Inner World*. London: Verso.

Ryan-Flood, R., and Gill, R. (Eds.). (2010). *Secrecy and Silence in the Research Process:
Feminist Reflections*. London: Routledge.

Salvage, J. (1990). The theory and practice of the 'new nursing'. *Nursing Times,
86*(1), 42–45.

Saxton, A. (1991). *The Rise and Fall of the White Republic: Class Politics and Mass
Culture in Nineteenth Century America*. London: Verso.

Scott, S., and Scott, S. (2000). Our mother's daughters: autobiographical inheritance
through stories of gender and class. In T. Cosslett, C. Lury and P. Sommerfield
(Eds.), *Feminism and Autobiography: Texts, Theories and Methods* (pp. 128–140).
London: Routledge.

Sedgwick, E-K (2003) *Touching Feeling: Affect, Pedagogy, Performativity*. Durham,
NC: Duke University Press.

Shore, C., and Wright, S. (1999). Audit culture and anthropology: neo-liberalism in

British higher education. *The Journal of the Royal Anthropological Institute, 5*(4), 557–575.

Shore, C., and Wright, S. (2000). Coercive accountability: the rise of audit culture in higher education. In M. Strathern (Ed.), *Audit Cultures: Anthropological Studies in Accountability, Ethics and the Academy* (pp. 57–89). London: Routledge.

Shukra, K. (1998). *The Changing Pattern of Black Politics in Britain.* London: Pluto.

Silverman, K. (1992). *Male Subjectivity at the Margins.* London: Routledge.

Singleton, V. (1996). Feminism, sociology of scientific knowledge and postmodernism: politics, theory and me. *Social Studies of Science, 26*(2), 445–468.

Skeggs, B. (1997). *Formations of Class and Gender.* London: Sage.

Skeggs, B. (2011). Imagining personhood differently: person value and autonomist working-class value practices. *The Sociological Review, 59*(3), 496–513.

Skeggs, B., and Wood, H. (2008). Spectacular morality: reality television and the remaking of the working class. In D. Hesmondhalgh and J. Toynbee (Eds.), *Media and Social Theory* (pp. 177–194). London: Routledge.

Skills for Health. (2003). A health sector workforce market assessment 2003: http://www.skillsforhealth.org.uk/files/323–skills%20for%20health%20.QDX.pdf.

Sloterdijk, P. (2005). Atmospheric politics. In B. Latour and P. Weibel (Eds.), *Making Things Public: Atmospheres of Democracy* (pp. 944–951). Cambridge, MA: The MIT Press.

Smith, P., and Mackintosh, M. (2007). Profession, market and class: nurse migration and the remaking of division and disadvantage. *Journal of Clinical Nursing, 16*(4), 2213–2220.

Smith, P., Allan, H., Henry, L., Larson, J., and Mackintosh, M. (2006). *Valuing and Recognising the Talents of a Diverse Health Care Workforce.* Guildford/Milton Keynes: University of Surrey/Open University.

Solanke, I. (2011). Infusing the silos in the Equality Act 2010 with synergy. *Industrial Law Journal, 40*(4), 336–358.

Spade, D. (2013). Intersectional resistance and law reform. *Signs, 38*(4), 1031–1055.

Speed, E., and Gabe, J. (2013). The Health and Social Care Act for England 2012: the extension of 'new professionalism'. *Critical Social Policy, 33*(3), 564–574.

Squires, J. (2006). Good governance and good for business too? Equality and diversity in Britain. In S. Hellsten, A. M. Holli and K. Daskalova (Eds.), *Women's Changing Citizenship and Political Rights* (pp. 199–216). Basingstoke: Palgrave Macmillan.

Stacey, M. (1988). *The Sociology of Health and Healing: A Textbook.* London: Routledge.

Staiger, J., Cvetkovitch, A., and Reynolds, A. (Eds.). (2010). *Political Emotions: New Agendas in Communication.* London: Routledge.

Star, S. L. (1991). Power, technology and the phenomenology of conventions: on being allergic to onions. In J. Law (Ed.), *A Sociology of Monsters: Essays on Power, Technology and Domination.* London: Routledge.

Staunaes, D. (2003). Where have all the subjects gone? Bringing together the concepts of intersectionality and subjectification. *Nordic Journal of Feminist and Gender Research, 11*(2), 101–110.

Stengers, I. (2002). A 'cosmo-politics' – risk, hope, change: a conversation with Isabelle Stengers. In M. Zournazi (Ed.), *Hope: New Philosophies for Change* (pp. 244–272). London: Lawrence and Wishart.

Stenner, P. (2007). The adventure of psychosocial studies: re-visioning the space between the psychic and the social. Inaugural lecture, University of Brighton, School of Social Sciences http://about.brighton.ac.uk/sass/contact/staffprofiles/stenner/inaugural_lecture.pdf.

Stenner, P. (2008). A.N. Whitehead and subjectivity. *Subjectivity, 22*(1), 90–109.

Stenner, P., and Taylor, D. (2008). Psychosocial welfare: reflections on an emerging field. *Critical Social Policy, 28*(4), 415–437.

Stephenson, N., and Papadopoulos, D. (2006a). *Analysing Everyday Experience: Social Research and Political Change.* Basingstoke: Palgrave Macmillan.

Stephenson, N., and Papadopoulos, D. (2006b). Outside politics/continuous experience. *Ephemera, 6*(4), 433–453.

Stevens, J. (1999). *Reproducing the State.* Princeton, NJ: Princeton University Press.

Stevens, J. (2011). *States without Nations: Citizenship for Mortals.* New York: Columbia University Press.

Straker, G. (2004). Race for cover: castrated whiteness, perverse consequences. *Psychoanalytic Dialogues, 14*(2), 447–465.

Straker, G. (2011). Unsettling whiteness. *Psychoanalysis, Culture & Society, 16*(1), 11–26.

Strathern, M. (1991). *Partial Connections.* Savage, MD: Rowman & Littlefield.

Sudbury, J. (1998). *'Other Kinds of Dreams': Black Women's Organisations and the Politics of Transformation.* London: Routledge.

Swan, E. (2008). 'You make me feel like a woman': therapeutic cultures and the contagion of femininity. *Gender Work and Organization, 15*(1), 88–107.

Swan, E. (2010a). States of white ignorance, and audit masculinity in English higher education. *Social Politics: International Studies in Gender, State & Society, 17*(4), 477–506. doi: 10.1093/sp/jxq016

Swan, E. (2010b). Commodity diversity: smiling faces as a strategy of containment. *Organization, 17*(1), 77–100.

Swan, E., and Fox, S. (2010). Playing the game: strategies of resistance and co-optation in diversity work. *Gender, Work & Organization, 17*(5), 567–589.

Tate, S. A. (2010). 'Supping it': racial affective economies and the epistemology of ignorance in UK universities. In M. Christian (Ed.), Integrated but Unequal: Black Faculty in Predominantly White Space. New York: Africa World Press.

Tate, S. A. (2011). Playing in the dark: being unafraid and impolite, European Journal of Women's Studies, 18(1), 94–96.

Tate, S. A. (2014). Racial affective economies, disalienation and 'race made ordinary', Ethnic and Racial Studies, 37(13), 2475–2490.

Temple, P. (2005). The EFQM excellence model: higher education's latest management fad? *Higher Education Quarterly, 59,* 261–274.

Thandeka. (1999). Learning to Be White: Money, Race and God in America. New York: Continuum.

Thien, D. (2005). After or beyond feeling? A consideration of affect and emotion in geography. Area, 37(4), 450–456.

Thornley, C. (2003). What future for health care assistants: high road or low road? In C. Davies (Ed.), The Future Health Workforce. Basingstoke: Palgrave Macmillan.

Tomkins, S. (1995). Shame-humiliation and contempt-disgust. In S. E. Kosofsky and

A. Frank (Eds.), *Shame and Its Sisters: A Silvan Tomkins Reader*. Durham, NC: Duke University Press.

Tomlinson, B. (2013). To tell the truth and not get trapped: desire, distance, and intersectionality at the scene of argument. *Signs, 38*(4), 993–1017.

Treacher, A. (2006). Something in the air: otherness, recognition and ethics. *Journal of Social Work Practice 20*(1), 27–37.

Turner, L. (2006). Face values: visible/invisible governors on the board and organisational responses to the race equality agenda. *Policy Futures in Education, 4*(2), 160–171.

Tyler, I. (2008). 'Chav mum, chav scum': class disgust in contemporary Britain. *Feminist Media Studies, 8*(1), 1–18.

Valentine, G. (2007). Theorizing and researching intersectionality: a challenge for feminist geography. *The Professional Geographer, 59*(1), 10–21.

Verran, H. (2002) A postcolonial moment in science studies: alternative firing regimes of environmental scientists and aboriginal landowners. *Social Studies of Science, 32*(5–6), 729–762.

Vertovec, S. (2007). Super-diversity and its implications. *Ethnic and Racial Studies, 29*(6), 1024–1054.

Walby, S., Armstrong, J., and Strid, S. (2012). Intersectionality: multiple inequalities in social theory. *Sociology, 46*(2), 224–240.

Walker, A. (1997). *Anything We Love Can Be Saved: A Writer's Activism*. London: The Women's Press.

Walkerdine, V. (2006). Workers in the new economy: transformation as border crossing. *Ethos, 34*(1), 10–41.

Walkerdine, V. (2010). Communal beingness and affect: an exploration of trauma in an ex-industrial community. *Body & Society, 16*(1), 91–116.

Walkerdine, V., Lucey, H., and Melody, J. (2001). *Growing Up Girl: Psycho-social Explorations of Gender and Class*. Basingstoke: Palgrave Macmillan.

Ward, L. (1993). Race equality and employment in the National Health Service. In W. I. U. Ahmad (Ed.), *Race and Health in Contemporary Britain*. Buckingham: Open University Press.

Webb, D. (2010). *Thinking About Suicide: Contemplating and Comprehending the Urge to Die*. Ross-on-Wye: PCCS Books.

Wengraf, T. (2001). *Qualitative Research Interviewing*. London: Sage.

West, L. (2001). *Doctors on the Edge: General Practitioners, Health and Learning in the Inner-City*. London: Free Association Press.

West, L. (2004). Doctors on an edge: a cultural psychology of learning and health. In P. Chamberlayne, J. Bornat and U. Aspitzsch (Eds.), *Biographical Methods and Professional Practice: An International Perspective*. Bristol: Policy Press.

Wetherell, M. (2008). Speaking to power: Tony Blair, complex multicultures and fragile white English identities. *Critical Social Policy, 28*(3), 299–319.

Wetherell, M. (2013a). Affect and discourse – what's the problem? From affect as excess to affective/discursive practice. *Subjectivity, 6*(4), 349–368.

Wetherell, M. (2013b). *Affect and Emotion: A New Social Science Understanding*. London: Sage.

Widgery, D. (1991). *Some Lives! A GP's East End*. London: Simon & Schuster.

Wiegman, R. (2012). *Object Lessons*. Durham, NC: Duke University Press.

Wilding, P. (1982). *Professional Power and Social Welfare*. London: Routledge.

Williams, A. (2000). *Nursing, Medicine and Primary Care*. Buckingham: Open University Press.

Williams, A. (2003). Challenging identities: working together differently in primary care. In C. Davies (Ed.), *The Future Health Workforce*. Basingstoke: Palgrave Macmillan.

Williams, F. (1989). *Social Policy: A Critical Introduction*. Cambridge: Polity Press.

Williams, F. (2000). A conceptual chart for CAVA Workshop Paper No 16, Workshop Four: methodologies for researching moral agency: http://leeds.ac.uk/cava/research/essay1.htm.

Williams, R. (2009). On structure of feeling. In J. Harding and D. Pribram (Eds.), *Emotions: A Cultural Studies Reader* (pp. 35–49). London: Routledge.

Willis, E. (1989). *Medical Dominance*. Sydney: Allen & Unwin.

Winnicott, D. (1975 [1958]). *Through Paediatrics to Psychoanalysis*. London: Karnac Books.

Winnicott, D. (2000). Transitional objects and transitional phenomena. In P. Du Gay, J. Evans and P. Redman (Eds.), *Identity: A Reader* (pp. 150–162). London: Sage/Open University Press.

Winnicott, D. W. (2005 [1971]). *Playing and Reality*. London: Routledge.

Witz, A. (1992). *Professions and Patriarchy*. London: Routledge.

Wright, K. (2008). Theorizing therapeutic culture: past influences, future directions. *Journal of Sociology, 44*(4), 321–336.

Wyatt, S., and Langridge, C. (1996). Getting to the top in the National Health Service. In S. Ledwith and F. Colgan (Eds.), *Women in Organisations: Challenging Gender Politics*. London: Macmillan.

Yuval Davis, N and Stoetzler M. (2002) Imagined boundaries and borders: a gendered gaze. *European Journal of Women's Studies, 9*(3), 329–344.

Zanoni, P., Janssens, M., Benschop, Y., and Nkomo, S. (2010). Guest editorial: Unpacking diversity, grasping inequality: rethinking difference through critical perspectives. *Organization, 17*(1), 9–29.

Zournazi, M. (2002). *Hope: New Philosophies for Change*. London: Lawrence & Wishart.

Index